Science of Mind Archives & Library Foundation

Extension Study Course in the Science Of Mind

Volume 3: Lessons 25-36

by Ernest Holmes

Extension Study Course in the Science of Mind
By Ernest Holmes
Questions and Answers by Reginald C. Armor

A complete commentary on the Science of Mind textbook by Dr. Ernest Holmes
Page numbers referenced refer to the Science of Mind textbook

Published by Science of Mind Archives & Library Foundation
573 Park Point Drive
Golden, CO 80401
http://scienceofmindarchives.org

Contents

Causes and Conditions

Office of the Dean

My Dear Friend,

You are now starting on your 25th lesson. You have completed one half of our course. We know that you have found it more than worthwhile and we want to be sure that you are using these lessons in your everyday life, for yourself and for others. Please remember these lessons are not written to show you how to escape from objective reality. Rather they are a dynamic system for learning how to enter into life and living.

It is not enough just to know these truths. We must do something with them. Our lives should become fuller, more happy and radiant. We should have better health and a more complete sense of well-being. Above everything else we should have what we all need, a definite toward assurance that Life is for us and not against us.

Yes, you are now halfway through your course but you are really just beginning what we hope and believe will be the most wonderful experience of your life. Won't you share it with others, for sharing with others is a beautiful experience. It takes time but it is worth it. We all want to feel close to people, to love and be loved, and to enjoy living together.

We all are engaged in the great adventure of living, and all around us there are opportunities for self-expression which includes others. We all are part of one stupendous whole which is God, the Living Spirit Almighty.

Sincerely,
Ernest Holmes

Lesson 25

Page 183 through page 187

As stated many times in this series of lessons, the practice of spiritual mind healing is based upon the theory that we are living in a mental universe, or in a spiritual universe governed by laws of intelligence. This practice is also based upon the theory that not only are thoughts things, but that combinations of thought produce definite results. Most of these combinations of thought are unconscious; that is, we are not consciously aware of their presence within us.

Turn to page 640 for a definition of *Unconscious Thought*, and you will notice that we all have subjective reactions with which the conscious mind is not at all familiar. In fact the largest part of our mental activity is in this subjective field. This subjectivity, in its place, is a part of the creative medium of Spirit which we call the world soul or the Universal Soul. Turn to page 633 for the definition of *Soul* and to Lesson 6 of this series for a discussion of this definition).

Thoughts as they become subjective tend to reproduce themselves. Naturally it follows that wrong thought impulses produce discordant physical manifestations, and that when such thought impulses are corrected, the corresponding manifestation will automatically change. Turn to pages 627-628 for the definition of *Repression* and a discussion of the principle that irritation and agitation are mental in their cause and that all emotional states, unexpressed, must inevitably find a distorted outlet

This is in line with the modern psychological theory held by the advocates of the different schools of psychiatry and psychoanalysis. Repressed or unexpressed emotions create such a disturbance in the psyche that both mental and physical reactions are distorted. It is the purpose of the physician practicing in this field to lay bare the psyche, by which we mean the subjective state of thought, so completely that these repressions, suppressions, and other forms of mental confusion shall be brought to the surface, and by becoming self-seen may be dissipated.

Psychoanalysis means the analysis of the soul, the psyche, or subjective mind. There is a Divine Urge (the definition of which you will find on page 586) toward self-expression. Whenever and wherever this self-expression is inhibited or wherever its energy remains unsublimated there is trouble. Turn to page 588 for the definition of *Energy* and to page 638 for a definition of *Transmute*, which has the same meaning as sublimate. From the use that we are making of the term, it means to cause psychic or subjective energy to flow off in some form of self-expression which will be constructive. The energy is there and something must happen to it.

All thoughts produce some energy in the psychic life, and the purpose of *Self-Analysis* as described on page 631 is to uncover the memory images of thought and transmute or sublimate their energy into some form of constructive self-expression. This is the chief end and aim of analytical psychology. You will find a more complete definition of *Psychoanalysis* on page 622. On the same page you will find a definition of the word *Psyche* as we use it in this course of lessons.

The psychic or subjective life is that part of the mind which is a medium between the Absolute and the relative. Turn to page 575 for definition of *Absolute* and to page 627 for the definitions of *Relative* and *Relativity and Absoluteness*). The subjective state of our thought is the medium between this Absolute or Unconditioned, and the relative or our world of experience. It is also the repository of memory and the channel through which the accumulated experiences of the race find expression.

Turn again to page 624 for the definitions of *Race Mind, Race Suggestion,* and *Race Thought* in order that your memory may be refreshed as to the exact meaning which we give these words in our vocabulary. It will be seen that the subjective state of one's thought is the accumulated storehouse of one's own memory plus the tendency of the entire human race. The hopes, ambitions, fears, trials, disappointments, and faiths of the ages are lodged in every man's psyche because his psyche is merely the place where he uses the Universal Creative Medium.

There is no such thing as *your* mind, *my* mind, *his* mind, *her* mind—there is *One Mind which we all use and One Law which reacts to us.* This Law is subjective to our conscious thought, that is, It reacts to it. Where It reacts to it we create what we call the individual subjective mind or we build around us an atmosphere in the Universal Subjectivity which contains the images of our thoughts, whether they are conscious or unconscious, and which also contains the tendency of the human race operating through us.

Thus we appear to be controlled by an invisible agency which is too great for us to cope with. As a matter of fact this invisible agency is merely a thing of thought, and being a thing of thought, thought alone can change it. This is fundamental and basic in the entire system of modern metaphysics and psychology. Mind in its conscious state can change mind in its subjective state; otherwise there would be no possibility of making conscious use of this Law.

Turn again to the paragraph beginning on page 430, *The Father Who Seeth in Secret* and to page 412, the second paragraph, which we have already discussed in Lesson 5. In this paragraph is the statement that life is a moving picture of subjective causes, but that we may consciously change these pictures, and by reversing their order and sequence reverse their manifestation in our conscious experience. This is what mental practice does.

As intimated in the first paragraph on page 411, statements of Truth are more powerful than statements of negation; indeed they definitely neutralize them. On page 338, the second paragraph, the thought is expressed that the aim of evolution is to produce a man who can consciously redirect the law of his being, for as the first paragraph on the opposite page (339) states, *surrounding all is a Divine Law obeying the dictates of this Eternal Mind.*

You see, man's mind is the Eternal Mind manifest in the human. The great mystics have taught us that there is a complete and final salvation for all people. If you will turn to page 334, the last paragraph, and read through to the end of the second paragraph on page 336, you will find a discussion of this teaching of the mystics, that evil is not an ultimate reality but only a passing experience.

To return to the lesson on page 183, *Thought which is built upon a realization of the Divine Presence has the power to neutralize negative thought*. This of course is a basic principle in spiritual mind healing. The practitioner redirects thought for the purpose of neutralizing the negation and affirming its opposite. In other words he begins with the basic principle of Perfect God and perfect man in a spiritual universe, and then remolds thought to meet the new pattern.

In the process of doing this he definitely meets and neutralizes certain specific lines of thought. For example, if the patient is filled with fear he treats him for faith. Involved within this new concept of Reality is a Law of Cause and Effect which has the power to create new conditions. Because the Law can deduce only, that is, because It must accept us at our own valuation, It immediately sets to work to create a condition in line with our new concept. You will find this idea explained in the last paragraph on page 354 and the first paragraph on page 355.

In spiritual treatment, as our text indicates, we are not so much concerned with the negative condition of thought as we are with the affirmative. We study the negative in order to know just what affirmative stand we should take. As stated on page 184, *Spirit is Changeless Reality*, and our personality is merely one of Its innumerable instruments for self-expression. However, the Spirit can give us only what we take. One of the most important ideas in this series of lessons is that Spirit is never bound by any form It has already taken. It is never caught in any form. It is manifest through the form.

Form is not a thing of itself. Turn again to page 594 for a definition of *Form*, which is also discussed in Lessons 8 and 24. The Spirit is not caught in any particular form, but the mind of man holds the solution of Spirit in a temporary form, which binds him until he recognizes its nature and sees that it is not a thing in itself.

Pure Spirit exists at the center of all form. This we discussed in Lesson 3, but as stated in the second paragraph, page 406, Spirit of Itself is formless even though It is ever giving birth to form. And the Laws of Spirit are perfect. Spirit is all that there is at this very hour, and all creation is spiritual. You will find reference to this in the fourth paragraph on page 407. Because the objective mind alone can consciously decide, it follows that all subjective decisions are merely conclusions built on already accepted premises, and as the last paragraph on page 400 states, the Spirit alone has the power of self-choice.

Treatment is for the purpose of entertaining spiritual or less-limited concepts. We do not use the Divine Mind as opposed to a human mind, but we do use a less-limited mode of thought; hence a more Divine approach to Reality. Of course there is only One Mind, but we use It in more than one way. We must remember that there is only that which Is and the way It works. The Universe is a spiritual, mental system, and this spiritual, mental system includes substance and form. Substance is forever taking form as it is impulsed by the creative thought of God or man. Man unconsciously creates his own destiny. In such degree as he realizes this he can recreate it consciously, subjecting himself no longer to a law of chance but to a law of certainty.

Spirit is not limited to any condition which now exists, but It can give us only what we take. Our taking is a mental act. As we reshape the inner images of thought the subjective Law will automatically re-form our conditions after the new pattern. We are dealing with an impersonal Principle, but this impersonal Principle is always Infinite, and one with the Infinite constitutes a majority. For every thought of heaviness we must bring a thought of lightness. We must think peace and poise if we wish to destroy confusion. Weakness will be overcome with a sense of power, as doubt is healed by bringing an opposite state of consciousness, which is faith.

It is necessary that our work be done with enthusiasm and conviction. For since the whole thing is a mental process it necessarily follows that whatever one's state of consciousness is when one gives a treatment, that state of consciousness is bound to manifest when the treatment takes effect and the thought becomes a thing. We may make an affirmation of success, for instance, and say, "I am a success," with such vehement realization that success follows, but the very vehemence of the declaration which we have made may, even while it is producing success, create a strain. In other words, we must be careful in getting rid of one devil that we do not create another. We are told to make known our requests with thanksgiving.

The spiritual universe is perfect, else as our text suggests at the bottom of page 184, it could not exist. The Truth is indivisible, and to daily meditate on the perfect life, as suggested on page 185, *is a royal road to freedom*. This is what is meant by being born again, an idea discussed in Lesson 4. Turn to page 471, *The New Birth*; also the Meditations *I See No Evil* on page 546 and *Within Thee Is Fullness of Life* on page 549.

Any statement which tends to lighten the consciousness is good; any thought which tends to broaden and deepen the consciousness is good. Your own thoughts are just as powerful as those of another. The ones suggested here are merely examples of how one can increase his consciousness. And do not be afraid of being too enthusiastic. Enthusiasm should always accompany the attitude of faith. (Read the section on *Quench Not the Spirit*, page 497.)

In practice one repudiates every negation and follows such repudiation by affirming its opposite. We must address the Divine Being within us, that Spirit which is God. The Secret Place of the Most High is at the center of every man's thought; the Tabernacle of the Almighty is man's consciousness of Good. We must come to realize that all the Power there is, is God; all the Presence there is, is ours right now. Then we must speak from the standpoint of this belief with confidence, trust, enthusiasm, and faith. We must act as though we already knew. This is the meaning of the saying, *Be firm and ye shall be made firm.* Turn again to page 502, *Now Are We the Sons of God*. We must awaken this consciousness within ourselves.

Next we are taught that we must turn entirely from the condition, for thinking of weakness perpetuates weakness. We must realize that the external or physical world is an effect. It did not make itself, it does not control itself, it is not conscious of itself. As stated in the second paragraph on page 393, and thoroughly discussed in Lesson 1 of this series, *The correct understanding that Mind in Its unformed state can be called forth into individual use is the key to all proper mental and spiritual work*. How wonderful to know that each one of us may use this Creative Power, the Law of the Lord which is written into the constitution of our own nature.

In treating we turn mentally from the wrong condition and seek to sense its opposite. *Disease and limitation are neither person, place, nor thing* (page 186). They are entirely in the nature of effect and not of cause. Our thought is in the nature of cause, which creates effects. We are governed by effects only because we have misconstrued their meaning. Again we must remember to judge not according to appearances but to plunge beneath the external surface and find the real cause of these appearances. Turn to the last paragraph on page 406, already discussed in Lesson 7. *Mind is the realm of causes. Conditions are in the realm of effects.*

We must not only refuse to look at the condition as it is, as though it had to be, but we must learn to look only at that which we wish to have come true in our experience. As our textbook says, the Infinite knows no difference between a million dollars and a penny. We are not dealing with the principle of big and little, good and bad, but with the Principle of potentiality. It can be anything to any of us. It can be to each one what he is to It. It must be to each one what he is to It. It cannot be less, It will not be more. Cause and Effect! Cause and Effect!! Cause and Effect!!!

It is the consciousness back of the word which gives the word power. We have discussed this many times in this series. A good treatment is filled with a sense of the Divine Presence. This is the greatest power for neutralizing evil which has ever been discovered.

We turn deliberately from the pain, the sickness, the fear, the doubt, the lack, the limitation, the want, the uncertainty, and in every instance we turn to the exact opposite. The greater the negation being experienced, the more certain it is that the exact opposite is an exalted freedom. There are not two powers in the universe. A sense of good reverses a consciousness of evil and therefore obliterates the form which the consciousness of evil created. As our text says, the illusion is never in the thing but in the way we look at it.

When we are making a demonstration we should pay no attention to what happens in the objective world. It is sometimes hard to follow this because it is so easy to get caught in objective conditions, and because we are always surrounded by them, most of us are coerced by what we see, read about, listen to, and think. Yet all the time freedom is expressing itself to us in the terms of our bondage. Our very bondage is a misuse of our absolute freedom.

We work out every problem, then, by realizing that the answer already exists in the Absolute, and if we learn to judge not according to appearances but according to the conclusion that God is all there is and is ever available, then the difficulty will dissolve and in place of the problem will come a satisfying answer.

Summary

A large part of our mental reactions are in the realm of the unconscious. This realm of the unconscious includes the mind of the ages; what all people have believed throughout human history. All are influenced by this sum total of human thought, perhaps in a sense partially hypnotized or mesmerized.

Back of this race suggestion is the Universal Mind which has never been influenced by our thinking. We have to think our whole lives back to this original starting point.

The inner but largely unconscious field of our thought, which is the sum total of all our thinking, is the medium between the Absolute or Unconditioned cause and our own personal experiences. It is silently attracting or repelling at all times. When you change your thinking, you will change your external conditions because they automatically reflect the sum total of your thinking.

Each individual is a creative center in the consciousness of God, from which point he may think volitionally while the Law of Mind in Action reacts automatically.

Sometimes in practice the practitioner starts from the external appearance and works back to the Absolute, and other times he starts with the supposition that God is all there is and draws his conclusions from that basis.

A spiritual mind treatment is always a getting back to the original source. In doing this a person must turn from all objective conditions that deny what he affirms and speak from the standpoint of the Spiritual Center of things.

Questions

Brief answers to these questions should be written out by the student after studying the lesson, and the answers compared with those which will be included in next week's lesson.

1. What do we mean by combinations of thought producing definite results?

2. What is the meaning of: (a) Psychiatry; and (b) Psychoanalysis?
3. What do we mean by repressed emotions?
4. What does the psychoanalyst do?
5. What do we mean by unsublimated energy?
6. What do we mean by: (a) Mind in a conscious state; and (b) Mind in a subjective state?
7. What do we mean when we say that Mind in its conscious state can change the action of Mind in its subjective state?
8. What seems to be the aim of evolution?
9. What type of thought has the power to neutralize negative thought?
10. Why do we, in treatment, sometimes find it advantageous to analyze negative thought?
11. Why is Spirit neither caught nor bound by any form It takes?
12. What do we mean by saying that subjective decisions are merely conclusions?
13. How would we substitute a law of chance for one of certainty?
14. Does some other person's thought have more power than your own?
15. Where is the Secret Place of the Most High?
16. Why does thinking of weakness perpetuate weakness?
17. Why does the Infinite know no difference between a million dollars and a penny?
18. Is it the words used, or the consciousness back of them, which gives power to mental treatment?
19. What consciousness has the greatest healing power?

Answers to Questions on Lesson 24

1. The process of spiritual mind healing is the technique of consciously entertaining ideas for the purpose of helping oneself and others.
2. The theory upon which the technique of spiritual mind healing is based is that we are surrounded by a Universal Medium of Mind which reacts to our thought with mathematical precision.
3. The theory upon which the technique of spiritual mind healing is based applies to all cases of healing by prayer and faith, regardless of the age in which they happened or the religious system under whose sign they occurred. If there is a Universal Intelligence which responds mathematically to one It must respond to all.
4. We do not create the power of Mind because it has always existed. We need not coerce it, since it is always responsive to thought.
5. Disease, discord, and unhappiness in human experience do not imply two ultimate powers, but One Power which can be used in two different ways.
6. It is possible for an ignorant use of the Law of Freedom (which is the Law of Cause and Effect) to create bondage because all thought is creative.
7. There is but one basic Law of Mind, and if our ignorant use of It has produced bondage, a reversal of Its use must produce freedom. The Law that produces bondage also produces freedom.
8. In spiritual mind healing righteous judgment means that we should disregard what appears as experience and recognize the absolute perfection of the spiritual man.

9. We do not deny that there is sickness, unhappiness, or poverty in the world. We affirm, however, that these negative conditions are effects and not causes, and being effects can be changed by a reversal of thought.
10. In stating, "There is one Life, that Life is God," we should add, "That Life is my life now"; otherwise we have not consciously unified with this Life in our own thought.
11. By race suggestion we mean the sum total of the thought of the ages. This has also been called carnal mind, race belief, karma, and by some psychologists, the collective unconscious.
12. Race suggestion affects us by creating a tendency toward repeating in our personal experience what the sum total of human thought has declared to be the truth about the average man.
13. Race belief is not necessarily evil or limiting, since human thought has also embodied the idea of goodness, harmony, abundance, and the like.
14. A person's attitude toward race belief, karma, etc., should be that neither the stars, other men's thoughts, nor even his own previous thoughts, have any more power than he permits them to have. This is true because he knows that he consciously uses the Mind which creates all destiny.
15. We say that the more spiritual the thought, the more power it has, because spiritual thought embodies more of the nature of Reality; it has a greater faith in the omnipotence of Good.
16. Spiritual thought is no different from any other thought. It is merely a more constructive use of the law of thought.
17. When we say that the Principle of Mind works creatively and mathematically we mean: first, by creatively, that the Law tends to create conditions which correspond to our thought; second, by mathematically, we mean that the Law works with mechanical precision.
18. When we say, "When we command, that which follows is automatic," we mean that having sown the seed of thought in the Principle of Mind we can depend upon Its mechanical reaction to do the rest.
19. The first man to be healed is the practitioner, because unless he rises above the belief in his own mind that the patient must suffer, he will not neutralize the cause of his patient's suffering.
20. When a practitioner feels strain or fatigue as a result of giving mental treatments it is because he is either consciously or unconsciously trying to will, force, or coerce the Principle that heals.
21. Spiritual mind healing is neither magnetic nor hypnotic, nor is it some form of mental suggestion. It is not magnetic as though it were a physical emanation from one person to another; neither is it a transmission of thought as practiced in hypnosis or mental suggestion. It is the action of the Mind Principle upon the thought of the practitioner rather than the action of the practitioner's thought upon the patient. (This is the most important point in this entire science.)
22. One would treat for proper physical circulation by recognizing and realizing that the energy of pure Spirit circulates through one's patient.

The Story of the Lost Word

It is said that once each year, during the great celebration in the temple at Jerusalem, the high priest would stand on the temple steps and, amidst the shouting of the multitude, proclaim the sacred name of God, which was the word of power. But he spoke the name only when there was such a din that no one could hear it.

It is important for us to remember this part of Jesus' instructions, for really it is no different than saying: If you want a garden, plant one; bury the seed in the ground and nature will take over and produce the plant. It is as though God said to the hen: Sit on the egg and I will give you a chicken.

How wonderful to realize that the lost word has been found, and found in the only place that you and I could use it—in our own mouths. How wonderful to realize that at last we have located the Divine Presence at the only place we could recognize it—within ourselves, and within everything. And how wonderful it is to know that at last we have reached our goal.

But this does not mean that we have reached the end of all things. Really, this truth we have found but marks the beginning of a new day, a new experience, a new life—a life no longer distraught by fear or haunted by doubts or filled with regrets of the past or misgivings over the future—a life that can be lived in its fullness today, and a life that will extend through all our tomorrows in an ever broadening arena of experience, an ever deepening realization of a Presence and a Power and a Peace that gives us complete security and an ever greater vision of the more that is yet to come.

Living without Fear

Fear is the great enemy of man. It is impossible for a person to do his best if he is filled with anxiety. We are speaking about morbid fear, the type of fear that devitalizes us mentally, emotionally, and physically.

It is these morbid fears that we wish to rid ourselves of and not the ordinary caution that is necessary to intelligent living. For instance, a person standing on top of a high cliff would naturally exercise the caution of not getting too close to the edge. But if one has a dread of high places for fear he might fall or be seized with an irresistible impulse to jump, then he has a morbid fear of altitudes. And if we could trace this fear back to its original cause we might possibly find that sometime in a previous experience he has been threatened by someone who may have suggested that he would be thrown off the cliff.

Or take the case of a child shut in a dark closet for discipline. It might be that later in life, after the child has become an adult, he would have a morbid fear of being in closed places. This is called claustrophobia, which means a morbid dread of being shut away alone. In adult life the one who had been punished by being shut in a dark closet might find it emotionally impossible for him to be alone even in an ordinary room where there are plenty of exits.

They tell us that an infant has only two fears—the fear of loud noises and of falling; that all other fears must be acquired. It was never intended that we should go through life filled with fear, doubt, and uncertainty.

Perhaps this is why Jesus laid such great stress on our need for faith and why he told his followers that they should not be afraid of what was going to happen tomorrow. But rather, that they should live today in a sense of confidence and peace and joyful expectancy. When tomorrow comes it will take care of itself. Today is the only day in which we can live. For when tomorrow comes it will be another today, and so on through all eternity.

But unless we do live without fear today we shall dread tomorrow. Those who live in the dread of tomorrow generally live in the morbid thoughts of what happened yesterday. Their minds are filled with things that were unpleasant in their previous experience and the unhappy events that they fear will transpire in the future. The present day in which they live is robbed of all peace and joy, and becomes a torture chamber sandwiched between yesterday and tomorrow. This so disturbs the mind that restful sleep is impossible. Such people seldom rise in the morning filled with buoyant hope and joyful expectation, and the natural enthusiasm and zest for living which we all need if we are to get the most out of life.

Yesterday is forever past. We cannot relive it. No matter how we may regret what happened yesterday, it is impossible actually to live it over again, but too often in imagination we do live it over again and again, and in so doing bring all the misery of yesterday into today. Learn to forget yesterday. After having carefully gone over it and learned by our mistakes, the thing to do is to correct those mistakes and forgive ourselves for anything that we have done.

And we must learn to forgive others. This is not always the easiest thing to do but it can be done. If a person can be made to see that he must forgive in order to be healed of unhappiness, he generally will make an effort to do so.

We usually give people some affirmations or affirmative prayers that will help them to do this. And particularly we encourage them to affirm that tonight they will sleep in peace and wake in joy and live in a consciousness of good. We try to get them to feel that there is nothing in the universe seeking to harm them; that while we all have made mistakes there is no God of vengeance, no Divine Power that could will or wish harm toward anyone. We are the product of the universe; we are the offspring of the Divine Spirit; we are some part of Its life shaped and formed and acting as man, as an individual, as a person. And how could the great and Divine cause of our being seek to destroy or in any way harm that life which is the offspring of Its own being?

This whole morbid thought that there is some deific power that is always testing us to see how much we can stand, or always restricting us lest we fail to recognize its overlordship, is one of the great psychological crimes of the ages. It really is man against himself, but we have come to interpret it as though it were God operating against man; as though it were the Creator seeking to blot out His own creation.

The person who has learned to forgive himself, simply and directly, and who has come to believe that God eternally forgives, and who has learned to forgive all others, finally comes to a place where he knows that the Divine is for him and not against him. He reaches a place where he knows that love is the great reality.

If you want to get rid of fear you need not take the time to consider each separate fear you may have—the fear of people, the fear of things, the fear of conditions, the fear of yesterday, today, and tomorrow. For all these varying forms of fear are rooted in one fundamental negation; we do not know that we belong to the universe in which we live. We do not realize that God needs us or He would not have put us here.

While it is true that we can trace specific fears to certain incidents that transpired early in life, and while it is true that if we do this we can remove them, most fears finally resolve themselves into a very few attitudes of mind, most of which are based on the belief that no one wants me, needs me, or loves me; that probably I am unworthy, unnecessary, and useless; that I am inadequate to meet life, I have not the strength or the power or the will to overcome obstructions, and I do not fit anywhere.

Most of our fears can be traced to these unconscious attitudes of mind which rise from our repressed desires to live more abundantly, and our inward sense of inferiority because we are uncertain of the future.

Well, the way to get rid of fear is through the cultivation of faith; a faith founded on the thought that God is all there is. If we learn to see God in people, in circumstances and situations, we shall find Him—*Seek, and ye shall find*. When we turn in complete confidence, with a simple, childlike trust and faith, to Life Itself, It will always respond to us.

It does not matter what the history of any evil experience may have been, or how long we may have harbored fear or resentment or doubt. In the very moment when we turn from it, it will depart from us. You see, eternity is here and now. God is everywhere. The Divine Spirit is in every person. And the movement of the Law of Good is in all human events. We alone block our good, and we alone can reaffirm it. We alone can readjust our lives to a new way of thinking until all our patterns of thought are changed.

In doing this we shall be making the best bargain we have ever made, for we shall be swapping fear for faith, doubt for certainty, hell for heaven. It is destined that we shall all do this, sooner or later, so why delay the day of our freedom from fear? This is the day that we should accept that Kingdom which is forever given. This is the day that we should get complete clearance from all of our yesterdays. This is the day that God has made. Let us be glad in it.

Meditation

Today shall contain joy and happiness; shall be filled with peace, and through it all there will be running the silent power of spiritual force, that which harmoniously and happily governs our thoughts and decisions and acceptances, so that everything will be done without effort.

So we lay all weariness aside and accept the life-giving, invigorating, dynamic power of the Spirit, knowing that it vitalizes every organ of our body, it flows with power and strength and purpose through everything we do, even as it leads us gently down the pathway at life.

Today is the day that God has made, and we are glad in it. And when the evening time comes, the cool shadows of peace shall fall across our pathway and the quiet of the night shall enter into our souls, the beatitude of the Spirit shall flow through us as a river of life. We shall sleep in peace, and wake in joy, and live in a consciousness of good, for God is over all, in all, and through all.

Practical Suggestion for Mental Treatment

Treatment and Feeling

That which is felt cannot be taught, while that which is taught may be felt. This is one of the most vital things in mental and spiritual science. A treatment has no power unless it has a meaning to the one who gives it, just as we know that a public speaker cannot convey a message which he himself does not understand.

If we wish to convey a message we must feel it, just as the musician feels the atmosphere of harmony back of his technique. Yet technique is equally necessary in order that he may give definite form to his feeling.

The practitioner recognizes the whole condition as a thing of thought, and in his own mind straightens out this thought about his patient. In so doing he reveals the eternal harmony back of the negative appearance. The straightening out of thought is technique. It may be taught, analyzed, taken apart, and put together again. It consists of words, phrases, thoughts, ideas, all of which are understandable, teachable, and learnable.

The essence of the treatment, the feeling which the practitioner has, his interior sense of the Divine Allness, of that Spirit which is closer to him than his own breath—this cannot be put into words, this cannot be taught. It can only be felt.

By using right words, statements, and phrases, and dwelling upon their subtle meaning, one may come to feel the meaning back of the words.

What Must Be Felt

What is it that must be felt in spiritual practice, the feeling which is beyond words, statements, and phrases? It is the *essence* of Life, the *Spirit* of the thing from which the mind automatically draws an intellectual conclusion. This feeling results in words which are an activity of the feeling, the enforcement of the Principle back of it. In this way the word becomes Spirit and life.

The practitioner assumes that the Truth is all there is; hence all appearances of evil are but wrong interpretations of the Truth. They are not the Truth in reverse, neither need we consider them as opposites to the Truth because the Truth has no opposites. Negation is a false statement of the Truth, a false belief about the Truth.

Treatment corrects the wrong use through its right knowing. Right knowing is an intelligent activity of mind which plunges beneath the surface and reveals Pure Spirit as the Invisible Cause of creation. The words that a practitioner uses should imply a feeling which lifts him above the appearance he wishes to change.

The practitioner makes a series of statements about the Truth. The feeling that he has must be that the Truth is all there is, and he must sense that the words that he speaks are the enforcement of this allness. Hence he must feel something which cannot be merely stated in words; he must feel the allness of his treatment, not as mental suggestion but as spiritual realization.

In such degree as he does sense this allness, his word will have power.

Treatment for the Sensitive Person

Fear and faith are identical mental attitudes. The energy used in the one is the same energy as that used in the other, since there is but one final Energy in the universe, and this final Energy is an energy of Spirit. Fear is a positive acceptance that we shall experience that which we dislike. Faith is a positive acceptance that we shall experience that which we do like. But they are identical in their mental content. The difference is in the direction.

We should not fight fear, but should convert fear into faith. If we realize that it is a mental attitude we can do this very easily. Looking at the thing which we fear and examining it carefully, let us convert this fear thought into one of faith, realizing that the energy of fear converted into faith will produce an opposite effect.

By way of illustration we might take a person who is afraid of being misunderstood. He is very sensitive and shuns human contacts. He must convert the energy of this fear into faith. Using the same energy he must declare that people now understand him, that no one misunderstands him, that everyone loves him, everyone desires his presence.

If he will look at the thing he is afraid of until he understands it, it will no longer have any element of fear for him. He can do this in such degree as he is conscious of perfection, and he must be actively conscious of perfection. He must state this consciousness of perfection in a definite manner.

The River of Life

Someone has said, *There is a river of life, clear as crystal, flowing through the body of humanity, uniting every part into one great being in Christ.* Jesus spoke of the well of water, from which if a man drank he should never thirst again. Throughout the Bible we have this simile of water, typifying the flowing power of pure Spirit. It is impossible to think of Spirit as being anything solid. It is always fluid.

In line with this thought it is interesting to note that modern physics has theoretically resolved all physical form into lines of energy, and these lines of energy must be directed by some intelligence or they would never take definite form. Therefore we say that the River of Life forever flowing through us is ever ready and willing to take the form which we give it.

It appears that we have the ability, at least temporarily, to pollute this Stream of Life with the consciousness of hate, despair, or any negative thought which denies its purity. But of course we do not really have the power to destroy, only to mold and remold.

It is fortunate indeed that this is true. For in spite of all our misdirection we are still being carried forward on the bosom of this Infinite to a harbor of perfect safety. We may rest in absolute assurance that good will be the final goal of all things.

We can hasten the advent of this good by definitely clarifying our thought and by daily meditating upon the invisible Source, the wellspring of Life within each one of us.

No Limitation or Compromise

Office of the Dean

My Dear Friend,
As our lesson states, we should place no limit on the possibility of our use of the Mind Principle. This of course is because we are in It and Its Law is operating through us. It is this Mind Principle that was in the background of Ralph Waldo Emerson's thought when he wrote the most beautiful series of spiritual essays ever written.

Emerson was, as you know, a New Englander, living in Concord, Massachusetts. He was trained for the Unitarian Ministry, but even at that time was too liberal to occupy the pulpit. Today he would be accepted in many churches. That he was the greatest intellectual thinker of modern times there is no doubt.

Emerson had the advantage of studying the great thoughts of the ages. He was thoroughly familiar with the great philosophers preceding him, and he had a mind equipped to understand their messages. For instance he said that there were but few people in any age who could understand Plato, but that to those few the works of Plato were brought as though God placed them in their hands.

It seems to us that our exposition of the persistent spiritual philosophy that has run throughout the ages would be incomplete without including Emerson, and so in this and in our next lesson we have added a commentary on Emerson's Essays on *History* and on *Spiritual Laws*, two of his most widely read essays. Please remember that they are but one person's opinion. We hope that you will enjoy them.

Sincerely,
Ernest Holmes

Lesson 26

Page 188 to the top of page 193

We should not limit the Principle of Mind. We should place no bounds to the availability of the mental Law and Its willingness to respond to us. We should realize that Its willingness is made necessary by the very nature of Its own being. Subjective Law cannot refuse to respond to us. Therefore we should not limit the possibility of our use of the Law. We should realize that It will work for us under all circumstances.

At the top of page 600 a more complete explanation of the use of the imagination and will is set forth. Imagination is the power of the word, while will directs this power for specific purposes. Through the right use of will and imagination man directs the creative agency along the lines of his own self-determination. If this were not true, man would not be an individual. The fact of individuality discloses this truth.

To learn to control our thought is to learn how to control destiny. It is to learn how to have destiny created for us, because the all-productive Law knowing nothing of lack, knowing only Its ability to perform, can as easily give us that which we call big as that which we call little. Big and little are in our own thought.

It is written that the law of the Lord is perfect and that perfect love casts out all fear. Turn to page 522 for a Meditation on Love and on Law. In this perfect Law of the Lord we have immediate access to the only Power there is; to that Power from which all things come and in whose mighty grasp all things are eternally held—the Power that binds all things together in one unitary wholeness. Mighty as is this Power, It is ours to use. However, to control one's thought is a high calling, and to find right patterns for thought is to be inspired from on High.

If you will turn again to the passage, *A Pattern for Thought* on page 496, which we discussed in Lesson 15, you will note that we are to think on those things which are of good report. We are to think on the positive rather than the negative, on the good rather than the evil. This is what is meant by the control of thought.

To learn to abide in peace is to know how to control one's thought, for peace *is* the power at the heart of God (page 444). This power comes to us through a recognition of our unity with the Whole. The search for the solution of the riddle of life, which is the great search referred to on page 445, finds its answer when the soul becomes peaceful, poised, and forever expectant of good. To achieve this end one deliberately turns away from everything that hurts, and with uplifted vision gazes steadfastly at the object of one's desire rather than its opposite.

No one can live for us; this we must do for ourselves. We cannot live by proxy. Each in his own way individualizes the Universal, outpictures through his own imagination the creative power of thought, and consciously or unconsciously creates the destiny which appears as his fate. Turn to page 593 for a definition of *Fate*.

Fate implies a predestined course one is compelled to follow, while the Karmic Law, which is the Law of Cause and Effect, implies a certain use of a natural law. Of course we do not believe in fate, but we do believe in Cause and Effect. Read again the definition of *Cause* on page 578 and *Effect* on page 588.

Be sure not to confuse the Karmic Law or the Law of Cause and Effect with Fate or with the Eastern concept of Kismet. To be a fatalist is to be already lost in one's imagination. If you think that you are controlled by any external force whatsoever, whether it be planets or peanuts, immediately disabuse your consciousness of this contradiction of the Universal Good and remember the saying, *Look unto me and be ye saved all the ends of the earth*. Only in this way can your words be as effective as were the words of Jesus.

Reality is more than an intellectual perception. It is more than merely a mathematical proposition. It is something that touches the very depth of our feeling, for who can analyze life or catch the infinite beauty in his finite grasp? That which we feel is greater than that which we do. Thus the creative arts have outlived the rise and fall of empires. Thus the thoughts of Jesus and Plato, of Moses and Aristotle, come down to us as though God Himself brought them. Somewhere along the line our intellectual perceptions must become *interior realizations*. We all have an interior awareness through which we intuitively know the Truth, just as we know that we are alive. This inner knowingness must be directed by the intellect for definite purposes.

When it comes to treatment you must know without doubting that as a result of your mental work some action takes place. Infinite Mind is the actor and you the one who uses Infinite Mind. As Browning said, *'Tis Thou, God, that givest; 'tis I who receive*. When the question arises in your mind, "Can I do this or can I not do it?" say, "Who is doing it, anyway?" Turn to the Divine within and think until you realize that you are some part of the Universe. It is not you but the indwelling Spirit, and to this Spirit be all power, all glory, all honor forever, Amen.

All of our searching after salvation must finally reach its climax in the one and only sure salvation, namely, the knowledge that there is no need of salvation; that *all that the Father hath is* ours. No one condemns us but ourselves and no one saves us but ourselves. Mind is the actor; you are the announcer. Go straight back to Principle and speak from It; not from the isolated sense of a confused personality but from a sense of the all-inclusive. Know that behind the words which you speak there is a Power which is perfect.

Turn to page 496 and read the second paragraph, *This Mind is God working in and through us*. If we would have access to the Power which Jesus used, we must acquire the Mind which he had, which is the Mind of Christ. To have the Mind of Christ is to have a conscious sense of unity with the Whole. The Spirit that raised Jesus, referred to on page 484, is the same Spirit which animates our thought, while the love referred to on page 476 as the central flame of the Universe must be the impulsion back of all spiritual mind healing.

We should approach our mental work without fear, with a certain amount of awe but with no superstition, knowing that the Law responds immediately and definitely, and that we have access to the only Power. First we must clear our own vision. Turn to page 435 under the heading, *Self-Healing Must Come First of All*. This means that the practitioner must clear his own thought before he begins to treat his patient. Therefore the starting point of all correct spiritual mind healing is to realize our unity with God, our oneness with the All-Power, the immediate availability of the Law, and the absolute necessity of Its responding to us.

As stated in the third paragraph on page 398, when we treat we should always be specific. *Treatment is a definite thing*. It is always given in a conscious state of thought. On page 381, the last paragraph, and the top of page 382 you will find a discussion of the thought that we must never lose a self-conscious state of mind. We must always be in complete control of any situation. We cannot be self-directive unless we are self-conscious, and we cannot be fully self-conscious while we believe that any influence, in the flesh or out of it, is controlling our thought. The only control we need to feel is that of the inner Self, the Christ.

Refer to the Meditation at the top of page 543, called *Whose Right It Is to Come*. You will find some very helpful thoughts on this subject. We are to be controlled only by the Spirit and we are to know that as a result of a treatment something really happens, for a treatment is the Power and the Presence of God acting through us in accordance with perfect Law.

We should be careful not to compromise with evil, lack, limitation, doubt, or fear. As our text tells us on page 189, we must be able to look a fact in the face and know that it is not fate. Emerson said that all facts are fluid; for there is one universal Law which controls all facts and that Law is the Law of Mind in action. We are using this Law when we give a treatment. When we speak the word for the healing of some person the Law at once sets about to produce the desired results.

We must not compromise with any undesired fact of experience. We must see beyond the fact to that which creates facts, to the Maker of all facts. There is no fact which cannot be changed. There is no fate which cannot be remolded. There is no appearance which cannot be made to disappear. What we see is always an effect of the Invisible. It is always a temporary form. The Spirit does not change, Reality *cannot* change, Truth cannot change, but facts of experience can change. It is this eternal change and rearrangement of facts which constitutes the play of Life upon Itself, the drama of human existence and the self-conscious expression of the Divine. The Truth Knows no opposites. Truth produces freedom. As our textbook says, *The results rest in the Eternal Law of Good* (page 189).

On page 190 is the statement that people have been healed throughout the ages through prayer and faith. This is because the belief of the one praying permits the Law to respond in a constructive way. The highest form of prayer or communion is a deep inner recognition of the omnipotence of Good, which we call the Presence of God. The more spiritual the consciousness, that is, the more exalted, the more power the prayer or treatment has. This again is Cause and Effect. But no matter how elevated the thought or how spiritual the consciousness, the Law of Cause and Effect can never be destroyed. We merely reverse our position in It. The position is reversed simultaneously with the change of thought.

The belief of the person praying decides to what extent his prayer is answered. To change one's belief and to substitute a better belief is a healing process. This is what a mental practitioner does. He treats to know that his patient is free from fear, from the sense of lack, pain, and limitation. He works to know that his patient's consciousness is a part of God and is whole. He seeks to uncover the spiritual man. As our text asserts in the second paragraph of page 191, man's freedom from sickness and trouble will come as he discovers his true identity, the meaning of Christ within him, the Truth about himself. *He that hath seen me hath seen the Father.*

In such degree as we reveal the real man we are realizing the Divine Presence, and as we realize the Divine Presence we are healed. Hence in practical application we learn to substitute positive thoughts for negative ones. In practice we resolve the objective condition into its subjective cause and by using statements, affirmations, denials, and realizations we build up a consciousness of the new idea, a conviction of greater certainty, a greater receptivity to Good, a higher faith. We state definitely that God is the only Power, Presence, or Principle there is; God is now in this man whom we are seeking to help, and as our text says (page 480), *believing in the Father, which is God, and in the son, which is ourselves, we shall receive. In this way, the Father is glorified in the Son.*

Turn again to the section on *Mental Expansion* on pages 489-90, discussed in Lesson 7, and refresh your mind with the idea that the image of God is imprinted upon each one of us. Also page 488, *The Law of*

God Is One of Liberty, which was discussed in Lesson 7. Bring all of these ideas together and immediately begin to treat someone, for the ideal must be made real through its practical application.

Sense the Divine Perfection in your patient, claim it, proclaim it, announce it, reaffirm it, believe in it, expect it to appear, know that everything unlike this Divine image is eliminated. In this way we become doers of the word and not hearers only. Review again the thought at the top of page 476. *The word has power only as it is one with Power*, which means that in exact proportion as we are conscious of the power of our word, to that degree our word is powerful. This again is Cause and Effect, invariable and immutable.

In the last paragraph of page 398 under the General Summary, the suggestion is made that we may grow in spiritual understanding. There can be no greater Allness than the Divine Allness, and it is this Divine Allness which we seek to realize in spiritual mind healing. It was a consciousness of this Divine Allness which gave Jesus his power through the spoken word. That word is already incarnate within each one of us. Each is surrounded by the subjective Law, which is the Silent Partner in every man's life. And each is also surrounded by the Universal Spirit, which is the source of all inspiration.

As stated in the paragraph at the bottom of page 347 and the first paragraph on page 348, the individual subjective mind is merely our use of the Law of the One Mind. We have discussed this over and over again, but it will stand much repetition. We are our own law whether or not we are conscious of the fact. If we have been thinking of ourselves in a limited way, isolated from good, separated from God, apart from harmony which is heaven, then we must reverse this order of thought. Never forget it is the Spirit which knows and the Law which obeys.

We have no objection whatever to any form of healing, for whatever destroys pain and human suffering is certainly good, and as such it is Divine. As mental practitioners we are dealing with a mental field, with the field of thought, of emotion, and of spiritual realization. Of necessity, we must confine ourselves to our own sphere.

But we should never think of denying the good which may come from any other field. All is good that does good, and humanity needs every aid and assistance it can possibly find. Our particular field is that of mental actions and reactions. We should joyously cooperate with any group which permits such cooperation, clearly recognizing the good they do, and refrain from criticizing any who refuse to cooperate with us. We judge not that we be not judged. We condemn not that we be not condemned.

Turn again to page 433 for a discussion of judgment. We should meet every man where we find him and we should also realize that every man's spiritual conviction is necessary for him or he would not have it. There is no reason why we should not cooperate with all forms of healing and all forms of religious belief provided they permit it, but where anyone refuses such co-partnership we should turn aside without condemnation, without any sense of sadness. Sooner or later that which is built upon a deep spiritual perception of Reality will no longer be hidden from the view of all men.

The highest form of mental healing is spiritual healing. The two should never be divorced. Therefore we must increasingly come to believe in the unity of good. Every treatment, as our text suggests (page 192),

10. In treatment we sometimes find it advantageous to analyze negative thought in order to know what affirmative mental statements we should make.
11. Spirit is in the realm of causation; form is in the realm of effect. Spirit, being Infinite, can create one form as easily as another.
12. By saying that subjective decisions are merely conclusions we mean that it is impossible for the subjective mind or Law to make any decisions at all. It is compelled by Its very nature to accept as a conclusion that which the conscious thought decides.
13. We substitute a law of chance for one of certainty by using the Law of Mind consciously and definitely, rather than unconsciously and chaotically.
14. One person's thought has as much power as another's provided he speaks with the same conviction and with an equal sense of his oneness with Power.
15. The Secret Place of the Most High is the center of man's thought.
16. Thinking of weakness perpetuates weakness, because any type of thought reproduces its kind.
17. The Infinite knows no difference between a million dollars and a penny because, being Infinite, It knows only that It is. Man's relative interpretation of It knows size. See definitions of *Space* and *Form*, Textbook Glossary.
18. It is the consciousness of what a person means by his words which gives them power in mental treatment.
19. A consciousness of the Divine Presence and Perfection made manifest has the greatest healing power.

A Commentary on Ralph Waldo Emerson's Essay on History

There is no great and no small
To the Soul that maketh all:
And where it cometh, all things are;
And it cometh everywhere.

The Universal Spirit knows neither great nor small. It is not comparative; It creates all and is present in all; all things are dear to the heart of Being; It is as manifest in the wayside flower as in a system of planets. The Infinite is not big in one place and little in another, but is equally distributed, omnipresent, ever available. It is both cause and effect—both creator and that which is created.

Emerson starts his essay on history with this bold declaration: *There is one mind common to all individual men*. The mind of God and the mind of man is one and the same. Somewhere in the cryptic depths of human nature the Divine Mind reveals Itself. This Mind is the one real agent behind all human endeavor, stimulating all individual thought.

Of the works of this mind history is the record. History is the Universal Mind as the individual life. History is an objective manifestation of subtle subjective and spiritual causes. The cause is hidden, the effect is obvious.

All the facts of history pre-exist in the mind as laws. The creative impulse is spiritual while its manifestation is always in accord with law. Behind the facts of history is the impulse of the Spirit emerging through law and order. Since every man's mind is rooted in the Infinite, the Universal Mind is to be interpreted to him through him, and in no other way.

This human mind wrote history, and this must read it. The Sphinx must solve her own riddle. The Mind which stimulated the acts of antiquity is the same Mind which is stimulating our present acts; It merges through all; It embraces all ages, encompasses all periods, is present at all times—uncreated It creates—unformed It gives form—unborn It gives birth; each hour of our day is an hour of Its day. The Universal Law which holds everything in place is the government of this Mind.

Of the universal mind each individual man is one more incarnation. All its properties consist in him. Every man contains the Divine properties. All are patterned after the Original Creative Genius. All are Divine by nature, not by choice.

It is through the unity of all minds with the One Mind that we are to interpret history. This interpretation is possible because there is within us the same motive that has stimulated other men's thought. We understand their motives through an understanding of our own mental reactions to life. We read the story of our own impulses in Solomon and Cataline. All human laws find their origin and ultimate reason for being in the Universal Mind. Hence the laws of justice and righteousness do not change, though we may reinterpret them, each in his own tongue. We understand what others have done because there is something in us akin to others, no matter in what age they may have lived. The Power which stimulates the poet, the artist, and the artisan is ours. We are at home with all people by reason of the Mind common to all men.

All that Shakespeare says of the king, yonder slip of a boy that reads in the corner feels to be true of himself. Of the infinite variety of characterizations possible to the Universal Mind, Shakespeare was a masterful interpreter, able to place himself in a thousand different lights before the One Animating Intelligence that It might personify Itself through innumerable forms for him. The boy, as he reads, instinctively senses himself in these characterizations. He enters into the play because the play has already entered into him. That which another wrote now emerges through him.

Mind knows no great, no small, no yesterday, no tomorrow. Since It is forever present, and is the Mind common to all men, *all the facts of history pre-exist in the mind as laws.* Emerson tells us, *the blow was struck for us.* The rich man reveals the opulence of our own being; the philosopher plumbs a deep in our own souls; nature gives us back to ourselves. Emerson felt the unity of all, the oneness of the Universal Spirit with the individual soul; he sensed the invisible tie that binds all to all.

The student is to read history actively and not passively—he should not think of history as a story of past events only, but as an active experience in his present life; it is a picture drawn for him, a movement created for his amusement. The stage setting is the world. Man creates the play, assumes the leading role, and at the same time is his own audience.

The crowning of a king, the laying of a cornerstone, and the building of a cottage are of like importance to the Cosmic Mind. We perceive the significance of others' acts only through a true appreciation of our own. The most trivial act which expresses the individual life has as deep a significance as the creation of an empire. Emerson gives a supreme importance to the individual life. A man must be conscious of his own worth; he must know that his place in the universal scheme of things is essential to its expression. Without man, God would be incomplete.

The world exists for the education of each man. Psychology teaches that our subjective reactions encompass the entire history of the human race; that our contact with the race mind is a tremendous influence in our lives. Emerson sensed that something about man which encompasses all ages. Thus to every man does it *abbreviate itself and yield its own virtue to him.* He must know that he is greater than the vast panorama of human existence and experience, whether he thinks of experience as extended into the past, unfolding through the present, or penetrating into the future.

The human drama is interior, never external; our appreciation of these interior facts constitutes the only validity they can have for us. We transcend them all. From this viewpoint alone can these facts *yield their secret sense.* The facts themselves are fluid.

History already is a stream merged with the ocean of life; it is rain mingled with the wave. The essential worth of any fact finds true significance in a combination of all facts, thus creating new tendencies toward greater accomplishments. As history is *but a fable agreed upon*, so present facts will soon melt into the general landscape of human experiences, each significant but not too important.

The perspective of eternity alone satisfies. Eternity alone encompasses all facts, is the melting pot of all experiences—the creator of all, it is the principle animating all. Creator and creation are one. God and man are one. Emerson says, *The genius and creative principle of each and all eras I can find in my own mind.* We shall misunderstand him completely unless we realize that he felt himself to be a projection of the Original Mind. To him the *human* is more than an *impersonation* of the Divine—*it is the Divine.*

All history becomes subjective; in other words, there is properly no History; only Biography. History is more than an external fact; it marks the evolution of personality. What we cannot see, know, and experience, we cannot understand. We feel historic events emerging through our own impulses, the result of our own passion. It is the history of our own lives; the facts only are external; they are already subjective in our being.

When the facts of history fit nicely into some niche in our own minds we understand their meaning. If we could remove the mask from the face of Sir Thomas More, The Reign of Terror, or the fanatic Revival, we should see things standing as proxies to ourselves. The soul encompasses all experiences, impersonates all characters, institutes all religions, and creates all governments. We stand on the mountaintop and descend into hell by the natural affinity of our own souls. We are both saint and sinner, the savior and the condemned.

Emerson is speaking of the Universal Mind incarnated alike in each; being a subjective unit It remains true to Its own nature even though incarnated in innumerable personalities. The thread of Its being runs in an unbroken stream of consciousness through our mentalities—each in all and all in each.

We have, as it were, been the man that made the minister. Our inquiries into antiquity are for the purpose of transposing the there and then into the here and now. The there and then, the here and the now, are alike to the Mind that stretches into the past, comprehends the present, and measures the possibilities of the future. The mind stands still while all movement takes place within it. Antiquity reveals what we might have done; current events portray our present states of thought; the possibility of the future is already inherent in our imagination.

We are satisfied when we uncover the ego. We find that all people have acted as we act. *The problem is then solved.* As our thought merges through appreciation of others into their environment and into the emotions stimulating their act, we understand the meaning of those acts. Moreover, we realize that each act was necessary for the occasion, adequate for the time, and justified by the necessity of the case.

Religion, poetry, art, philosophy, science, invention, the minister and his congregation, Jesus, the Church and image worship, all reveal the eloquent soul expressing itself through multiform practices. Looking deep into our own nature, *we have the sufficient reason.*

The progress of the intellect consists in the clearer vision of causes, which overlooks surface differences. While the intellect remains on the surface of life viewing dissociated facts and measuring differences of opinion, it fails to penetrate the unitary cause, the thread of beauty running through all. To the man whose vision penetrates through externals all things become holy—*all men divine.*

All have one common origin in the *one mind common to all individual men*; unity passes into multiplicity that the One may be expressed through the many. Every man's life is divine at the root. The philosophic problem of the One and the many is solved when we understand that the many emerge from the One. Infinite potentiality produces limitless variations of Itself; the cause is generic, the expression individual, but since all effect is rooted in one cause, unity runs through variety binding all together in one common wholeness.

Genius studies the casual thought. Emerson sees through the hard fact into the *soft and fluid.* Nature is hard fact; its cause is a fluidic presence, solidifying into definite form for the purpose of self-expression. The fact is transitory, the fluid eternal. Time is but a measure of eternity melting at each end into the backward flow of the past and into the onward flow of the future. The present is but a point in this eternal flow.

In the attempt to place our finger on the hard fact of the present we find the flow of an invisible cause already moving the present into the past and introducing the future. The finger points to one place, the flow knows no place, no time—only being. Man places the time, as with events, and *far back in the womb of things sees the rays parting from one orb.*

Nature wears a mask which, could it be lifted, would reveal the central principle forever the same—*through countless individuals*. Through all the variations of nature runs *the eternal unity*, the everlasting will and purpose of the universe, the omnipresent good. Half concealed, nature reveals herself through an inner sense which all have but few use.

The mask is lifted, the many melt into the One, the One emerges through the many. The vast panorama of human existence, all types, all species of the kingdoms of organized life, fuse together in one stupendous whole. Identity and form remain, yet constantly change and evolve. A thing is never twice alike. Creation is a constant process impelled by a continuous urge, propelled by a dynamic power, and held in place through an Infinite will and purpose and an immutable law.

There is at the surface infinite variety of things; at the centre there is simplicity and unity of cause. As an individual can imagine innumerable situations and still maintain the integrity of his individuality, so the Unitary Cause never departs from the simplicity of oneness even though It passes into a variety of forms.

The psychology of any people is revealed in their art, literature, and government. The psychology of one age bears a likeness to that of another. *Nature ... hums the old well-known air through innumerable variations.*

It is the spirit and not the fact that is identical. If all facts were identical, nature would become a monotony without variation, the unity would be bored by its own sameness, and life would be unbearable. It is the spirit which is identical; the fact is a passing fancy. Our emotions may change and the shifting scenes of time flow on into newer and greater experiences, into diversified results and accomplishments, but always the soft presence of the interior spirit reveals its identity.

While we never appear to be the same in any two instances, we are never other than the same. The Eternal thing within us which is God is the *chain of affinity* revealing us to ourselves. A universal theme runs through all literature. The naturalist melts into the tree, the lover of animals finds a communion of soul with them, the geologist reads in the rocks an identity with himself, and the artist awakens to self-revelation through his art.

Common souls pay with what they do; nobler souls with that which they are. Being is greater than becoming. We sense in great and noble souls an interior source, an inner calm which comes to them through constant communion with the Universal Spirit. The presence of beauty bespeaks its own loveliness. It is not alone through external acts that man is revealed; he is truly revealed when the actor melts into the act, when action becomes an eloquent gesture of the immovable soul.

In the man, could we lay him open, we should see the sufficient reason. Emerson based his philosophy on the theory that life flows from within. He says, *It is in the soul that architecture exists*. The true poem is the poet's mind. The subjective state of man's thought decides the tendency of his objective experience, sets a gauge to the possibility of his achievement, and controls his destiny.

The soul is the medium between the Absolute and the relative. Everything begins with an idea. Emerson draws no line between the word of God and the word of man. He believes the difference is not in essence but in degree. Could we lay a man open, we should find a subjective imagery exactly balancing his objective accomplishments.

The Original Architect dwells in nature. Our patterns are instinctively drawn from her mind, but since the two minds are one we need not leave the precincts of our own thought in drawing from the deeper reservoir. The Creator is forever passing into creation, Being is forever in a process of becoming.

The trees have souls, the Intelligence which creates the forest and the flower builds the temple—*a blossoming in stone*. Nature individualizes herself. The Divine passes into the most commonplace object. *The mountain of granite blooms into an eternal flower*. The whole theme is unity in variety—variety within unity.

All public facts are to be individualized, all private facts are to be generalized. The race is composed of individuals. The race acting as a whole is a generalization of individual minds. The individual acting as a unit is an individualization of the race mind. All are rooted in the fundamental unit. To interpret the stream of consciousness running through human events is to understand history. Individual biography is understood, the motives and incentives of personal action, when we link the individual stream of consciousness with the collective and the universal streams.

The insistent demand of nature arouses our curiosity, stimulates us to accomplishment and pushes us from one position into another with an irresistible demand. Unity must pass into variety. All nature is unified at the center. The man who is *en rapport* with her finds a table spread before him in the wilderness, is at home on the sea, has fellowship with the forest and *everywhere falls into easy relationship with his fellowmen.*

Everything the individual sees without him corresponds to his states of mind. We search in catacombs and libraries that we may discover the self. We are the Greek, else we could not understand him. We have already passed through the whole category of human experience.

Emerson speaks of the *strict unity with the body*. The spiritual nature referred to is the invisible prototype of the human form, having the eyes which cannot squint and a body shapely and symmetrical in form. This body the Greeks reveal in their sculpture.

Bard or hero cannot look down on the word or gesture of a child. It is as great as they. Because the child acts instinctively from natural causes he acts truly. Emerson was always searching for the instinctive act in man, the primordial genius, the Original Creative Cause. His admiration was not for the antique but for the natural. *A great boy, a great girl, with good sense, is a Greek*. The simplicity of naturalness draws the veil before the fact of antiquity, melting all times into one common eternity, into one universal identity.

We measure time not in Egyptian years but through experience; the same incentive runs through the ages. Periods of time, destinies of nations, the achievement of individuals, the triumph and defeat of societies all merge and find an outlet through every man's mind, only to flow on into ages still unborn, into the eternal sea of never-ending existence.

When we understand Plato we can converse with him. When we understand the mind common to all individuals, language becomes universal, time is not, all periods flow to one center which our own soul individualizes.

I see that men of God have always, from time to time, walked among men. All are incarnations of the Original Spirit but some have penetrated more deeply than others into their own natures. These *disclose to us new facts in nature*. The man who reveals us to ourselves inspires us. The man who discovers himself has power to inspire the *soul of the commonest hearer*. We cannot unite great souls like Jesus with the history of sensuality or materiality, for material history as a whole has not penetrated the same depth, has not dipped so deeply into the Infinite.

The Infinite is still accessible through the finite and the day comes in the evolution of our own consciousness when *our own piety explains every fact, every word* which Jesus uttered. The instinctive desire to worship or to commune with the true Spirit is alike in ancient and modern. As the mind penetrates spiritual causes, objective differences disappear, and the unity which remains unites Moses, Zoroaster, and Socrates with our own minds. They no longer belong to antiquity and each man can say, *They are mine as much as theirs.*

The priestcraft of the East and West, of the Magian, Brahmin, Druid, and Inca, is expounded in the individual's private life. Religion is a universal sentiment. We are one with all its forms because we are universal. There is neither East nor West for the soul. Our own private lives and inward emotions explain the passion and performance of every other man' s life. The religious emotion should not be stifled too much by the intellect.

The child finds himself tyrannized over by the *cramping influence of a hard formalist*. The grown man discovers that the formalist is himself tyrannized over by his own fears. The child has become a man, the man is still a child.

Through generations of misconception we trace the cause of profane worship. Having traced this cause to its original source the road leads again to our own door—to superstition, to fear, and to misunderstanding, the foundation of which false structure is built on the cornerstone of dualism.

How many times in the history of the world has the Luther of the day had to lament the decay of piety in his own household! Luther illustrates every man's life. The lips proclaim that which the heart does not feel; the intellect announces that which the soul rejects, and our everyday life too often contradicts our spiritual aspirations.

A man is complete when he strikes a balance between his intellectual and spiritual qualities. We hedge ourselves about with misrepresentations, with superstitions and fears. Emerson's great theme is, lay bare the soul, loose the spirit, find the cause, be yourself, live the life, and trust in the integrity of the universe.

Universal man wrote by his pen a confession true for one and true for all. This refers to generic man. It has a meaning identical with the Christ spoken of in the New Testament, and in modern metaphysical terminology is referred to as the perfect or the God-intended man.

A great literature bears some relation to and in some way reveals this Invisible Presence, this spiritual completeness. When we look deep into the soul we have experiences which transcend mere intellectual deductions. From such inner communing follow our highest outward actions. The soul reveals wonders undreamt of by the intellect. As the soul awakes the intellect, man *verifies them with his own head and hands.* The inner impulse seeks to become objectified. The head and hands are instruments of the soul. The law of thought association and correspondences is always at work.

True imagination is not fanciful daydreaming. True imagination is fire from heaven. We must distinguish between the idle caprice of the mind and intuition, between reality and hallucination. Many fables were based on intuitive perceptions of truth and were prophetic; they foreknew and foresaw much that was to happen in the further evolution of the race through the arts and sciences, government and religion.

The soul beholds these eternal truths in their unified beauty—the adoration of them is spontaneous and worship becomes an interior communion rather than an external act. External worship is crude and mechanical, *the obligation of reverence is onerous.*

The fire from heaven is the candle of the Lord burning on the individual altar in the sanctuary of our own souls; it is never independent of the Original Flame. *Every man is a divinity in disguise, a god playing the fool.* Man is a divine being wearing a mask—largely unconscious of his own divinity, occasionally awakened by some flash of consciousness which temporarily reveals the self to the self and proclaims the eternal incarnation of a son begotten of the only God.

At such times man's language is divine and his music celestial. When the shroud of separation falls like a black mantle over his shoulders, his eyes become dimmed, his ears stopped, the heavenly music ceases, the vision vanishes, and like a child crying in the night he returns to earth and separation.

When great souls come among us we fail to recognize them. Too often our heavenly vision becomes shortened by our external environment. The suggestion of separation and materiality smothers but cannot quite extinguish the Divine spark. When we touch the Original Cause our strength is renewed, the transcendent vision illuminates the consciousness, the harmony of celestial music unites us with the heavenly choir and has power to *clap wings to all solid nature.* We see through the specific form and penetrate the universal identity—Proteus assuming any form he wills. From the essence of universal substance any and all forms appear. We too have come up through all these forms, and though our faces are turned toward heaven there is often a downward pull on the soul.

We must be careful to keep the vision clear. In the process of our evolution we have not yet entirely shaken off the weight of downward tendencies—*ebbing downward into the forms into whose habits thou hast not for many years slid.* One would infer that Emerson believed in an ascending gradation of consciousness. In this he did not differ greatly from the theory of the modern evolutionist.

We are to keep our faces toward heaven, for the central spark in the human is truly divine. The facts, forms, and events of human evolution are winged. Each fact asks us who we are, and if we take the event too seriously, if the fact becomes too solid, if we *cannot answer by a superior wisdom, we are held in bondage*. It is not by the fact or the form that we are held, but because the fact or the form temporarily extinguishes the true spark. We forget who we are, hence serve the fact and are held by the form.

When we see the spirit in all facts and forms everything falls into its logical place, everything glorifies the eternal unity. Man masters the fact, impersonates the form, both of which serve him. Man has the power to transcend his environment and enter this hour into the full recognition of his true nature. He does this not by repudiating human existence but by understanding it.

The Universal nature, too strong for the petty nature of the bard, sits on his neck and writes through his hand. There is a power overshadowing us, an urge stronger than we are impelling us onward. This Divine Urge is not fully understood even by the most evolved. It sits on his neck and compels him to write.

Not fully understanding it and yet conscious of its subtle presence, he writes extravagantly. Unable to understand its meaning he is compelled to set down the symbol. The intuition transcends reason; the spiritual faculty announces; it does not argue. There is a heavenly language mingled with the babble of tongues. The *shoes of swiftness* bespeak the presence of the invisible Spirit. The garland of virtue fades on the brow of the unconstant. Truth alone rises triumphant. Its approach is silent. *Who seeks a treasure must not speak*. It is to be found everywhere. Nature incarnates herself in countless forms. When we unmask nature we behold the constant amid the complexity.

Out of the human heart go, as it were, highways to the heart of every object in nature. There is something in us akin to *the whole chain of organic and inorganic being*. The greatest life is the one that includes the most. Inclusion and not exclusion is a helpful key to the philosophy of Emerson.

The objective world is the fruitage of the subjective. *He cannot live without a world*. Nature fits man for an objective existence. But we are not to think of this objective existence as being actually external. Man is really united with it. The objective world is the fruitage of spirit; it is rooted in pure cause. Spirit and matter are two ends of the same thing.

Man must act. He must have a stake to play for. An unexpressed life is a fancy, a phantom, an empty dream. Cut man off from action and he is lost. Being plays with becoming. The Spirit shapes itself into innumerable forms for the purpose of self-expression, self-recognition, and self-gratification. Man's center is in Being; the play of life upon itself goes on through man—the building blocks for the game consist of empires, Alps to climb; his sciences, his religions, his philosophies, all are playthings.

There is also the reaction of man to man, of thought to thought, of imagination to imagination, of emotion to emotion. The deep of nature and of the individual mind calls to the deep within us. We learn not by hearsay, not through theory, but by experience.

When the depths of our nature is stirred, latent possibilities spring forth into accomplishment, being passes forever fresh and new into a glorious becoming. There is something in us corresponding to everything we contact in life. From this viewpoint, *The mind is One—nature is its correlative, history is to be read and written.*

History no longer shall be a dull book. It shall walk incarnate in every just and wise man. Emerson's reference to the soul means the Universal Spirit or Over-soul. He tells us that It brings Its entire being to each newborn man—he is the epitome of Its being; he incarnates It. It enters into him. This incarnation is not by proxy, not by hearsay or the reading of books, but through living.

Man is a microcosm containing within himself the same qualities, essences, and attributes of the Macrocosm. He is priest. saint, savior, and sinner. He is darkness and light, literature, law, and government. He is the interpreter of the Universe, the ambassador of God, the woman worshiping at the tomb, the Christ proclaiming his own divinity, the child at play, and the philosopher interrogating the Universe. He is both question and answer, problem and solution, imagination, will, and purpose, fused into unity, manifest through variety—the light of the morning stars and *all the recorded benefits of heaven and earth.*

The transcendent perception of Emerson's mind made him hold our slight knowledge rather cheaply. His mind encompassed a larger order than the average man is wont to envisage. The wisdom of antiquity, the morals of Confucius, the compassion of Jesus, to him were not dead facts but living presences. History was more than a record of human experiences; it was a revelation through each individual of the *one mind common to all individual men.*

He wrote from this larger viewpoint, this almost impersonal and yet personified viewpoint when he said:

I am the owner of the sphere,
Of the seven stars and the solar year,
Of Caesar's hand, and Plato's brain,
Of Lord Christ's heart, and Shakespeare's strain.

What We Understand About Healing

Office of the Dean

My Dear Friend,
One of the principal things we should come to realize in Spiritual Mind Healing is that there is a self-existent and creative Mind Principle. It is present in and through everything, and responds to us at the level of our recognition of It. This is why we say that Creativity is self-existent, which means that It exists everywhere because God or the Creative Cause exists everywhere.

The fact that we have not seen this Creative Law and the Divine Presence should not confuse us, since no one has ever seen anything other than external effects. We never see love, truth, beauty, consciousness, energy, harmony, or gravitational force, but we do not doubt their existence.

Because we are surrounded by self-existence our work should be done without effort. There is no compulsion in it; rather it is a thing of receptivity.

We think you will enjoy the exposition of Emerson's Essay on Spiritual Laws. This essay is one of the grandest visions of Reality ever put into print. We suggest that you get the Essays and study them, since they are among the world's greatest literature.

Sincerely,
Ernest Holmes

Lesson 27

Page 193 to *Spiritual Mind Healing,* page 198

One of the principal things to remember is that Mind energy already exists. We use this energy as we do that of electricity by individualizing it for conscious and specific purposes. We never create energy. We merely make use of a power which already exists.

On page 645 read the definition of *Vitality and Energy*. You will find that the Vitality of God is self-existent. It is not vitalized by something else but already has the power of life within Itself. So a mental treatment has the power of life within itself. It has the ability to manifest itself in form; otherwise there could be no Science of Mind. The application of this science rests entirely upon the supposition that we are surrounded by a Creative Law which receives the impress of our thought and acts upon it.

No one has ever seen this Life Principle. The very fact that we live proves that It exists. (See Lesson 3 and the definition of *Mind* on page 612. We use a Power which exists before we make use of It. Through the imagination and intuition we feel the existence of Reality and through the directive power of the will we consciously decide what this Reality, which we feel, is to do for us.

We may use this Power for helping ourselves or for helping someone else. There would be no difference in the actual use of the Power; the only difference would be in the *direction*. For instance, if you were going to treat yourself you would say, "This word is for *me; I am* thus and so." If you were going to treat

John Smith you would say, "This word is for John Smith; *he is* thus and so." In treating someone else you talk to yourself about him, stating that the Truth is the law of his being.

In the third paragraph on page 193 of the textbook occurs the statement: *True spiritual work will strengthen the will without exhausting the mind.* If our mental work tends to tire us we may know that we are resorting to some form of mental coercion, some form of will power or compulsion which is a denial of the Divine Presence as Spirit, and of the Law as a medium for the operation of our thought. We plant the seed in faith, believing, and the Creative Genius of the Universe produces the plant. By conscious thought we give direction to the Law, which of Itself has no direction but which, once being instructed, tends always to create an objectification of the thing thought of, and to bring it into the experience of the one for whom it is directed.

Our idea of concentration in mental work is not one of compulsion, nor is it one which would lead us to imagine that we are gathering together forces of which we are to make use. Concentration, from our viewpoint, means mental attention. To think of it from any other standpoint is to suggest to our thought that we are dealing with some reluctant power.

The more simple and direct you are in your approach to this science the better results you will obtain. Jesus taught no system of concentration, but rather suggested the simplicity of one's approach to Reality. In the midst of those who proclaimed the powers of darkness and of light Jesus made this simple statement: *Believe, and it shall be done unto you*.

The conscious belief must become a subjective acceptance before it can produce a definite result. Hence our belief is not always productive of good. Sometimes we only *think* we believe. We must have the will to believe and we must center our attention—which is real concentration—on the thought that our entire being accepts our belief. *We concentrate our attention. The Law creates the form* (Paragraph 3, page 194).

It is the office of the will to determine what the creative imagination shall undertake, for we certainly are always creating something through the use of our thought. In seeking to demonstrate what we wish instead of what we do not wish we should remember that we are not dealing with two powers but with One Power which may be used in two ways. There is a limited way of using this Power, and a less limited way.

While there are no degrees to the Power Itself there are degrees in our use of It. To create that which we call big would be no more difficult for this Power than to create that which we call little; and conversely and paradoxically, that which we call little is no less than that which we call more. It is self-evident that the Infinite cannot know size, but It does contain the potentiality of all form.

The creative power and processes of our thought go on whether we are aware of it or not. We are always causing something to happen when we think. We should study our mental reactions and see whether or not we are demonstrating freedom or bondage. As stated on page 487, we should learn to bless and curse not, for the Law of Cause and Effect is always at work.

On page 453 under the heading *When the Blind Lead the Blind*, we find that we must be careful what thoughts we entertain. Our thought should be founded upon the perception of the unity of good, the absoluteness of the Law, and the availability of Spirit. All of our statements in treatment should be based on the supposition that the Law immediately responds to our thought. We should always be sure that we have faith, and equally certain that our faith is based upon some degree of understanding and therefore provides the way for our complete acceptance.

We must be careful to determine whether or not we wish to experience the result of what we are thinking. (See the first paragraph on page 195.) I am sure that if our whole desire is constructive it can produce only good, peace, and joy. This is the criterion for a correct use of the Law of Cause and Effect. When Jesus said, *Love your neighbor as yourself*, he certainly implied that whatever good a person desires for someone else he has an equal right to desire for himself. If you hate yourself and then follow the admonition of Jesus to love your neighbor as yourself, you would hate your neighbor. Many good people fail to recognize the significance of the thought that they, as well as their neighbors, are already in the Kingdom of Heaven.

One thing is certain, salvation must begin at the center, not at the circumference of our experience. We should make every effort to demonstrate peace, poise, power, prosperity, and happiness for ourselves. Then from the lamp of this experience we shall more clearly see how to light the pathway of another's thought. Nothing is more certain than that we can give only what we have.

Many good and sincere souls have walked down a stony pathway of self-resignation thinking that in doing so they honored God. But we ought never to forget that even sincerity may be subject to illusion, and that there is no God who can be glorified by the suffering of any man. The good we desire for others we should desire for ourselves, and the good we desire for ourselves we should desire for others.

If a person has time to give only one treatment in a day, that treatment should be given for himself that his light may shine before men, for if the light within him is extinguished how great is his darkness! There is nothing selfish in this idea. We are one with the Whole and the Law follows our word, and our word is, in a way, the sum total of our thought processes. Surely we are compelled to choose what path we want to follow. As suggested in the second paragraph on page 196, we live in a universe of Love and of Law.

We believe that back of our objective personality there is an identity which is spiritual. This identity has been discussed in Lesson 17. There must be a spiritual man not separated from the physical man, but which is the invisible cause of the physical. In moments of cosmic consciousness and illumination the great mystics have been aware of this Divine man.

For a complete definition of *Mystic* and *Mysticism*, turn to page 613. The mystics have had an awareness of the spiritual universe and thus have experienced cosmic consciousness. You will find this described on page 341. They have apparently plunged through the physical universe and recognized, possibly even seen the spiritual. They have all told us that man is a spiritual being, and could he know himself as he really is he would discover that he has the same power which Jesus exercised.

On page 337 Jesus under the heading *Evolution*, you will find that Jesus became the Christ because of his conscious recognition of his unity with Good. He had completely balanced the Law and the Word in his experience. (Read again the definition of *Law* on page 605, and *Word* on page 646. In such degree as we gain conscious control of our subjective reactions we shall exercise authority over the Law.

We believe that there is a perfect idea of man, but we also believe that our human concept may practically obliterate this idea. Of course it cannot destroy it; it merely covers it up so that the perfect man does not appear. All spiritual mind healing tends to uncover this perfect idea, to reveal it to the intellect. In spiritual mind healing, when a person gives mental treatments he begins with the assumption that man already is perfect. Conforming his argument to this theory he makes mental statements which tend to prove his theory.

For example, you may say something like this: "Man is a spiritual being and a perfect being; hence he is not subject to poor circulation, overaction, inaction, or wrong action. Because he is a spiritual being he is perfect now." Turn to the bottom of page 524 for an example of this—*No Over-Action nor Inaction*. You are in this way conforming your statements to the idea of a perfect God, a perfect man, and a perfect relationship between God and man.

Just as the manifest universe is a result of the contemplation of Spirit, so our world is a result of our contemplation. Being ignorant of this we perpetuate the very conditions we seek to erase. We should think of ourselves as perfect, as complete in every part, as governed and guided by Love and Wisdom, Truth and Beauty. As man recognizes his Divine Nature he becomes to his world what God is to the Greater World.

In spiritual mind healing *the practitioner talks to himself* in order to convince himself of the perfection of his patient. He brings forward every argument imaginable which bears evidence to his patient' s perfection. Over and over he may affirm this. He makes any statements to himself which will convince himself of this truth. As this inner realization dawns in his own thought he finds his patient responding.

Turn to page 485 under the heading *The Inner Light*, for this statement: *When the* soul *knows freedom, the* Law *will free the body*. Soul is the subjective part of man, for this is the medium between the Absolute and the relative. The Absolute is the Unconditioned and the relative is the form which this Unconditioned takes. (Read again the definition of *Absolute* on page 575 and *Relative* on page 627.)

The subjective images of our thought are continuously reflecting some condition into our physical bodies or into our environment. We may change the subjective images of thought. They are the medium between the Unconditioned, the Absolute, the Uncreated, or the Power of God if we wish to put it that way, and what takes place in our experience.

Treatment changes the subjective images of thought, and in so doing heals the mind of false beliefs. The mind healed of these false beliefs immediately reflects a better condition. *The practitioner heals the mind of his patient through the act of healing his own thought about his patient*. Because there is but One Mind, that which he realizes rises to the consciousness of the one for whom it is directed with as much healing power as the practitioner realized when he spoke this particular word. That is what is

16. What do we mean by having a spiritual experience in our thought?
17. What is spiritual self-awakening?

Answers to Questions on Lesson 26

1. We can be certain of the willingness of the Principle of Mind to respond to our word because Its nature compels It to give back to us an objective manifestation of that which we think into It.
2. *Big* and *little* are in our own thought because the Principle of Mind which responds to our thought knows neither big nor little.
3. Karma means cause and effect, a principle which we consciously use, while fate means something over which we have no control.
4. In treating a person who believes he is controlled by planetary influences, know that the Spirit within him is the same Spirit which creates the planets.
5. Our intellectual perceptions become powerful when we have an inner realization of their meaning, and they become creative when we direct this realization for some definite purpose.
6. If you doubt your ability to treat effectively, at once reassure yourself that you are using a Principle which must respond to your word.
7. To have the mind of Christ means to be consciously aware of one's unity with the God-Mind.
8. The impulsion back of spiritual mind healing is Love.
9. We should approach our mental work directly and simply, with neither fear nor superstition, and with a calm sense of the absoluteness of the Power with which we deal.
10. A practitioner must clear up his own thought first because until he does he cannot think clearly about his patient.
11. In treatment, thought should be conscious if it is to be directive; it must be specific in order to accomplish definite results.
12. The answer to prayer is determined by the belief and inner realization of the one praying.
13. Man's true identity is his Spiritual Nature, which is already perfect.
14. When we refer to man's Spiritual Nature we mean that he is rooted in, is a part of, and unified with a perfect Law, a perfect Presence, and a complete Wholeness.
15. The realization of man's Spiritual Nature is the background of all spiritual mind healing.
16. The kind of statements which help us better to realize the Spiritual Nature of our patient would be similar to the following: *There is One Life; that Life is his life now. This Life is complete, harmonious and perfect within him. This Life permeates every part of his being and eliminates everything unlike Itself.*
17. Our Silent Partner is the Law which acts upon our word, and the Divine Spirit which inspires us to speak the word. The Spirit knows, Law obeys.
18. The spiritual practitioner never objects to any form of physical healing. He should cooperate with all, but confine his work to his own field.
19. The spiritual practitioner should have no objection to any religious belief, but should gladly cooperate with all.

20. The highest form of mental healing is spiritual, because spiritual realizations furnish the highest mental concepts we can attain.

A Commentary on Ralph Waldo Emerson's Essay on Spiritual Laws

Emerson viewed the universe, both visible and invisible, as a spiritual system; the material universe being a counterpart of the spiritual. Man is a part of this spiritual order, so indivisibly united with it that the entire cosmos is or may be reflected in his mind. Evolution is an awakening of the soul to a recognition of its unity with the whole.

He believed in a spiritual system transparent through the material; in a soul element running through all nature; in a universe governed by law; in a parallel between physical and spiritual laws; and in the interpretation of the spiritual through the physical. In his Essay, *Powers and Laws of Thought*, he states: *I believe in the existence of the material world as the expression of the spiritual or the real.*

In *Spiritual Laws* he says: *When the act of reflection takes place in the mind, when we look at ourselves in the light of thought, we discover that our life is embosomed in beauty*. Even the common things of life assume a natural goodness, beauty, and dignity when viewed as a whole. Experiences, like beads, are threaded on the continuity of the perceiving soul, each fills a natural place, none is too important, none isolated, all are necessary—the mind transcends all its conceptions.

Experiences which seem disconnected and tragic are viewed by the soul as incidents, for *the soul will not know either deformity or pain*. The soul itself transcends all experiences, gives the lie to contradictions, bridges every chasm and finds completion within itself. Man is robbed when he conceives of himself as being separated from the whole. *All loss, all pain is particular: the universe remains to the heart unhurt.* There is something within us which transcends the hurt; there is an abiding trust at the center of our being, a faith unshaken. Sorrow and grief disappear in the light of this central sun—*For it is only the finite that has wrought and suffered; the infinite lies stretched in smiling repose.*

This thought reveals Emerson's belief that suffering is a result of ignorance, that the Spirit Itself is above suffering, and exists in a state of perpetual tranquility. In no sense is this to be confused with a denial of the objective universe or with the belief that one must renounce the world if one wishes to enter into a state of peace. Emerson draws no line between the physical and the spiritual; his idea is not division but unity, not separation but wholeness, not God *and* man, but God *in* man—God in everything. From the viewpoint of this larger order he thought and wrote.

Emerson had an implicit trust in a universe whose integrity he never doubted. He infers that our troubles are borrowed; that theological problems are conjured up from the ignorance of our own consciousness, phantoms which we ourselves create, idols of our own misconceptions, bogies of our own fancy. *A simple mind will not know these enemies*. The man who has nature as his priest, whose altar is the sanctuary of his own soul, finds a communion simple, direct, and complete—a strength and solidarity *in that which he is*.

Viewing the universe as a spiritual system, the Spirit as a unitary wholeness, and man as a part of this natural order, Emerson finds no virtue in fighting the devil. Goodness is natural and normal. Virtue is not an opposite of evil, but is instinctive righteousness; it need not be analyzed. Like a flower it blooms on the tree of life, never comparing itself with the soil from which it springs; it keeps its face toward heaven.

The purpose of nature is greater than human will. The urge for self-expression emanates directly from nature and accounts for much that we often call the volitional act of man. Therefore men of great genius have sung, *Not unto us, not unto us*. The necessity of the times produces the man. The universal urge flows through the individual genius, and where the channel is unobstructed produces a Shakespeare. We can furnish no adequate theory to fit these facts, no method to gain this insight; it forever remains the secret of that spontaneous nature which gives unto all men *the power to stand and go*.

We are begirt with spiritual laws which execute themselves. In the light of these laws we find that our petty differences, our *frauds and wars*, are miscreations that mark a wrong approach to good—that sorrow and the *gnashing of the teeth* are results of limited vision. The soul will never find its true place in the natural order of the universe until it blends and unites with this natural order. Trouble is self-imposed. Peace forever lies calm and serene at the center.

Love should make joy but our benevolence is unhappy. Emerson was greatly opposed to the average man's concept of duty, particularly pertaining to spiritual things. The unnecessary sacrifices arising from a false sense of duty belie and belittle the magnificence of the Spirit. The spontaneous joy of love finds no true expression through a benevolence which is self-imposed. When we worship from a sense of duty the altar is profaned. There can be no set rules for the spiritual life. The instinctive urge in the child will find its own logical outlet. Questions need not be answered until they are asked; water reaches its own level by its own weight. That which is inherent in us will find its outlet if we allow it. *When the fruit is ripe, it falls*.

Even our mechanical laws are subject to a spiritual order and operate under that universal law which is the government of all things. There is too much resistance to nature, too much fight and struggle, too little acquiescence. We create vast systems of thought destined to failure because they contradict the natural order.

Man does not live by will but by a higher law which controls everything. *Belief and love* are the mainsprings of existence and *relieve us of a vast load of care .... There is a soul at the center of Nature and over the will of every man, so that none of us can wrong the universe*. When we are in line with spiritual laws we are propelled into right action and easy accomplishment. When in our ignorance we oppose these laws they react against us. Thus through misconceptions we find the return circuits of the law imposing the hardship upon us which we have set in motion toward another.

Living by faith and *by lowly listening* our lives are carried on with the stream of existence, freed from pain. Heaven organizes itself in us and we live naturally as the rose, breathing the pure air of Spirit, living in the light of that Eternal Sun which is forever ascending, forever sending forth rays from the Universal Soul whose center is everywhere.

The incarnation of the Universal in the individual is the mainspring of Emerson's thought. Each is an individualized center of God-conscious life and divine action. Each is a unique individualization. When man obeys the dictates of the inner voice he finds every pathway open before him. *He has no rival.* The *general soul incarnates itself in him.* Through him, the unity of this general soul passes into unique variation of itself. No two people are alike.

The more we study our own individuality and seek to build a superstructure upon the foundations of our own thought and endeavor, the more power we have. *The height of the pinnacle is determined by the breadth of the base.* To believe that anything less than this divine calling is worthy is to fall under the illusion of separation from the whole, and to deny the realization *that there is one mind in all the individuals.*

When man follows the genius of his own individuality, *he creates the taste by which he is enjoyed. He provokes the wants to which he can minister.* This is another way of saying that cause and effect are but two ends of the same thing, and that both cause and effect are spiritual; one follows the other as the night the day. A man is himself, gives expression to the universal mind, and does his best work when he gives complete attention and enthusiasm to his endeavor, when he is able to *let out all the length of all the reins.* Anything less than this stultifies the mind, stunts the effort, inhibits the Spirit, and limits the man. Self-expression is the keynote of life. Man exists for the purpose of providing an extension of consciousness through which the Universal may work.

Accept your genius and say what you think. Take yourself for better or for worse. Rely on that inner impulse, that intuitive perception, that spiritual genius which lights every man's path to the gateway of good. Find the divine in the most commonplace things of life. Elevate the human with a positive faith. Trust the integrity of your own soul. Fan the human spark into a blaze divine, and *perceive that anything man can do may be divinely done.*

Do away with the illusion of hope and the morbidity of fear. Realize that no good can be solid unless it is an extension of the self. Play with the gifts of life, *and scatter them on every wind.* The gates of the eternal reservoir are forever open and the *infinite productiveness* knows no drought. The supply is always equal to the demand, man is always united with the Divine, and searching deeply into his own nature he finds that *in himself is his might.* Man's mind is a magnet, *a selecting principle, gathering his like to him, wherever he goes.* The natural affinity of the soul irresistibly draws that which belongs to it. The power compelling this movement is an impulse of the Spirit acting in accord with immutable law. Not by conscious choice but by divine necessity man gathers his own.

What your heart thinks great, is great. The soul's emphasis is always right. To Emerson there was neither great nor small. Hence the most trivial incident, provided it fitted nicely into the scheme of everyday life, became important. The friends which our consciousness attracts to us belong to us. Through them the Universal Mind speaks a divine language. The transparency of those incidents which we understand reveals the universal nature to us. That which coerces our attention and intrigues our consciousness has a peculiar meaning. That which truly belongs to us cannot be withheld. That which we ought to know we shall know. *It will tell itself.* The sympathetic understanding of individuals proclaims a larger unity in which all individual souls have their being. In the bonds of this unity there are no secrets.

There is a *perfect intelligence that subsists between wise men of remote ages*. There is a timelessness in the universal Mind which includes all epochs. When *like-minded men* think, disregarding the age in which they live, they tap the same universal stream of consciousness, read the same meaning, discover the same laws, imbibe the same spirit, and proclaim the same truth, each in his own tongue. Thought passes through the individual stream of consciousness back into the universal, to be reinterpreted by other individuals who grasp its meaning. Thus the individual universalizes himself; thus the Universal individualizes Itself.

Since there are no secrets withheld from the Universal Mind, and any individual may tap this Mind at the level of his own consciousness, it follows that apparent secrets are merely things with which we have no affinity. Once the affinity is gained the secret is proclaimed, but *no man can learn what he has not preparation for learning, however near to his eyes is the object.* We are living in eternity now. We are surrounded by a limitless intelligence this moment, and the potentialities of the Infinite are already incarnated in us. Not until we are ready will the Divine secret be disclosed. When our eyes are opened we shall see: *God screens us evermore from premature ideas*. The good we desire will be ours when we are ready for it; when we unite our individual good with that universal good which includes all. We awake from the dream of isolation and separation to discover that we have never been apart from our good. We have only failed to perceive it.

Not in nature but in man is all the beauty and worth he sees. Nature, without anyone to experience her beauty, remains empty. The pride of creation, on this planet at least, is the consciousness of that being who beholds her splendors. Nor can location or environment make the man. Those places which man hallows with his presence are sacred, not because of the concrete and material fact but because man weaves into the fact a design which his imagery brings to it—a pattern spun from an inner creative source, the incarnation of the Almighty in the human. A noble person carries with him the light of the stars and all the gifts of heaven. The veil of the temple is rent when we are prepared to enter the Holy of Holies, no matter where the place may be.

He may see what he maketh. Each lives in a world of his own making. To the pure, all is pure. Evil beholds the image of its own false creation. Emerson instinctively foreknew certain psychological facts which are now common knowledge, and anticipated our present theory of dream psychology. *Our dreams are the sequel of our waking knowledge*. The peaceful mind, trusting in the universe and believing in the eternal goodness, is calm in the midst of confusion and finds perfect rest in sleep, but the mind distraught by the events of the day, fearful of the future, and morbidly introspective of the past, or the mind distraught and evil in its imagination, finds no repose—is continuously tormented by itself.

Asleep or awake we shall never see anything more fearful or more lovely than our imagination pictures it. Our concept of life is, in imagination, an outline of our introspections. *The good, compared to the evil which he sees, is as his own good to his own evil.* Emerson never departs from the thought that man is the center of his own universe. Any apparent circumference is a true radiation of this center. As a man thinks, wills, and purposes, so he is. He is a free agent in a universe which denies him nothing, but reflects back to him an exact representation of his own beliefs.

Emerson's exaltation of the individual in no way denies his dependence on the universe, for he continually reiterates the thought that man lives by virtue of his relationship to that universal wholeness which is incarnated in all.

He may read what he writes. The revelation of another man is to us but the measure of our own thought. We must bring to the author that which we expect to take away. The depth which his thought reaches finds an equal deep in our own minds; reveals us to ourselves. Hence any author *is a thousand books to a thousand persons*. The great thinkers of the ages are eagerly sought by the few who can understand them.

We are all universal; there is a place in each which has a possibility of responding to the most divine concepts. Deep truths remain hidden until the mind is ready to receive them. We draw from each other that which we are. *Every society protects itself*. The presence of our physical bodies in any company is no guarantee of an affinity of mind. It is the affinity of mind and spirit which attracts, compels, and binds.

What avails it to fight with the eternal laws of mind, which adjust the relation of all persons to each other by the mathematical measure of their havings and beings? The laws of mind are mathematical measures. Unnatural relationships exist only by false coercion. Ultimately the soul readjusts false relationships and draws its own to it. *He shall have his own society ... how beautiful is the ease of its victory!*

When a person whose mind is related to us, *a brother or sister by nature*, comes into the atmosphere of our consciousness the union is complete, this circulation of consciousness now binds the two into one *so softly and easily, so nearly and intimately, as if it were the blood in our proper veins*, because the eternal laws of mind fulfill their purposes. Thus the inevitable law of attraction, which man cannot resist, accomplishes its end. Thus the self is forever wedded to the self.

We are attracted to those who meet us on the level of our own evolution, *on the line of my own march*. He whose consciousness appreciates and understands the gods finds himself in their company, while a gross mind still wallows in the mire from which an instinctive urge seeks to extricate it. Companionship and society reflect the soul. When we meet the great through due appreciation and affinity of soul, we meet them not as candidates for greatness but because we too are *native of the same celestial latitude*.

A subtle meaning is written into the closing lines of this paragraph, referring to the punishment which follows *the neglect of the affinities by which alone society should be formed*. An evil person finds no enjoyment in the company of natural goodness. We find no comfort outside ourselves and those conditions and persons which the affinity of our souls draws into the atmosphere of our experiences. If we were in hell and our minds dwelt on heavenly things we should immediately find ourselves in heaven. If we were in heaven and our mind dwelt on evil we should immediately find ourselves in hell. *Let him be great, and love shall follow him*.

He may set his own rate .... a man may have that allowance he takes. Emerson is not speaking of external possessions but of inner gifts. The world is not at all concerned over us, but leaves us sternly alone to work out our own salvation. Ultimately we are accepted at our own valuation, provided these values are true and not false ones.

The measure of our own worth is measured back to us and the measurer is not a man, but *the eternal laws of mind. . . . He teaches who gives, and he learns who receives*. There is no teaching unless the teacher has the ability to impart himself. Seldom do we find persons who have overcome the objective barriers and who directly impart themselves. Such will always have an audience, no matter what the topic of their discourse. Anything less than this surrender of the soul is *an apology, a gag, and not a communication, not a speech, not a man*. A discourse carries with it a conviction equal to the depth of the one giving it—equal to the emotion behind it. Without argument it finds acquiescence. Almost without words it bridges the gulf between individual minds.

The inner feeling from which the spoken word is propelled strikes a depth which no rhetoric can measure. The orator is the oration. The speech is the speaker, the sermon is the preacher. Without the artist there can be no art. A complete surrender of the intellect to the inner genius makes possible this subtle soul communion, strikes fire from heaven and kindles a like flame in the imagination of other people.

The effect of any writing on the public mind is mathematically measurable by its depth of thought. How much water does it draw? Authors who cause us to think, live in our minds. They awake in us the same concepts, the same emotions and hopes which they themselves have experienced. He who writes from the sincerity of his soul, who gives an answer to the deep questionings of his own mind, is answering the questions of other men's minds, for *there is one mind common to all individual men*.

There can be no mistake and no chance in *the final verdict upon every book*. Those books come down to us which deserve to live; they are brought by a law of natural affinity and placed in the hands of those ready to receive them *as if God brought them in his hand*.

The great man knew not that he was great. Greatness, like virtue, is natural and flows from the spontaneous mind without effort. Honesty and sincerity are not warriors pitted against crime and ignorance, but are lights shining in the darkness. As the light knows naught of darkness, so virtue knows no vice. Greatness cannot contemplate meanness. The pure soul radiates purity. Good cannot understand evil, and beauty sheds its radiance upon ugliness and is unaware of any seeming opposite.

Men who have towered above the average, whose spirit has been exalted above the commonplace, whose inner awareness has given them a heavenly companionship, have been simple and direct both in speech and manner. They have done what they did because they must, not even by choice but through the spontaneous acclamation of their own natures. They may have been egoists, but never egotists. Our institutions are founded on the thought of these minds.

Truth has not single victories; all things are its organs. Behind the infinite variations of nature there is a unitary cause. Even a lie announces our ability to speak. Disease is not an evil of itself, but in its own nature is perfect. There is but one substance from which all things are formed. This substance is ever available, ever ready to spring into form.

Human character evermore publishes itself. It will not be concealed. It is impossible to hide the self; everything we do reveals our character to those around us, whether we talk or remain silent. *When a man speaks the truth in the spirit of truth, his eye is as clear as the heavens.* The liar uncovers himself. We cannot cheat nature nor even fool man very long. That which we really are penetrates the mask we wear and though we take every precaution to conceal insincerity, we shall fail. Nature is so organized that we cannot fool her.

The *mind common to all individual men* carries the inner impression of our thought to those with whom we are dealing and subjectively moves their thought to a sure knowledge of our motives. Hence the unbelief of a lawyer becomes the unbelief of the jury, *despite all his protestations.*

A man cannot convince others if he is not convinced himself. He cannot give that which he does not possess. He cannot proclaim with conviction what he does not believe. A man cannot lie as he would tell the truth, for his own knowledge of his falseness finds a corresponding impression on his hearer.

The lie may last for an hour, but truth stands forever, and in the long run *a man passes for what he is worth . . . Never was a sincere word utterly lost. Never a magnanimity fell to the ground, but there is some heart to greet and accept it unexpectedly. A man passes for that he is worth. What he is engraves itself on his face, on his form, on his fortunes, in letters of light. Concealment avails him nothing; boasting nothing. There is confession in the glance of our eyes, in our smiles, in salutations and the grasp of hands. His sin bedaubs him, mars all his good impression. Men know not why they do not trust him, but they do not trust him. His vice glasses his eye, cuts lines of mean expression in his cheek, pinches the nose, sets the mark of the beast on the back of the head, and writes, O fool! fool! on the forehead of a king.*

Virtue is the adherence in action to the nature of things. Virtue is natural. Good is prevalent in nature, and the reason why *God is described as saying, I AM,* is that God is all-inclusive. The Eternal is absolute, complete, and perfect. It should not be said that God is good as opposed to evil, or timeless as opposed to time, for this suggests opposites to the Divine Nature. Creator and creation constitute one indivisible wholeness, whose name is *I AM.*

It was a perception of the allness of Truth and man's complete unity with it that enabled Emerson to say, *The lesson which these observations convey is, Be, and not seem.* An external attempt to be thought great is a pretense, while to Be is to be great. The Divine incarnates Itself in us. When we live from this God nature we live in the truth which *makes rich and great.*

The petty differences of opinion, the confusion of complicated concepts, the experiences which give the lie to the Divine Reality, are of the wisdom of this world. They are false judgments based upon a belief in duality. But when *we take our bloated nothingness out of the path of the divine circuits* we are free. This *bloated nothingness* is the false valuation which we place upon things. Wealth, conceived of as an entity, is a bloated nothingness. The ambition to promote oneself is bloated nothingness. Much of our apparent knowledge, our intellectual ponderosities, may be classed as bloated nothingness.

When the external formality of worship violates the spontaneous expression of an instinctive faith, worship becomes a bloated nothingness. The pride of fame and name is a bloated nothingness. Only that which promotes the welfare of the soul is profitable. Only that which allows the *divine circuits* to flow unobstructed gives freedom. We are to *lie low in the Lord's power and learn that truth alone makes rich and great.*

Be a gift and a benediction ... Common men are apologies for men ... God loveth not size; whale and minnow are of like dimension. One of Emerson's deepest thoughts was that the Infinite knows no great and no small. Thus a dignity may be placed upon the slightest act, a compensation found in the smallest pleasure, a true greatness arrived at through the contemplation of a simple truth.

The man who thinks great thoughts is a great man. He is *dear to the heart of being*, because he has allowed the Spirit a free expression through his mind. The possibility of greatness sits at the doorway of every man's consciousness, silently seeking admission. Thus the humble is exalted, the valley is lifted to the mountain top, while *deep cries unto deep .... real action is in silent moments.*

This thought was expressed by many great men preceding Emerson. External acts flow from inner concepts; all our institutions are founded on thought. The *silent thought by the wayside as we walk*, which Emerson says *revises our entire manner of life*, is the illumination one receives who penetrates objective confusions and subjective differences of opinion. This state of being is apparent throughout all his writings, an inner awareness of the relationship of the individual mind to the Universal Spirit.

When a person has sensed this inner unity in the small moments of his waiting hour he finds that the *aim of these moments, is to make daylight shine through him*. The light of Spirit will henceforth radiate through his every act. He is twice born. All things take on a new meaning. Life has a greater significance. His heart now knows that which his intellect could never explain. Nor can the wisdom of man confuse, dim, or obliterate this inner light.

Until this moment comes, *he is not homogeneous, but heterogeneous and the ray does not traverse.* While we believe in a spiritual world in one place and a material world in another, in a God external to our souls, in a heaven to be desired and an immortal existence to be obtained, we are not thinking from the standpoint of unity but of duality. Confusion and blindness follow the *life not yet at one*.

Action and inaction are alike to the true. Emerson held the moments of contemplation to be as valuable as those of action. Having theoretically dissolved the material universe, or having resolved it into a spiritual universe, drawing no line between cause and effect, he felt it worthwhile to contemplate his relationship to the Infinite. But unlike many who taught a complete repudiation of the material, he joined life with living, found prayer and performance to be two ends of the same thing, found in nature an answer to the call of the soul, believed action to be good when necessary and inaction to be equally good in those moments when the soul silently wedded itself to its source. *Heaven is large, and affords space for all modes of love and fortitude.*

The fact that I am here certainly shows me that the soul had need of an organ here. The objective world is a necessary expression of the Spirit. We would not have bodies if we did not need them, and we should not question the integrity of the soul which has projected the body.

We must learn to accept ourselves for better or for worse—to trust the Divine Nature inherent in our own being and to live from this Divine Nature alone.

The ancestor of every action is a thought. The external badge, the prayer meeting or philosophic society is evidence of this fact. The Creator is within. Hence, *the rich mind lies in the sun and sleeps, and is Nature.*

Let us, if we must have great actions, make our own so. Only that is great to us which we make great. The greatness of others is ours when we ourselves are great. *All action is of an infinite elasticity*. A potential possibility is inherent in everything which the Infinite projects, and since we are incarnations of the Infinite we are equipped with limitless possibilities. When our minds are *inflated with the celestial air*—when we are in accord with the Divine Nature, we are powerful and complete.

Since man is an inlet to this celestial air he need not *go gadding into the scenes and philosophy of* others, for he has within himself the same scenes and philosophies. We unduly honor those whom we call great, and extend to them *a very extravagant compliment*, when we feel that our entire time must be spent in studying their lives, thoughts, and actions, rather than in the contemplation of our own being, in the careful searching of our own souls for the Infinite Originator. When we do this we find that the texture of our own souls is *identical with the best*.

This over-estimate of the possibilities of Paul and Pericles, this under-estimate of our own, comes from a neglect of the fact of an identical nature. It is this identical nature which Emerson emphasizes in all his writings—this mind common to all individual men. Because of this identical nature the spiritual background of every man is the same. The source of all life is One, though its manifestation be varied. These varied manifestations are but the play of life upon itself. Hence *if the poet write a true drama, then he is Caesar*, for looking back into the depth of being itself, the poet, Caesar, or nature, all are God. It is through the power of this God Being inherent in us that we live, imagine, and create. *These are all his, and by the power of these he rouses the nations.*

Again Emerson says: *But the great names cannot stead him, if he have not life himself*. The great names are to him what he brings to them. Life is what we make it, height and depth, hope and despair, heaven and hell. When a man believes *in God, and not in names and places and persons* then *suddenly the great soul has enshrined itself in some other form*, pure, original. The great soul, which is the Divine Nature, comes to us in the silence of our thought, comes in the performance of our act, in the contemplation of our being and in the outward swing of completion. Flowing into the receptive mind it floods the intellect, surges through the emotion and finds an extension of itself in us, as the Universal passes into action through the human.

Through all the multiplied forms of life runs one thread of unity, *the subtle element*, the Divine stuff of every form. The One passes into the all—the all is resolvable again to the One, while those spiritual laws

is doing. He has a definite intention in mind and if he does receive subjective impressions from his patient he receives them only to correct them, provided they are negative.

The chief characteristic of this form of spiritual mind healing is different from that of Eastern systems of thought. There is nothing occult, esoteric, or mysterious about it. It is a conscious and definite act of the self-knowing mind. A person is never under the control of any power or presence, in the flesh or out of it, but is working in his own thought. It is true that the practitioner often tunes in to the stream of consciousness of his patient, and in so doing often discovers what thought should be reversed, but he should never be influenced by it.

On page 422, General Summary, you will find a discussion of the idea that each one of us maintains a stream of consciousness in the One Mind. In this universal medium, past, present, and future are one. What we subjectively contact at times is a mental vibration of thought which sometimes carries with it a picture of the person, the incident, the thing, or the place where the thought was created.

Because, as stated in the last two paragraphs of page 421, *Man is Universal on the subjective side of life*, and because mental telepathy or thought communication takes place through the medium of Universal Subjectivity, it follows that it is entirely possible to contact innumerable streams of consciousness. If you study these paragraphs carefully and thoughtfully you will arrive at a definite understanding of what this means.

Turn to page 618 in the Glossary for a definition of *Psychic Phenomena*. While we do not deny the various forms of psychic phenomena but seek to understand them, we do affirm that spiritual mind healing is always a conscious act in the thought of the practitioner. He does not sit in the silence wondering what is going to happen. As our text states, he neither hopes, wills, longs, asks, nor merely desires. He does a definite piece of work in his own thought, in his own consciousness.

As stated in the previous lesson the practitioner starts with the assumption that his patient is always a spiritual entity, perfect and complete. He now uses the method of argumentation or mental realization to bring out in his own mind a recognition of the spiritual perfection which he has claimed for his patient.

Turn again to the bottom of page 332 and read through page 333 and reimpress your consciousness with a vision of true individuality as described in this text. Then on page 477 and the top of 478 under the heading, *The Light of the World*, read again the saying of Jesus where he refers to himself as the individualized *I AM*. This is the conclusion at which you are trying to arrive in your own mind about your patient. He is a spiritual entity and as such, from the spiritual standpoint, he is perfect.

As one becomes acquainted with this spiritual viewpoint, senses and assimilates its meaning, its atmosphere, the Mind Principle which is activated re-forms the substance of the body after a new, harmonious pattern. The practitioner is not desiring this to be so; he is knowing that it is so. He is talking to himself about his patient. In a certain sense he is taking the entire belief and experience of the patient into his own consciousness. Here he transmutes negative thought into a positive mental state.

The practitioner does not treat every organ of the physical body, but affirming the spiritual perfection of the entire body, he devotes the larger part of his treatment to handling the specific condition which needs to be changed or neutralized. He does this by a conscious reversal of thought. He is not trying to send out a thought; he is trying to become conscious of an idea of perfection, and because the medium of mind is universal the statements made by the practitioner set a power or law in motion which instantly seeks an outlet in the direction specified, that is, for the person whose name is mentioned in the treatment. We can always direct this law for definite purposes.

In this system of spiritual mind healing we seek, in so far as possible, to eliminate superstition and to cooperate with all other forms of healing. Our work is done entirely in the field of mind. There is no reason why we should not work side by side with any physician, psychologist, or anyone else who is seeking to alleviate human suffering. To deny oneself the privilege of doing this is to resort to the rankest of superstitions, to the grossest form of ignorance. Emerson tells us that limitation is the only sin there is and we are quite sure that he is right. There is no sin but a mistake and no punishment but a consequence—Cause and Effect.

The practitioner must be careful not to assume a sense of personal responsibility for the recovery of his patient. His responsibility rests in an obligation to do his work systematically, intelligently, and sincerely. He should not wonder if his work is going to be effective or if his patient receives the treatment, or if the treatment he has given is the right one.

Any mental argument which arises in a person's mind denying that he has the power to use his word successfully for helping others would be a negative suggestion. Being born of thought it can consciously be changed. Therefore if something says to you that you cannot do this, that you do not have the power, that you do not know enough, that you are not spiritually evolved, or have not had enough experience to give successful treatments, at once recognize this thought as merely a mental suggestion. It is an inertia of thought, a denial of good, and as any modern psychologist would tell you, thought inertia actually assumes the aspect of an entity although it never is one. Its argument tries to deny us the privilege of using the spiritual Principle of Truth.

We must be constantly on guard to detect this subtle argument and bombard it, as it were, with the truth, until there is no longer left any belief in negation to argue about. Thus, as stated at the top of page 200, *the practitioner must treat himself to know that the word he speaks is entirely independent, even of himself.* In such degree as each realizes that he is working through a medium of Law he will have this kind of independence. It was this perception of the Law as obeying his word that gave Jesus his power.

If you will read on page 604 the sections under the heading *Knowledge* and also *Knowing No Other*, you will get a good description of this inner sense which you must have if you are to speak with authority. It is your business to give the treatment and the business of the Law to execute it. You must become aware that there is a Truth, a Power, which recognized and called upon meets every need. In such degree as you have implicit faith and confidence in your treatment you will be successful.

In treating people be certain that you are giving definite time, thought, and attention to each case. Never pass this up lightly as though you merely held a thought for them, for this is one of the greatest mistakes you could make, both for yourself and those you are seeking to help.

Too many people say, "Hold a thought for me," not knowing what they mean nor realizing that a practitioner must give definite time to each case every time he treats. This profession can never be based on an intelligent procedure without having this clearly understood, both by the practitioner and the patient. People must know that treatment is definite. Every case is specific and no two can be treated exactly alike. Therefore a practitioner takes only as many cases as he has time to give adequate mental attention.

Disease is never an entity. The mental practitioner treats disease as being an impersonal thought force. It is neither person, place, nor thing of itself. It has no real, eternal law to support it. It is, however, a definite experience in the life of the one who has it, and this experience must be separated from the one who suffers from it.

The practitioner, then, separates the belief from the believer. Of course this is entirely a process of thought in his own mind. For instance he might say, "This disease, being neither person, place, nor thing, having no law to support it, does not belong to this person and cannot operate through him. The individual being spiritual and his spirit being perfect, no form of discord can attach itself to him."

Even at the expense of seemingly monotonous repetition, the practitioner uses any argument or any line of thought, any affirmation, any denial, or any statement whatsoever which confirms his own conviction. Over and over again realize that you as a practitioner treat no one but yourself. Heal yourself of what is wrong with your patient and he will tell you that he is being benefited by your work. This is the meaning of, *And ye shall know the truth, and the truth shall make you free*.

Spirit is perfect, so the spiritual man needs no healing, but the psychological man needs a healing and so does the physical man. The practitioner must use any statement which convinces his own mind that his patient is a spiritual and perfect entity right now. Naturally those statements which have been fraught with great spiritual significance through the ages will have a deep meaning. In the last analysis each man's philosophy more or less hinges around his idea of God. Our conduct is subconsciously conditioned by our spiritual ideals. A man without spiritual ideals would make an ineffective spiritual mind healer.

Neither the Universal *I AM* nor the individual *I* are ever sick. The physical *Myself* does not manifest this inner perfection and the psychological *Me* is often disturbed by some discordant thought. When, however, the psychological man reflects the images of thought which descend from heaven, by which we mean a harmonious state of consciousness, then the physical will respond. That is the way in which spiritual mind healing affects the physical body.

The practitioner must recognize only perfection. You should begin to use this Principle at once if you have not already done so. Do not wait for a greater understanding but begin today to declare this truth. Begin today to say that you know, and you know that you know. Claim that you do know how to use this spiritual power.

Turn again to the definition of *I AM* on page 598, which has already been discussed in Lesson 3. When Jesus said, *Before Abraham was, I am*, this is what he was referring to, and this was also the *bread* of which he was speaking in Matthew 4:4. For a further explanation of why Jesus so effectively used his healing power turn to page 427. The Universal *I AM*, which is God, is perfect, and the individual *I*, which is Christ, is also perfect.

On page 541 read the second and third Meditations. Dwell on them thoughtfully and with a great sense of their reality. Let the meaning of these words sink into your consciousness until you know that there is a *witness within you* and that the voice of truth does speak through you. Then realize that your word is law. You do not will it to be so, you do not compel it, you do not insist that it shall be law. You quietly recognize that it is the law for that thing whereto it is spoken.

It is not enough to say that truth is; you must *know* that you speak the truth. Thus Jesus said, *All power is given unto me in heaven and in earth*. We too are Sons of God, so this Power is also ours. Begin to use the Principle today and It will begin to work for you today.

In mental practice never locate disease. This is because thoughts are things. If we place the disease in some particular location, because our work is in the field of mind alone the mind locates that disease where we have placed it and tends to hold it there. Spiritual mind healing takes place in thought. We cannot be too careful to separate the belief from the believer, for the spiritual man has no disease, and this is the only man we talk about in our treatment.

While most disease may be assumed to be mental in its origin, it does not necessarily follow that it originates in our conscious thought. Because we are all more or less subjectively united with race mind any of us might take on certain conditions which do not belong to us. This is another reason why we must mentally separate the disease from the one suffering from it.

The very fact that in analytical psychology so much care must be taken to probe the psyche or the subjective mind in order to discover the origin of the psychosis proves that subjective mental reactions are not necessarily conscious; neither have they necessarily ever been conscious. Therefore if we tell a person that his disease is in his thought we should carefully explain what we mean; otherwise our statement may seem cold and unsympathetic. Remember, we should have sympathy with the patient but not with the disease.

Summary

Spiritual mind healing is a conscious act of thought. It does not depend on the psychic impressions it receives. It is a concise and definite statement in the Law of Mind which acts upon it. The spiritual mind healer never tries to receive impressions. He endeavors rather to rise above them and initiate a new chain of causation. Treatment is not a desire, a hope, or a longing, but words spoken from an inner awareness of spiritual reality.

The practitioner talks to himself about his patient or whatever he is treating. If an argument rises in the mind of the practitioner denying that he has the power to do this, he must meet the argument by rising entirely above it into a field of unrestricted thought.

It is important to realize that you treat no one but yourself. This method is to be followed in every form of treatment, no matter what you are working for.

The basis for this treatment of course is that there is a spiritual man who needs no healing. It is the business of the practitioner to recognize this inner perfection.

The practitioner must realize that his word is the law of elimination to anything that does not belong to the spiritual man. Therefore he must have complete conviction that there is a spiritual man and that the person he is working for is this spiritual man.

We do not deny that the physical or the mental man may be ill; we do affirm that the Spirit is perfect, and we do seek sincerely, deeply and simply to identify the person we are working for with the Living Spirit.

Questions

Brief answers to these questions should be written out by the student after studying the lesson, and the answers compared with those which will be included in next week's lesson.

1. Why should a mental and spiritual practitioner never enter into a psychic or subjective state of consciousness in treating?
2. If a practitioner finds his consciousness disturbed by negative thought while treating, what should he do?
3. From what source may negative subjective impressions rise?
4. What is meant by *tuning in to a stream of consciousness*?
5. Explain the saying, *Man is universal on the subjective side of life*.
6. What do we mean by transmuting negative thought into a positive state?
7. In mental treatment for physical healing, is it necessary to treat each organ of the body separately?
8. How many patients should a mental and spiritual practitioner treat in one day?
9. What should a practitioner do if someone asks him to "hold a thought" for him?
10. What is meant by *healing oneself of what is wrong with one's patient*?
11. How does a mental practitioner straighten out his own thought about his patient?
12. What do we mean by our conduct being subconsciously conditioned?
13. Distinguish between the Universal *I AM*, the individual *I*, and physical *Myself* and psychological *Me*.
14. Would we say that it is the individual *I*, the psychological *Me*, or the physical *Myself* which is sick, impoverished and unhappy?
15. What is the *witness within you*?
16. Why do we never mentally locate disease in giving mental treatment?
17. Assuming that most disease is mental in its origin, does it necessarily follow that it originates in our conscious thought?
18. Why should a mental practitioner be sympathetic toward his patient but never with what ails him?

Answers to Questions on Lesson 27

1. Mind energy is an ever-present, self-existent, creative potential which surrounds us at all times.
2. We use mind energy by consciously thinking. Our thoughts provide the mold which gives this energy definite intention.
3. (a) In using mind energy for self-help one would say, "This word is for me. I am thus and so" (making whatever claims one believes to be true about one's Spiritual Nature). (b) In using mind energy for others one would preface one's statements by saying, "This word is for (name of person being treated)."
4. In treating others the practitioner never addresses them mentally; he speaks to himself about his patient.
5. If spiritual healing tends to exhaust the will or tire the mind we may be certain that we are unconsciously using mental suggestion, coercion, or will power, instead of relying completely upon the action of Principle upon our word.
6. The office of mental concentration is not creative; it merely centers the attention on the definite desire and directs it.
7. When we say, "While there is a limited use of the Law, there are no degrees to the Power Itself," we mean likening the Law to the ocean. We can individually dip up as much as our buckets will hold. The ocean would represent the sea of mind energy, while our buckets would represent our ideas.
8. To base faith on understanding means to be aware that there is a creative Law of Cause and Effect which must respond to our word; and to have a conviction that we can and do use this Law.
9. We may be sure that our use of the Law will produce good if we use It for constructive purposes only.
10. Loving one's neighbor as one's self does not imply self-effacement, for it indicates that we should love the self as well as the neighbor.
11. If you have time to give only one treatment a day you should give it to yourself, because unless your own thought is straight you cannot think clearly about anyone else you may desire to help.
12. By balancing the Law and the Word we mean the recognition of the fact that our word is personal, while the Law is impersonal. One is the complement of the other, and both are necessary to complete wholeness.
13. In treating to relieve poor circulation declare that your patient is a spiritual entity and that there can be no overaction or inaction in him. His circulation is established in pure Spirit and is now manifest in his physical being.
14. We do not know exactly how the reaction takes place, but experience has demonstrated that it does. We assume that this action takes place through the Law of Cause and Effect and in the medium of the One Mind. In this medium, what is known at one point is simultaneously known at all points.
15. Scientific mental and spiritual treatment changes the subjective images of thought, which in turn produce the desired conditions within the physical body or the body of affairs.

16. By having a spiritual experience in our thought we mean something more than conviction, belief, or acceptance. We mean an inner sense of completion; a dynamic sense of the unity of all life.
17. Spiritual self-awakening is an individual experience which is felt. Its meaning cannot be put into words.

The Prayer of a Successful Business

Let us assume that our business is praying to us for right action, even as we turn to the All-pervading Presence for Its inspiration and guidance. Our business is saying:

MAKE ME GLAD; INCREASE MY ACTION;
DRAW EVERYTHING TO MY ATTENTION THAT I OUGHT TO KNOW
IN ORDER THAT I CAN PROJECT MYSELF IN EVERY DIRECTION
WITH THE CERTAINTY OF SUCCESS.

MAKE ME TO SEE MYSELF AS EVER EXPANDING.

I PRAY THAT I MAY SERVE ALL WHO COME NEAR ME.

I KNOW THAT EVERYONE WHO COMES HERE
SHALL FEEL MY LOVE AND FRIENDSHIP.
THEY SHALL SENSE A WARMTH AND COLOR WITHIN ME.
THEY SHALL FEEL AT HOME AND THEY SHALL FEEL SATISFIED.

I BLESS AND PRAISE EVERY ONE WHO COMES HERE
AND REJOICE IN THEIR PRESENCE.
I DRAW THEM TO ME WITH THE IRRESISTIBLE POWER OF DIVINE UNION.
I SERVE THEM AND AM SERVED BY THEM.

I MULTIPLY. I INCREASE. I EXPAND. I REJOICE. I PROSPER.

I AM ALL ACTION, ALL POWER, ALL PRESENCE.

I AM SUCCESS AND HAPPINESS AND FULFILLMENT.

There is no business activity outside the field of the Universal Mind, and because you know that you have a business or are running one, the Law of Mind also knows it. This treatment is but a way of demonstrating your complete partnership with a Power with which you are already one.

Thinking Affirmatively

There is a Power for good in the universe greater than you are, and you can use It. We all believe this. The question is: Why do we not use It more effectively? If all things are possible to faith, why do we not have more faith? If affirmative prayers are answered, why do we not always pray affirmatively? Let us try to figure out just how we can more effectively cooperate with the Law of Mind in Action.

First let us begin with the thought that we are all united with invisible forces which are creative; that already we are one with a Universal Mind which can do anything.

Next let us consider that we are centers in this Mind, and that the sum total of all our thoughts is either silently attracting good to us or repelling it from us.

And third, let us know that we can change our thinking, and in so doing cause the Law of Good to act affirmatively for us instead of negatively.

Let us start with the first proposition. We are surrounded by a creative Mind which reacts to our thought. This is the basis of all faith and all effective prayer. This is why Jesus told us that when we pray we should believe we already have what we desire. When Jesus said that it is done unto us as we believe, he implied that there is a Power that can, will, and must react to us. But this Power has no choice other than to react to us in the way we think. This Power acts as a law operating on our beliefs. This is why he said that it is done unto us *as* we believe.

Up until the time of Jesus it had been believed that God might help us, that there were concessions He would make if we pleased Him, or if we performed certain rites or ceremonials. Jesus changed these suppositions into certainties. He said simply and directly that there is a Power that operates on your belief, the way you believe. Therefore, he added, be sure that you believe that you already have what you desire and then the Law of Good will bring it to you. But even the Law of Good, which is all-powerful, can bring you only as much good as you take. This taking is an act of your own mind; it is an act of faith.

No one else before Jesus had made such a claim. Only within the last hundred years, or less, have people come to realize that he was talking about a spiritual Principle in which we all are rooted, which operates on our faith, our conviction, and our acceptance.

It is the very simplicity of his claim that causes us to overlook its deep and dynamic meaning. Jesus was really saying this: You are surrounded by a Mind, a Power, an Intelligence or a Principle that receives the impress of your thought and acts upon it exactly as you think. Your thought is like an image held in front of a mirror. Thought itself is a law, reflecting back to you what you think.

Now we come to our second concept: We are thinking and active centers in this Mind, and the sum total of all our thoughts is either silently attracting our good to us or repelling it from us. This shows the part we are to play in our use of the Power greater than we are. Because it is the sum total of all our thinking that we must consider. And in doing this, one of the first things we learn is that about ninety percent of our thinking is unconscious.

Psychologists now tell us that eighty-five percent of our accidents are unconsciously invited; that at least seventy-five percent of our diseases are unconsciously created; that our success and failure in life is largely unconscious, and, of course, our happiness or our misery is almost entirely so.

You see, scientific investigation verifies what you and I are talking about. Most of our thinking is unconscious. Here is where habit patterns of thought are laid down from infancy. It should be our purpose to find out what these thought patterns are, and when they are unhappy or morbid or filled with fear, to change them so that the natural, normal flow of the Life Force Itself shall be resumed.

So we come to our third idea: We can change our thinking, and in so doing cause the Law of Mind to act affirmatively for us instead of negatively. Jesus gave us the perfect technique for doing this.

He told us that when our faith is in the good it will obliterate evil; that is, good and evil are not equal powers. Good always overcomes evil. The affirmative attitude will always overcome the negative. This is why we are now told to accentuate the positive and forget the negative. Just keep on thinking about peace and let confusion go. Affirm the good and forget the evil. This is a sound teaching.

So Jesus told us that when we pray we should become quiet, enter the closet of the self, close the door of the senses, and here make known our requests. But when we do this we should be certain that we accept the answer and then we shall get it. *When ye pray, believe that ye receive ... and ye shall have...*

This whole idea is so simple that it often eludes us. We are surrounded by a Creative Mind which reacts to our thinking. The sum total of all thinking decides what is going to happen to us. We can change our thinking and cause the very law that limited us to bring us freedom. What more could we ask? What more could be given than this?

The Bible says, *If ye know these things, happy are ye if ye do them* (John 13: 17). So let us proceed to the doing.

Going back to our first statement that we are surrounded by a Mind Principle which acts creatively on our thinking, let us make this the basis of our belief. Whether we call this Mind or Principle or Spirit or God or a Law, makes no difference. The only thing that matters is whether we accept this self-operating Power around us, a Power which actually can and will do whatever ought to be done for us if we believe in It. And do we accept the fact that the sum total of our thinking decides what is going to happen to us?

Our first proposition is one of faith. We must believe. It is natural to have faith and to believe, but when we find that we lack these qualities we now know what to do about it, because belief and faith are mental attitudes. So if we practice affirmative prayer daily, by saying: "I do have faith; I do have conviction; I do believe; I do know and understand that there is a Power greater than I am; I do realize that I can use It; there is nothing in me that can doubt, deny, or limit this Power; my whole being accepts It, both consciously and subconsciously" then we shall be preparing our minds to pray affirmatively, which means to pray effectively.

If there is a Principle of Mind that reacts to our thinking or to our belief, it naturally follows that if we say, "It cannot," then It cannot because we do not let It. If we say, "It won't," then It cannot because we do not permit It. And if we limit It to a little good It cannot give us a greater good. The Power Itself is absolute; the way we use It is relative.

We can practice believing because thoughts are things, and when we say, "I believe," and, "There is no doubt in me," we do two things—we affirm our belief and by so doing build a positive acceptance in the mind, and at the same time we reject our doubts by denying them. This is the way thought works.

Realizing that ninety percent of our thinking is unconscious, we should daily affirm that there is nothing in us that denies the good we affirm; that every experience we have ever had up until now, which denies that good, is wiped out of mind and memory as a negative force; that we are forgiven our mistakes and encouraged to go on and do better.

We are now ready to entertain our third basic concept and see if we cannot actually bring ourselves to believe that we possess the good we desire even though we do not see any possible way for it to happen. This also can be reduced to a simple method. You can say to yourself, "I do accept this good. I do believe my prayer is answered. I do affirm the presence of love, friendship, happiness, prosperity, health, peace—whatever the need may be and nothing in me denies, rejects, or refutes it. I do accept it."

You will find after you have done this for a while there will come a gradual acceptance of your affirmation. And you will learn that as the subjective reactions of your thought build up an affirmative attitude, things will begin to change in your environment. It may take a little time, but you now have courage, knowing that you are dealing with a definite Principle and that It cannot fail.

We are all surrounded by a certain amount of skepticism and doubt, and perhaps many people think what we believe is all nonsense. This should not disturb us in the least. We are to know that we are working independently with God and the great Law of Good. Whether we are working for ourselves or our family or our friends or the whole world, every affirmative spiritual statement we make will have some power. An invisible Law of Good will be acting upon it.

You have no one to prove this to but yourself. But if you do prove it to yourself, no doubt your friends will begin to ask you what it is all about. You have no authority for what you do other than the authority of what happens when you do it.

We have nothing to give to the world unless we have first proved it. The blind cannot lead the blind. But alone with Truth, one man can pass from weakness into strength, from fear into faith, from defeat into success, and even while he is still living, from a state of continual death into a realization of everlasting life.

Meditation

I know there is a Power of Good which is responding to me and bringing into my experience everything that is necessary to my unfoldment, to my happiness, to my peace, to my health, and to my success. I know there is a Power of Good that enables me to help others and to bless the whole world.

So I say quietly to myself: There is one Life, that Life is God, that Life is perfect, that Life is my life now. It is flowing through me, circulating in me. I am one with Its rhythm. My heart beats with the pulsation of the Universe, in serenity, in peace, and in joy. My whole physical being is animated by the Divine Spirit, and if there is anything in it that does not belong, it is cast out because there is one perfect Life in me now.

And I say to myself: I am daily guided so that I shall know what to do under every circumstance, in every situation. Divine Intelligence guides me in love, in joy, and in complete self-expression. Desiring that the Law of Good alone shall control me, I bless and prosper everything I am doing; I multiply every activity; I accept and expect happiness and complete success.

Realizing that I am one with all people, I affirm that there is a silent Power flowing through me to them, which blesses and heals and prospers, makes happy and glad their pathway.

And realizing that the world is made up of people like myself, I bless the world and affirm that it shall come under the Divine government of good, under the Divine providence of love, and under the Divine leadership of the Supreme Intelligence. *For thine is the kingdom, and the power, and the glory, for ever. Amen.*

Getting Along With People

No one can live to himself alone. Other people are so much a part of our lives that we cannot think of living without them. People who feel themselves excluded from society are maladjusted.

On the other hand, much of our trouble comes because of others. In our relationships with others two things must happen if we are to be happy. We must be with others, enjoy them and act with them, without in any way seeking to control their actions.

This is not always the easiest thing to do, particularly with our closest friends. But you may be certain that the one who has the largest number of friends is the one who can work and play with them while at the same time letting them alone.

This is true even in the family life. For the family is made up of the individual members of its group who must live in close relationship with each other and work and play together, while at the same time remaining individuals. It is a fortunate child who is born into a family that understands this and that gives the child as much freedom as possible while at the same time teaching him to cooperate with others.

The over-protected child loses his self-confidence; when he grows up he lacks self-assurance. While the child who feels neglected, unloved, and unwanted is likely to grow up with the unconscious feeling that everything and everyone is against him. He is apt to develop either an over-aggressive or an under-aggressive attitude toward life. When his attitude lacks the proper amount of aggressiveness he continually lives in dependence on others and gets along well only with those who are protecting and caring for him. When his attitude is over-aggressive he finds it difficult to get along with others for he generally seeks to dominate them.

The well-adjusted person is one who has been permitted to be an individual but who also has learned to cooperate with others. This attitude probably was formed way back in the early family life. For it is here that we become conditioned for the years ahead.

But we cannot be born again physically, nor can we actually return to the days of our infancy. However, modern psychology does, in a sense, do this for the poorly adjusted person. He is taken back in imagination to infancy and his mental and emotional reactions which well up from the under part of his mind and memory are brought to the light of day.

This is a slow and expensive process. Few people could afford either the time or the money to go through with it. Moreover, there are not enough analysts in the world to handle even a small fraction of the ones who need help.

But there is another thing that we can do, something that Jesus knew about—something he referred to when he said, *You must be born again*. And when they asked him how it could be possible for a man to be born again he said, *You must be born of the Spirit*. This is the new birth that comes through a new outlook on life, a new way of thinking, a new sense of our relationship to our environment, to the people around us, to ourselves and to God.

It was this relationship to God that Jesus placed first, for he said that if you find this, everything else will be added. Today we know that the psychological, emotional, and mental readjustments which are necessary to our well-being will be made if we experience this new birth that Jesus was talking about.

In order to do this we must have a firm conviction that all people live in God, and we must have a deep realization that we are all one in this Universal Spirit which is God.

There is a place where we begin and leave off physically, but there is no place where we begin and leave off mentally or spiritually. Our minds merge with the minds of others, and as they meet, some silent force within us attracts or repels automatically in accord with our accepted thought patterns.

If we do not merge with others in cooperation, in unity, and in happiness, we may be certain that there is something in us that still feels it has been rebuffed.

Here is where the adjustment has to be made. What we must do is to see that we ourselves are adjusted to others. We neither wish to dominate them nor do we wish them to dominate us. We wish to get along with them happily. They have opinions that are different from ours. We must be flexible enough to recognize that their opinions are right for them, even though they do not fit into our scheme. This is what Jesus called nonresistance.

When he spoke of nonresistance he did not mean that we must agree with every person's opinion. He meant exactly what he said—do not resist it, let it alone, do not even try to dominate it. If we do not resist it, it will depart from us, it will not disturb us. If we can get over this idea of trying to control other people's thoughts or actions and still live with them in happy relationship, we shall be well on the road to adjustment. And above everything else, if we can trace our own origin back to its original source, which is God, and do the same for everyone else, we shall find that we are getting along with others.

If you want sunshine, step out into the sunshine. If you have locked yourself away in a dark closet, why not come out into the light? If you have been feeling that everything is against you and no one really cares for you, know that God is in everyone, and meet the God in others and see what happens.

It is remarkable how Jesus approached this subject. It is as though he had said, "You think that you were born of flesh and blood. You think that your parents gave you life. You think that everything that has happened to you since you were born is held against you. You think that all the negative thoughts you have ever had are operating against you. You think that all the fears and failures and doubts and uncertainties you have been carrying around for years are something over which you have no control. Why not try something else?"

"I have a method which will work for you if you will let it. Just forget all the past. Forgive yourself and everyone else for everything that has ever happened. Try to feel that everyone is doing about the best he can. Come to realize that while you were born into this world through your parents, you really are a spirit. You really are born out of Life. The thing that entered into you when you were born was God, the living Spirit. Why not get back to the true center of your being and think and act and live from the point of view that you are one with everything because you are one with God?"

Jesus gave to us the secret of complete adjustment when he said, *Seek ye first the kingdom of God ... and all these things shall be added unto you.*

Go back in your thought and your imagination to this central idea: I am one with God; all people are one with God. We all live in God. When I meet others it is God in them I meet—God individualized, God personalized, God as my friend.

Jesus added the Spirit to the knowledge of what today we call psychology, or the way the mind works. He did not deny that people are unhappy or badly adjusted to life. He did say: You do not have to be this way. Seek first things first and everything else will be added. And by first things, to which everything is added, he meant—find God in yourself. That is why he said, *Blessed are they that do hunger and thirst after righteousness: for they shall be filled ... Knock, and it shall be opened unto you ... Seek, and ye shall find.*

If people look drab or uninteresting to us it is because of the way we look at them. If we have not received joy from others it is because we have stifled joy at the center of our own being. Joy must go forth to meet joy. Love must go forth to meet love. All people are rooted in God, and it is only as we go down to the roots of our being that we unify with others in spirit and truth. Everything that follows is the play of Life upon Itself.

Meditation

Because I am one with God, I am one with all people. Because I am one with Life, I am one with everything that lives. I feel my union with people and with nature. I feel that I belong to Life.

I love life and I enter into the joy of living. I enter into companionship with others, into cooperation with them. And I know that something within me reaches out and embraces the whole world. Something within me blesses everything it touches, brings life and happiness and joy to everyone. Something in me acts as a healing balm, restoring everything to its natural and native perfection.

As I silently listen to the Spirit within me and think of Its perfection, I know that I am being born again—born into joy and hope and gladness, born into love and faith and assurance.

Silently I release every negative thought from my mind. I loose it and let it go. And I, too, pray *that they all may be one; as thou, Father, art in me, and I in thee, that they also may be one in us.*

Practical Suggestion for Mental Treatment

The Family Life

In treating against family confusion, work to know that there is no confusion. The family is a collection of perfect ideas.

It may be difficult at times to sense this, but the practitioner is not dealing with the manifestation of discord as though it were a thing of itself, but only as though it were a wrong combination of thoughts operating through persons who are already spiritually unified with each other, desiring each other's good, and being kindly disposed toward each other.

What the practitioner handles or dissolves is the belief that good ever can be divided against itself. The idea of argument and criticism cannot enter this family life. It certainly cannot upset the equilibrium of the Spirit which indwells every member, joining them together in a community of Spirit. They have a partnership with each other and with the Eternal.

The practitioner must also know that there is no sense of jealousy or any other kindred thought which can operate in the family life. He resolves all of these so-called people into the One Spirit and re-forms them in his own imagination into the image of perfection. He sees them emerge as unified manifestations of wholeness. The household of God is a household of peace and happiness, and nothing enters it but love, joy, and understanding.

This treatment, effectively pursued, will dissolve confusion. Sometimes it will produce a change in the family life, but it will heal if it is persisted in.

The Presence Is Peace, Joy, and Beauty

All people desire a personal God, and in our system of thought we may be certain that Spirit is personal to everyone who personifies It. If the Spirit is omnipresent and undivided, It is at the very center of our being, and each of us is a unique representation of this omnipresent One.

Kipling said, *Each in his separate star shall draw the thing as he sees it, for the God of things as they are.* Most certainly God is personal to everyone, and the wonderful thing is that each represents God in a unique way. Each individualizes God and no two individualizations are identical. Thus the personality of God is not only real to us, but it is uniquely real.

To sense the Divine Person back of each act and the Divine direction back of each thought is both scientific and sensible. Moreover, without such a sense there would be no warmth or color in our work. Every treatment should be filled with the atmosphere of helpfulness, proceeding from our realization that we are recognizing God in our patient, the God who is personified through him, personal to him, individualized in him.

Instead of denying that God is personal to each one of us we emphasize such personalness. Indeed it is one of the chief cornerstones of this whole spiritual structure, this whole philosophic system of thought.

Not only is there a Presence within us which directly responds to us; there is also a Law operating through us which obeys the will of this Presence. Since this Presence is peace, joy, and beauty, and since It must be harmony and wholeness we may be sure that these qualities seek expression through our activities, seek manifestation in everything that we do, say, and think, or as Jesus said to the woman at the well, . . . *for the Father seeketh such*.

We Work Only in Consciousness

Office of the Dean

My Dear Friend,
As our lesson states, the spiritual man is as perfect as God because he is an incarnation of the Spirit. It is the psychological and the physical man who is sick. This in no way denies either the physical or the mental, but goes beyond them to the spiritual. It is the Spirit that we affirm.

We seek complete cooperation with those who work with the physical. From this standpoint our work is something added to other forms of healing. Our work is in the field of thought alone and deals with the Law of Mind in Action. The basis for the whole treatment is Perfect God, Perfect Man, and Perfect Being. God is assumed to be the only Person and the only Power there is.

The statements we make in the treatment are to reveal the spiritual man. In doing this the practitioner starts with the idea of his own spiritual perfection and from this level of consciousness announces the Truth about the one he is helping. He then must turn resolutely from everything that denies that which he affirms.

As you will notice in one of the supplements to this lesson, there is a Door that you alone can open, and you must make every effort to open this Door. It is the Doorway to the Secret Place of the Most High within yourself. Every man's life is hid with Christ in God. That is, the spiritual side of his nature is already one with peace, poise, power, and perfection.

Try always to keep this Doorway open.

Sincerely,
Ernest Holmes

Lesson 29

How to Heal, page 202, to *The Medium of Healing,* page 208

In spiritual mind healing we seek to separate discordant mental beliefs and discordant physical conditions from spiritual man. Spiritual man is not sick. This is self-evident if we recognize that the Spirit of man is God. Spiritual man cannot be sick any more than God can be sick. It is the psychological man and the physical man who is sick. Our treatment is in the field of mind, while the work of the physician is in the physical realm.

The mental practitioner should do his work in the field of thought only. He cannot do this while he feels that he must treat a physical condition. For even though he knows that as a result of his mental treatment the physical condition should change, unless he is able theoretically to resolve things into thoughts there would be no basis upon which he could proceed with his metaphysical work. Unless a thing is mental in its origin it cannot be handled mentally with any hope of success. Only that which is mental can be mentally handled. This is self-evident.

So the spiritual mind practitioner deals with thought. Hence our text states that he does not treat the physical body as a thing in itself, nor disease as belonging to the spiritual man. He treats man as a spiritual being immune from discord. In doing this he is not denying in any sense of the term that people are really sick. He is not denying that people are poor or unhappy. He is affirming, however, that there is a higher realm of causation which we may enter and, as it were, letting down fire from heaven, cause the light of eternal Truth to dispel the darkness of the belief in separation from the Infinite.

To plunge beneath the surface and find the mental equivalent for right action is to discover the spiritual prototype which will produce a corresponding reaction in the physical body or in the environment. It was this that Jesus was so well able to do.

As suggested on page 476 under the heading, *The Meat Which Perisheth*, starvation takes place on more than one plane. The higher always governs the lower. When consciousness functions in unity with the eternal harmony the reaction tends to produce physical well-being. The spiritual practitioner starts with the assumption that God is all the Power and all the Presence there is; that man is in God and God is in man; that there is a Perfect Divine Presence at the center of every man's being. This Divine Presence is man's life and in reality is the only life there is.

It is about this spiritual Reality that the practitioner makes his statements, claiming for the spiritual man everything he believes to be true about God, and declaring that the Truth is manifest in and through him now, in every part of his being. The practitioner seeks mentally to separate the disease from the one suffering from it. In changing the mental concept from a material to a spiritual basis he heals the psychological man, that is, he heals the subjective state of the thought of the man who is suffering. This subjective thought of the patient's consciousness acting in accordance with the Law of Cause and Effect, correspondingly affects his physical body.

First the practitioner recognizes *his own* spiritual perfection, for it is from the level of his own self-awareness that he speaks for his patient. As water will reach its own level by its own weight, so consciousness will externalize at its own level by its own recognition. No treatment is complete without a realization of peace and a silent recognition of the Divine in man. It is this consciousness of wholeness which is the real power of a treatment. We should not refuse to go through the mental process necessary to reach this conclusion. That is the only way in which we can arrive at a definite Science of Mind and furnish people with a definite technique and teach them how to help themselves and others.

It is essential that the worker in this field should always keep his feet on the ground even though his head may be in the clouds. This is more than a theory; it is the practical application of a dynamic principle to the problems of everyday life. There is nothing mysterious about the process; neither should it be thought of as difficult. It should be easy. The silent recognition of one's perfection or the perfection of another should not be brought about by strain, but through mental relaxation.

To believe that good destroys evil need not produce a controversy in mind. It is a conclusion to which we should come without controversy. To argue that God is all in all should not be laborious, even though it is a definite and conscious act of the mind. To think peace instead of confusion is not to argue with confusion nor to combat it, but rather to rise above it without any sense of strain. The state of consciousness which produces the desired result must be more harmonious than the state of consciousness which produced the discordant result and being more harmonious it should be more restful.

In this form of treatment the practitioner should attempt to explain away all discordant facts as though they had no right to exist in the kingdom of harmony. He must have a firm conviction that they really do not have any place there. He sees them as wrong answers, but always he must be certain that he has the right answer. Hence our text declares that mental treatment is a direct statement of belief coupled with the realization that the desired good is already accomplished.

To realize that our good is at hand is to recognize the omnipresence of God. Read the definitions of *Omnipotence, Omniscience* and *Omnipresence* on page 615; also the definition of *Only-All* on the same page. To recognize this *One* Perfect Presence is to become conscious of God. To recognize that this One Presence runs through everything and from Its unity produces multiplicity is to understand the secret of the ages. (Read the definition of *Multiplicity* on page 613.)

The practitioner turns resolutely from the undesirable condition, carrying it back into a spiritual realm where it actually has no existence. As a result of this treatment he realizes that the condition disappears in the light of Truth. He is looking into the center of Reality. Read the definition of *Light* on page 607 and of *Life* on page 606. It is into this consciousness of light and life that the practitioner lifts his thought about his patient. This is what is meant by the Christ-consciousness or that consciousness in which one is aware of his unity with the Whole.

Now read again the definition of *Unity* on page 640. The Bible says that God is all in all, over all, and through all. It is in the silence of our own soul that we recognize this unity. (See the definition of *Silence* on page 632.) Combining this idea of life, light, and unity you will see exactly what a practitioner must do as he seeks to lift his thought about his patient to that consciousness which is the Creator of all appearances.

The practitioner realizing that the spiritual man needs no healing, works in the realm of his own thought until he is conscious that his patient is this spiritual man right now. As he clears his own thought about his patient, the patient becomes benefited. Consequently, spiritual mind healing is a result of clear thinking. Under the argumentative method it is a systematic process of reasoning which presents the Truth about man's being and in presenting this Truth repudiates that which ought not to be. (Read again the definition of *Truth* on page 639.)

The Law of the Spirit makes us free, as the Scripture says. You will find a discussion of this under the heading, *There Is No Condemnation*, on page 484. The practitioner should never mentally condemn his patient. The patient suffers, but the practitioner must not connect that suffering with any so-called sin or mistake which the patient has made. If he is going to separate the belief from the believer (a phrase which occurs frequently because of its importance in our technique of treatment), he cannot do so while he feels that there is any reason why the spiritual man should experience discord.

While there is no doubt that we suffer *from* our mistakes and *by* them, and that we shall cease suffering when we cease making such mistakes, it is also true that to condemn ourselves or others is to act in opposition to the real Truth of being. Jesus tells us to judge not that we be not judged. This we discussed in Lessons 5 and 26, but you may turn again to page 433 for a recapitulation. Under the heading, *The Altar of Faith*, on page 430 we are told not to resist evil and to love our enemies. We are to make every endeavor to plunge mentally through all forms of discord and thoughts of hatred to the place where love and peace abide.

On page 414, the second paragraph, is the statement, *Thoughts are more than things; they are the cause of things*. Our work is done in mind alone. We must never lose sight of this. Hence the practitioner must endeavor to see his patient as a spiritual entity *now*, perfect *now*, complete *now*, in heaven *now*. Read again, *Now Are We the Sons of God*, pages 502-3. It is this spiritual concept of man's Divinity which the practitioner uses as a mental equivalent for physical healing.

As a result of this belief in man's Divinity, the Law of Cause and Effect is set in motion in a new way, a new polarity is established, and a new manifestation takes place. This manifestation is the result of a new mental image, and the new image is the result of a change of thought. The practitioner does not say, "Here is a patient whom I must heal." From a spiritual viewpoint he has no patient to heal. The man who comes to him is not a patient but is a perfect being coming to be recognized as such. He may not be aware of this, but the practitioner must be or he will not be practicing spiritual mind healing.

The practitioner has nothing to do with the patient's thought, as though discordant thought belonged to someone. Probably one of the most difficult things for people to see in this form of practice is that the practitioner straightens out *his own thought* about his patient's belief. Because there is but one mental Law, the patient's belief about himself is straightened out at the same time. Of course the reaction to the practitioner's thought takes place in a subjective field, as we have already discussed in Lesson 28.

Mental healing is a result of clear thinking followed by definite statements, or as suggested in the last paragraph on page 418 under the General Summary, *With right glance and with right speech man superintendeth the animate and the inanimate*. But as stated at the bottom of page 395, *the engine of the Subjective Mind must be guided*. This is what treatment is for.

Any statement which will do this will be helpful. Turn to the Meditation at the bottom of page 543, *My Word Comes Back to Me*, and meditate earnestly upon the meaning of the thoughts expressed there. See if you cannot realize that *your* word is the law of harmony, triumphant over every discord. Have implicit confidence in that word.

It is not at all necessary that you use someone else's thought in doing this. Your own thought has the same power. These meditations are merely suggested ways of thinking. It is certain that the personal mind must be re-educated if we are to transmute our old mental equivalents of lack, want, limitation, and fear into the new order of thought, that upper atmosphere of our being which knows only the Good, the Beautiful, and the True. The spiritual transmutation of thought from a lower to a higher basis is absolutely essential in spiritual mind healing. Again we must realize that the Law of Cause and Effect is never broken. As suggested on page 460, history proves this. Love alone destroys hate and overcomes all things unlike itself.

In order to clear up any belief in duality, reaffirm your position in the unity of Good. State again that your word is the law unto the thing whereto it is spoken. Repeat again, "God is all. There is but One Power."

When we say, "Claim that no form of race suggestion can operate," we mean that we are protecting ourselves from the suggestion of human belief around us. For instance, if you were treating a patient who believes in fatalism you would have to heal him of such belief just as definitely as you would have to treat him if he had tuberculosis, because it is just as much of a disease. If he believes in hell you have to heal him of that, for it also is a mental disease.

Our work is based entirely upon the supposition of the unity of Good, the oneness of God, man, and creation, and all the evidence must support the belief in this unity. It is absurd to suppose that the Intelligence which operates the planets is controlled by them, just as it would be absurd to suppose that the artist who paints a canvas steps into it and is lost in or absorbed by it. Our whole thought is that God is all there is and there is nothing else, for God is over all, in all, and through all. God is both transcendent and immanent, both overdwelling and indwelling, in us and around us.

All beliefs in a power opposed to Good are to be considered hypnotic, mesmeric, and as false mental suggestion. They do not belong to anyone; therefore you must treat to know that they are removed from the consciousness of those who suffer from them. They are to be handled just as deliberately as belief in any other form of disease.

When you are giving a treatment, you are thinking (fourth paragraph, page 204). You are using that kind of thought which directly contradicts the negative and as directly affirms the positive. For every thought of evil you bring a thought of good, for every belief in lack you bring a consciousness of abundance. Your affirmation covers the denial and neutralizes it. You will be surprised as you gradually discover how definite is the reaction to definite thought.

As suggested at the top of page 205, our thought must rise higher than the disease and supply a spiritual consciousness which is the direct opposite of the mental and physical confusion. For instance, if you are treating someone who feels very much alone in the world your consciousness of his unity with God must be greater than his belief that he is isolated from Good. In such a case you would make a statement something like this: "This man is included in the All-Good, he is a part of the All-Good, he is one with all people, and because he is one with all people, all people are one with him."

Read again the Meditation on *Unity* page 549 and turn also to the Meditation at the bottom of page 520. Combining these two, work until you create an awareness of complete unity and you will surely demonstrate friendships for the one for whom you are working. This is what is meant by going beyond the disease and supplying a spiritual consciousness which will heal it.

Do not wonder whether your thought goes *out* or *in*. Merely *know* that you operate in the same Mind in which your patient lives and that your statement in Mind about him produces a corresponding reaction in his physical body and in his environment. There is no sensation in treatment (page 207). This is another thing we should be careful to understand. There is nothing you have to feel in giving a treatment other than the conviction of the Truth of your own statements.

Sometimes the people for whom you are working will say they felt your treatment. This is perfectly all right. If, on the other hand, they say they did not feel anything, do not be disturbed, because generally speaking, nothing is felt immediately, but the Law is at work just the same. Remember that all you have to feel is a conviction of the truth of your statement.

Summary

The spiritual mind healer seeks to separate the belief from the believer. This can be done only in the mind of the practitioner.

This method of treatment could have no effect were it not true that everything originates in a field of Creative Intelligence which acts upon Itself. This is but another way of saying that there is nothing in the Universe other than Intelligence and what It does.

We seek to plunge beneath the surface and find the mental and spiritual equivalent. Spiritual mind healing is not mental soaring in the clouds of superstition or mystery, but rather bringing the Great Reality down to earth.

The end and aim of this form of treatment is to recognize, appreciate, and feel the Presence of Perfect Spirit and Perfect Action.

Any arguments used are but systematic methods of reasoning which present the truth about the spiritual man.

The patient's thought is straightened out simultaneously with the inward realization of the patient's consciousness. From this standpoint mental healing is a result of clear thinking and from this standpoint clear thinking means basing our whole proposition on the theory that God is all there is.

Spiritual treatment is not something you feel as much as it is something you know, although a deep feeling does go with it, an inner spiritual realization and recognition of the Divine Presence. To feel this Presence and to state its reality and to know that your word is the law of elimination to everything that contradicts it, is the basis for all spiritual practice.

Questions

Brief answers to these questions should be written out by the student after studying the lesson, and the answers compared with those which will be included in next week's lesson.

1. How does the mental and spiritual practitioner treat to heal the physical body?
2. In mental and spiritual treatment does the practitioner deny the physical body? Does he deny poverty and unhappiness?

3. What do we mean by the higher realm of causation?
4. What is the mental equivalent for right action?
5. What is meant by *the meat which perisheth*?
6. What is the real power of a mental treatment?
7. What is the mental technique for spiritual treatment?
8. In mental treatment do we combat negative conditions?
9. What is the secret of the ages relative to unity and multiplicity?
10. What is meant by the mental practitioner lifting his thought about his patient?
11. What do we mean by a practitioner mentally condemning his patient?
12. Why should a practitioner never mentally condemn his patient?
13. What is *the engine of the subjective mind*?
14. How can we re-educate our minds?
15. How should one treat a fatalist?
16. How should we treat one who has a consciousness of loneliness?
17. What general line of thought should be embodied in all mental treatment?
18. In treating mentally does our thought go *out* or *in*?

Answers to Questions on Lesson 28

1. A mental practitioner should never enter a psychic or subjective state of consciousness in treating because it is his office consciously to direct thought rather than to be influenced by it.
2. If a practitioner finds his consciousness disturbed by negative thought while treating he should declare that such negative thought cannot operate either through him or his patient.
3. Negative subjective impressions may rise from one's own consciousness, the consciousness of those around him, or race suggestion.
4. By "tuning in" to a stream of consciousness is meant that we tune in to the kind of thought with which we mentally identify ourselves, such as fear or faith, failure or success, happiness or sadness, sickness or health.
5. The statement, *Man is Universal on the subjective side of life*, means that while his objective personality occupies definite space and deals with specific sequences of experience, that part of his consciousness which is subjective functions in a medium where there is neither past, present, nor future.
6. By transmuting negative thought into a positive state is meant building up within one's consciousness a state of thought which automatically neutralizes the negative.
7. In mental treatment for physical healing we need not treat each organ separately. We should, however, declare that the entire body is a Spiritual System, giving special attention to the particular need.
8. A practitioner should treat in one day only as many patients as he can handle, giving the necessary time to each case.
9. If someone asks a practitioner to hold a thought for him he should explain that this practice is not holding thoughts. Each treatment is a definite piece of work, with beginning, middle, and ending.

10. By *healing oneself of what is wrong with one's patient*, we mean that the practitioner straightens out his own thought about his patient.
11. A mental practitioner straightens out his own thought about his patient by using any mental argument or line of thought which convinces his own mind that his patient is a Spiritual Entity.
12. By our conduct being subconsciously conditioned we mean that our habitual subjective thought patterns tend to control our objective actions and reactions.
13. The Universal *I AM* means God, or the Impersonal Self. The individual *I* means the personification of the Universal *I AM*. The physical *myself* means the human body. The psychological *me* means the mental life of the individual.
14. We should say that it is the physical *myself* and the psychological *me* which is sick, impoverished, and unhappy. The individual *I* is always as perfect as the Universal *I AM*.
15. *The witness within you* is the realization of the true nature of your own being.
16. We never mentally locate disease in giving mental treatments, because in mental treatment we deal with only the spiritual man, who has no disease.
17. Assuming most of our diseases to be mental in origin it does not necessarily follow that they originate in our conscious thought, since the greater part of our subjective reactions are below the threshold of consciousness. We have ample proof of this in analytical psychology. In the metaphysical field we hold that we may unconsciously accept race beliefs.
18. A mental practitioner should have sympathy with his patient, recognizing his true nature. He should never be sympathetic with what ails him. He should turn from the wrong condition and declare for its opposite, which is wholeness.

The Door That You Alone Can Open

It is said that at the entrance to Solomon's Temple stood two pillars called Jachin and Boaz, and that those who wished to enter the Holy of Holies must first pass between the two pillars. These pillars are symbolic of the Law and the Word, or the Universal Presence and the Universal Principle. The Temple represents the self. In order to understand the true self we must first realize that the Universe is built on the two great principles of Reality, the Personal as Presence and the Impersonal as Law.

It is also said that the High Priest met at the Temple doorway all those who had passed between the pillars, and conducted them to the Holy of Holies. The High Priest represents the Divine incarnation in every man. This is the High Priest who must conduct us to the Holy of Holies in which reposes the Ark of the Covenant. Ark means a vehicle containing the Life Principle, while Covenant means the eternal laws of God that are forever established. In this Ark is the Scroll of Life upon which is inscribed the name of God, the *I AM*.

Whether we look at this as a fable or a reality makes no difference. It was most certainly someone' s attempt to describe the nature of the Universe and our relationship to It, and how we are to discover the secret of secrets which is a knowledge of the Spiritual Truth about our own being.

First of all we must come to realize that the Universe is a balance between the personal and the impersonal, the Principle and the Presence, or the Law and the Word. Or if we wish to put it another way, the mechanical and mathematical, and the personal and spontaneous. This is the nature of Reality as proclaimed by the great of every age. This is the first and basic Principle of our whole science, philosophy and religion.

We are some part of the Whole, but we must discover our true relationship to It. If we are to be admitted to the Temple which is the self, and find entrance to the Secret Place of the Most High within us which is the Holy of Holies, we must meet the High Priest who is our own spiritual being or the incarnation of God within us. The door to the Temple must be opened by the self. You are the only person who can open this door for yourself, and I am the only one who can open it for myself.

At first this may seen difficult or altogether impossible because we all like to believe that someone else can live for us or be happy for us or find God for us. Such is not the case. Each individual is a unique institution in the Universe.

There was never a you before just like the you that you are, and there never will be another one. Nature never duplicates her creations even though she multiplies them. There is a doorway or an entrance through which the mind must pass on its way to spiritual realization, and that door can be opened by none but the one who is to enter. Within each of us is the Secret Place of the Most High, the Holy of Holies, the Ark of the Covenant, the Scroll of Life, the Sacred Name of God.

There is only a certain amount that can be taught; the rest must be learned through the doing. Every man must discover God in his own way, but always within himself.

Now there are many approaches to the door, and no doubt many entrances to the Holy of Holies. Every great spiritual leader has found a door through which he has entered. As we study the spiritual systems of the ages we discover that the approach has been varied but the Temple of the Spirit is One. God is all there is, and there is none beside Him. This statement includes everything.

In all the kingdoms that exist, in all the planes that exist, and deep within the self, hidden and yet felt, there is a High Priest ready to conduct us to the sacred and secret chamber of the self, where God and man are one. The search for union passes into the realization, not that we are just with or in, but that we are *of* God. One with, or one in, implies separation. The great realization is that we are *of* that which is; we are some part of It.

Many have found entrance to this door through deep spiritual meditation, some through high inspirational enlightenment; others by just sitting still and letting something happen to them, symbolized by the Descent of the Holy Ghost.

The end, the aim, and the whole purpose of our study is not for the salvation of the individual life, because life cannot be lost, but for the discovery of the self which the Scripture tells us is hid with Christ in God. We have studied our techniques and we have come to understand something about how the Science of Mind works and how to use it, what to do, and why. These, however, are but guide posts on the way to the real discovery of the self, the self that is hid with Christ in God, or the Son begotten of the only Father.

The opening of the door to the Temple often calls for patience and waiting, painstaking and watchful prayer and meditation, for continual communion with that which is both the Oversoul and the Inner Spirit. The end and the aim of our search is to discover that Universe which is individualized in each one of us, and that individuality within each one of us which now has the possibility of expanding to the universalization of the self.

Your Spiritual Bank Account

We all know that we have to have money before we can spend it. And how comfortable it makes us feel to have a good fat checking account, an account big enough to draw on in emergencies without impoverishing us when it comes to paying for our ordinary needs.

Let us talk about another kind of checking account which is equally important. We are calling it *Your Spiritual Bank Account* because we believe there are great spiritual forces that we can draw on and deposit in our own minds, and which can be used in any emergency, in any stress or strain of life.

Life has enough of everything and to spare. It contains love and faith and peace of mind and joy. Would it not be wonderful if we could build up a spiritual bank account and hold it in reserve—an account which we knew would be sufficient to meet any emergency in our lives? For we are always being called on to meet emergencies—times when we need more love and tolerance, more kindness and understanding, a deeper faith and a higher hope.

These are the real crises in our lives. And at such times, unless we have a vast amount of good stored up, we not only become impoverished, but we sometimes become destitute of hope. And then despair takes the place of hope, and fear takes the place of faith. This is what we want to avoid.

How would it be if we all opened up a spiritual account with the Bank of Life, and realizing that we were drawing on the Infinite, each day deposited enough hope and happiness and faith to more than meet any emergency that might possibly arise? The wonderful part about this is that we know Life contains all these things and It wants to give them to us. It is intended by the Divine scheme of things that we should have them.

How would we go about to open up such an account and be sure that we had enough of these qualities on deposit so that our checks would be honored whenever any emergency arose? We know that we have to deposit money in the bank in order to draw checks. We know that the money is in a safe place and that the checks will be honored unless we overdraw the account. In our ordinary affairs we have to earn the money, and in a certain sense this will be true of our spiritual bank account. But the earning of the supply or the substance for our spiritual bank account is a little different, for we earn the ability to draw on the Bank of Life only through having practiced love.

This is where many of us fall down because we do not quite realize that love is the base of everything. We have had so much experience that seems to contradict this that we become skeptical and cynical and sometimes wonder if love, after all, is the greatest reality in life. And yet we know that we could not live without love, for life is absolutely meaningless unless its whole motivation is built on love and givingness.

Why can we not think of it this way: God has already made the initial deposit—and a big one—for everyone who is ever born into this world, because God has given Himself to us. He has imparted His own life, and in a mysterious way which is beyond our comprehension has endowed us with the capacity to love. If God is love—and no sane person can doubt this—and if each one of us has, as we must have, immediate access to the love of God, then we earn the ability to draw on the Bank of Life in such degree

We shall earn the ability to draw on this bank through constant meditation and prayer and communion with the Infinite, using statements in our meditations similar to the following:

> *God is love and all the love there is, is mine now. I shall endeavor to see something lovable in everyone I meet, in every situation in which I find myself, and as I do this I shall accumulate a great storehouse to be deposited in my bank. And then when some experience comes along which seems unkind or unlovable, I shall be able to write a check on my Bank of Life which will cover every liability of hate or of unkindness.*

And here is one of the great secrets of nature—the person who has taken the time to harmonize himself with love will find that when some incident that seems hateful or discordant arises in his experience he can draw on a reserve force which he now has. He can actually apply this to the situation when it arises.

If you have accumulated a certain amount of love and then meet some situation where discord and strife seem to enter, get quiet inside yourself and say, "I am bringing love to bear on this situation—a love which comprehends and includes everything, a love which has no hurt in it, a love which is not afraid, a love which is calm and confident and sure of itself."

Right here is where the Law of Mind in Action comes into play. When you apply your thought of love directly to discordant situations, and there is nothing in you which is afraid, your thought of love applied to that situation will heal it. If you have deposited enough love in your checking account you will find that you can meet the situation, your check will be honored by the Bank of Life, and the situation that confronts you will be healed.

First of all you must have a firm conviction that God is love, and an equally firm conviction that when you apply this principle of love to any human problem the very words you speak in your meditation or treatment or prayer will operate as a law in the condition that confronts you, and will neutralize or overcome everything that opposes it.

This is not an act of will. It has nothing to do with holding thoughts. It has nothing whatsoever to do with concentrating your mind or influencing people. It has to do with this one thought: God is love. God has deposited love at the center of every man's being, whether he knows it or not, and this love which I now use is not only the greatest sentiment in the world; it is the supreme power, it is the perfect law, it is a reality.

And because you have deposited a love which can see around everything that contradicts it, and because you have ample love left in your own thought, you will find that the love you use, acting as law, will definitely overcome the fear and the hate and the sense of insecurity that comes where there is a sense of lack of love.

Perfect love alone can cast out all fear. Love is always greater than fear. Fear is not really an enemy of love. All that fear can do is cast a shadow across your pathway. But this shadow is dissipated when you look at it with love. You are not dealing with two opposing forces but with only one force, which is absolute and positive and conclusive.

But first you must have made the deposit with the Bank of Life. You must have spent much time with yourself straightening out all the little animosities and resolving them into the one great love which is God. God never fails and love never fails and you will never fail if you use the love that God is.

And now let us think of some other things we want to deposit in the Bank of Life. Perhaps one of the most important, next to love, is faith—faith in God, faith in ourselves, faith in what we are doing, and faith in those around us. A person without faith is so insecure, so shaken by circumstances, that he becomes unstable in everything.

Let us see, then, if we cannot draw upon the great reservoir of all faith which comes only through implicit, complete surrender of all our fears, whether they be big or little. Faith is natural; fear is unnatural. Faith is positive; fear is negative. Faith is affirmative; fear is a denial of life. And we need a great deal of faith if we are going to meet all the fears and uncertainties that we are sure to encounter.

Only a little faith cannot do this. Just as we cannot pay a thousand dollar debt with five hundred dollars, so it is impossible to meet a trying circumstance unless we have sufficient faith to cover all the fear. As a matter of fact, we have as much faith as we use. We have as much faith as we believe.

When Jesus stood before the tomb of Lazarus he was confronted with the fear of death. He was confronted with the weeping and the wailing of the family. In a certain sense he was confronted with the whole human belief in death. And you will remember that they told him he dare not roll the stone away from the tomb of Lazarus.

This stone is a symbol of the obstruction that confronts us sometimes when we attempt to use our faith for definite purposes. How often we look at the stone. How often we think of the tomb, with the dead inside. How seldom do we realize that there are no obstructions to Divine Power.

But Jesus lifted up his voice in communion with God; he raised his thought above the fear of the moment. He could not have done this unless he had spent much time drawing on the Bank of Life and depositing large amounts of faith to his own account. For on another occasion he said, *This kind goeth not out but by prayer and fasting*—by communion with God. Jesus had spent so much time alone with God that what to us seems unreal was to him the one solid reality—God is Life, God is Power, and this Life and this Power are available right now.

Jesus must have gradually accumulated a storehouse of faith, and when the emergency arose he was able to stand calm and certain, uncaught by the fears of others. He looked up and not down, and offered what seems to us to be the greatest short prayer of the ages: *Father, I thank thee that thou hast heard me. And I know that thou hearest me always*. What sublime confidence! What infinite trust! What limitless assurance!

God always came first with Jesus—*Father, I thank thee*. How many of us have enough faith deposited in the Bank of Life so that when fear confronts us we can boldly proclaim, "My faith is sufficient. My trust is complete. My assurance is absolute. Father, I thank thee that thou hearest me." There is no doubt here, no uncertainty, no hesitation.

And I know. . . What power and possibility is caught in the two simple words—*I know*. There is no question, there is no doubt, *I know that thou hearest me always*. Not once in a while; not by and by; not yesterday but here, today, as I face this tomb. In the midst of all this doubt and fear and uncertainty, I know.

And now carefully note what happened next. It is written that Jesus cried with a loud voice: *Lazarus, come forth*. He could not have said this with such assurance if he had been depending on his human will power. He was standing still and watching the glory of Life with a calm assurance that his words were honored by a Power greater than he—that Power which we all have access to, Life Itself.

There are many other things that we must accumulate and deposit in the Bank of Life besides love and faith. Important among them is joy and happiness. For Life intended us to be glad. There is always a song when we know how to sing it, and always a joy if we can find it.

And, of course, we need to deposit a large amount of peace, a peace that rides above the storm of confusion and doubt and uncertainty that so often confronts us. If you listen to peace you will hear it, and it will flood your whole being. Then when you meet confusion, just write out your check on the Bank of Life and do not be afraid to sign it in the name of God. This is God's bank. And just as surely as you do this you will discover that your words of peace, acting as a law of good, will draw upon a Power greater than you are and liquidate the confusion.

This is practicing the Presence of God, coming to know that we are in partnership with the original Banker, the One who made the Bank of Life, but the One who, in a certain sense, must wait for us to join in this divine partnership.

There is a Power that honors our faith. There is a Love that meets love with love, a Law that meets faith with faith and good with good. We did not create this Law, this Power, this Divine Presence. We had no more to do with it than we did with the creation of the North Wind or the North Star. It was there before we recognized it; it would be there if we had no existence. But it does not seem to be there until we believe in it and use it.

Let us, then, be certain that we open up our account with this great Bank of Life. For here, and here alone, is the real substance that we can draw upon to purchase every good and beautiful thing that life has in store for us. Here alone is peace and joy and certainty. Here alone is freedom from fear and doubt.

Deliberately close all your accounts with the lesser banks, throw away the old checkbooks, and forget them, and learn to turn daily to the one and only supreme source, which is God.

Meditation

Believing that God is all the Presence there is, I am learning to feel this Presence in everything and in everyone.

Dwelling on the thought that God is Love I permit my mind to become filled with the consciousness of this Love. I permit this Love to envelop everything and everyone, bringing with it a sense of peace and joy and certainty.

Realizing that God is Life I open my whole thought to such a complete inflowing of this Divine Life that I see it and feel it—the one perfect Life which is God—in people, in nature, animating every act, sustaining all movement. My faith in this Life is complete, positive, and certain.

Knowing that all things are possible to faith, I say to my own mind: Be not afraid. Faith makes your way certain. Faith goes before you and prepares the way.

Believing that God is in everyone, I meet this God in people and I am one with everyone I meet.

Knowing that God is peace I open my mind to the quiet influence and the calm certainty of this peace.

And knowing that God is joy I meet every situation in happiness. I commit my life unto that Power which can do all things with complete assurance.

Practical Suggestion for Mental Treatment

The Radiant Presence of Love Dissolves Fear

To understand that love overcomes both hate and fear is one of the chief requisites of a scientific mental practitioner. Love does not overcome hate and fear by argument or force, but by some subtle power of transformation, transmutation, sublimation, invisible in its essence but apparent through its act.

As light overcomes the darkness, as the presence of heat causes the atmosphere of the room to change until it is warm and comfortable, so the radiant presence of love and peace dissipates fear, hate, and confusion.

In every series of treatments the practitioner should bring out these points of Being relative to his patient. His patient is dominated by love and appreciated in love by everyone who contacts him. Fear and hate cannot motivate him, cannot operate through him, cannot do anything to him, do not belong to him, and are no part of him. Nothing enters his consciousness but a sense of peace.

The practitioner does not fight evil. He knows there is no evil. He knows there is no reversal of his thought; that the statements which he has made about his patient are the Truth about him. He knows that the Truth does absolutely, positively, immediately and permanently uproot, cast out and forever obliterate every negation about his patient. He knows that his patient is not controlled by material laws nor governed by others' thoughts. He covers him with love.

Love is the victor in every case. Love breaks down the iron bars of thought, shatters the walls of material belief, severs the chain of bondage which thought has imposed, and sets the captive free.

Spiritual Conviction Is Essential

A man without spiritual conviction cannot hope to make the same use of the Creative Power of his thought as the one who has it. We must deliberately play with the idea that the Kingdom of Heaven is at hand, that the Kingdom of God is within.

We must reorganize our thought on this basis, taking as our central theme the conviction that pure Spirit is ever at the center of our being. We should keep the door of our thought open to the Invisible Guest who would enter and sup with us; to that *I AM* which is the Resurrection and the Life.

Jesus intimated that one may pass from death into life even while in the flesh. One may die from one experience and be born into another in this world. We are learning how to do this by mentally letting go of the old and taking hold of the new.

Our mental vision must be guided by the star of hope and not the illusion of despair. We are to know that the Spirit triumphs over everything, love is all-conquering, joy becomes supreme.

We could not have a more definite statement or a more direct teaching. Wherever the mental vision is set, there at the end of that vision is either freedom or bondage, joy or grief. If our concept of love and our belief in its beneficent presence is greater than our fear of its opposite we shall win.

The mental argument is within our own minds. We alone are the arbiters of our fate. Fate becomes not a thing of itself but a certain use of the Law, and we are to use this Law in love, in faith, with confidence. The Spirit is love, joy, peace!

The awakening of our thought to the Divinity within us should not be a dreary process but a joyous one. There should be great spontaneity in it, a sense of exhilaration and jubilation. Thus alone can life more abundant enter into us.

Loose the Consciousness

It is certain that none of us receives as much benefit from this science as we might. We do not permit our consciousness to range in the field of greater possibilities.

A certain time should be taken each day for the enlargement of consciousness. This is done by reminding our imagination that the field with which it deals is limitless, that Mind is the creator and the sustainer, that Mind is infinite, ever available, and always responsive to us.

There should never be any sense of finality in our self-discovery. No matter how much good we experience today, we should expect more tomorrow. Expectancy always speeds progress; anticipation of better yet to come helps to dissolve the overload of burdens which we now carry with us.

We must learn to loose our consciousness. Nothing is too good to be true. The Kingdom of Harmony is already an ever-present Reality, but as far as we are concerned It waits to be perceived, and only as much good can come to us as we mentally receive.

We must increase our receptivity, continuously extend and expand our comprehension. We should declare a hundred times a day:

> *Good and more good is mine. An ever-increasing good is mine. There is no limit to the good which is mine. Everywhere I go I see this good, I feel it, I experience it. It crowds itself against me, flows through me, expresses itself in me, and multiplies itself around me.*

Bibles of the World

Fragments from the spiritual history of the race
revealing fundamental UNITY of religious thought and experience

HERMES—The Mind is of God's very essence (if such a thing as essence of God there be) and what it is, it and it only knows precisely.
The Mind, then, is not separated off from God's essentiality, but is united into it, as light to sun.

JUDAISM and CHRISTIANITY—The Lord is nigh unto all them that call upon him, to all that call upon him in truth.
The righteous cry, and the Lord heareth, and delivereth them out of all their troubles.
Yea, I have loved thee with an everlasting love; therefore with lovingkindness have I drawn thee.

ISLAM—This is the goodness of God; He bestoweth it on whom He will; God is of immense goodness.
O Hearer of prayer. Prayers are granted of Thee before they are uttered. Thou openest the door to admit hearts every moment! How many letters Thou writest with Thy Almighty pen!

CONFUCIANISM—All are equally men, but some are great men, and some are little men. How is this?
Those who follow that part of themselves which is great are great men.
Those who follow that part which is little are little men.

SIKHISM—The inaccessible and illimitable God
Dwelleth in men's heart,
The body is the palace, the temple, the house of God.
Into it He putteth His eternal light.
Those who do excellent works are called excellent, the gate of God.

The Medium of Healing

Office of the Dean

My Dear Friend,

Here we are, well along in our course. You now know that spiritual mind healing as we teach it is based on the theory that there is but One Mind Principle which we all may use. When you give a treatment you are using this universal and impersonal Law of Cause and Effect or the Law of Mind in Action.

Be sure that you never depart from this simple but profound and adequate theory, and above everything else be certain that you do not confuse the Law of Mind in Action as a principle, with the personalness of the Indwelling Spirit which is God.

Another thing that is of great importance is that spiritual mind treatment, as our special article in this lesson states, is neither well-wishing nor wishful thinking. It is a definite and concise statement in the Mind Principle that governs all things.

You as a person make the statements. The Principle as a Law acts upon them.

I trust that you are getting along beautifully and that you have already received definite and concise evidence of the reality of this Principle acting in your experience.

May the good God bless and keep you.

Sincerely,
Ernest Holmes

Lesson 30

The Medium of Healing, page 208 through page 214

Do not forget that our Principle is based on the theory of One Mind acting in and through all people. This Mind as pure Spirit is God the Infinite Knower, but this Mind as Law is a mechanical force.

In treatment we are using this Law, and we must at all times be conscious that our word is the law of the thing unto which it is spoken. When you give a treatment you are making definite statements about someone; therefore, whether the person is physically present or absent makes no difference whatsoever. The medium through which the treatment operates is always present, the Law is ever available, and the inspiration of the Spirit within you is always accessible.

Be sure that your treatment is specific and definite. Not only must it have a high sense of spiritual realization but it must have an equally definite sense of conscious direction. As a result of the treatment which you give, some definite action is to take place for yourself or for someone else. You must be certain in your own mind that this action *is* taking place. Your word is the enforcement of the Law. It is more than a conscious recognition of the Law. It is a conscious use of It. Mental treatment is never vague. A scientific practitioner is one who has a conviction of the Law with an inspirational faith in using It, and who is definite in his use of It.

Statements such as, "God is," "God is all there is," "God is perfect," and "God is right here," are powerful because they arouse an inspirational enthusiasm and deep spiritual conviction in the mind of the one who uses them. They stimulate imagination to the acceptance of a greater good, but once the imagination is thus stimulated and a conviction thus generated we must give conscious direction if we hope to make a demonstration. The Law is the actor but It can act for us only at the level of our recognition. It is the doer but can do only what we believe that It can do, and in accepting the belief that It can do, we must accept that It already has done.

It is easy enough to see that there are different approaches to this Law, different methods of using It, and different people may have different convictions about it. For instance, many will tell you that all you need to do is to have a great sense of realization. You need not dispute this because you do need to have a great sense of realization, but this realization undirected will never do anything other than give you a sense of peace. This of course is good, but you desire also a definitely stated good. Never forget that the Law undirected will do nothing of Itself, for the Law Itself has no intention, no purpose to execute.

Turn again to page 403, second paragraph, beginning with *The Law of Mind is not selective*. If the Law is not selective and has no definite choice of Its own regarding you, then you must choose for It.

But someone will say, "This is blasphemous." However, the same person would not say it is blasphemous to plant poppy seed with the expectation of raising poppies; he would call that natural, since the creative soil is not selective. It is creative without selecting what it creates. A failure to understand this has been one of the many drawbacks in the Science of Mind.

Ignorance and superstition insist in confusing the Law of Mind and the personalness of God the Spirit. But the moment a person sees that the Spirit within him uses the Law he is freed from his particular superstitious reaction. There is no natural law known to man which is selective. That is, no law chooses for itself; we always choose for it. Our treatment, therefore, is always directed for some specific purpose. We always know whom we are treating; there is never anything vague about it.

The third paragraph in our lesson referring to deductive and inductive reasoning has already been fully discussed, but for the sake of clearness turn again to the definition of *Inductive Reasoning* on page 601 and *Deductive Reasoning* on page 583, and realize that neither God as Spirit nor God as Law reasons inductively. The reason for this is that God as Spirit is already Omniscient or All-knowing, and the Universe as Law is already Omnipotent.

Read the treatment on page 563, *I Represent the Principle of Perfection*. Each one of us is a point in the Infinite, and by virtue of that fact each is a center of God Consciousness. It is because of this that our word, as power, will never do anything in particular for us until we direct this power. Therefore when you give someone a treatment say, "This word is for (speak the name, designating who the patient is as separated from some other individual)" then all of your statements are made about him. These statements are formulated in such a way that they clearly bring out in your own thought what you consider to be the truth about him. In this way your word becomes the law of his experience.

As suggested in the second paragraph on page 209, we should not confuse the idea of subjective or subconscious Law with the idea of this Law being unintelligent. For while we consciously direct this subconscious or subjective Law, and while It has no purpose other than the one which we give to It, It is nevertheless infinite intelligence compared to our conscious thought. It has the ability to bring means to ends, to bring means and ends together.

As stated at the top of page 414 and discussed in Lesson 5, our thought must be independent of any existing circumstances. Since the Law is to create a condition which will exactly correspond to the thought, the practitioner must be sure that he arrives at the right mental conclusion. The Law will execute that conclusion. There is neither hard nor easy, big nor little to the Law. It knows only Its ability to do. It is conscious only of receiving the impulse to do, to execute.

We could hardly say that the soil knows or is conscious of its ability to create a tree, yet it does know how to create it. Since the Law is not selective It cannot of Itself decide what It is going to create, nor can It reject that which is involved in Its creative medium. But once having received an impulse It does set about to produce a logical and an inevitable result.

Turn to the paragraph on page 393 starting with the statement, *The invisible essence of Mind is Substance*, and read again the explanation of this paragraph in Lesson 9. This will refresh your mind with the idea that when you give a treatment your sole responsibility is to be sure that you arrive at a state of realization in your own thought. You must be sure that you consciously use the God Power within you and that you definitely direct It. This is what constitutes scientific mental practice.

As our lesson states on page 209, paragraph 3, *the very force which makes us sick can heal us, the force which makes us poor can enrich us*. If this were not true we should be dealing with duality; we should be setting one power against another with small hope of success. The secret of the whole thing is right here. From the standpoint of the Universal, Law Is and we use It.

It is to each of us what we are to It, no more and no less. Turn to page 469 for a more complete explanation of this, which we call the reciprocal action between the Universal and the individual. Life is to each one of us what we are to It. As we have frequently discussed in these lessons, we are surrounded by this Law of Cause and Effect which reproduces the images of our thought. It does this automatically and mechanically, without any sentiment; hence it will bind or free us according to the way we use It. Our use of It is an expression of our Divine Individuality. Its response to us is by way of an immutable Law of Cause and Effect.

If you will turn again to the first paragraph on page 406 which was discussed in Lesson 7, you will find still another way of conveying the thought that Spirit guides and the Law executes. That we use such a Law is the central theme of our entire thought. As our text states, the Law being deductive cannot refuse us anything. Hence we do not look for a law of health and a law of disease, but One Law.

There is, then, nothing to oppose a treatment. Never feel that you have an adversary, visible or invisible, conscious or subjective, for you have not. The imaginary adversary is a phantom, an illusion of false belief. With the realization that God is all the Power and all the Presence there is, make your declarations with complete conviction that nothing opposes them. You should not say, "This thing is easy, while that thing is hard," but rather endeavor to realize the truth about any and every situation, sensing that the knowledge of truth is synonymous with freedom.

We come next to the thought as to whether or not our mental work tires us or exhausts our will power. We have already shown that will power has nothing to do with our form of mental healing. The Principle works independent of our thought, even though it is our thought which directs It. Our whole endeavor should be to conceive that we are dealing with such a Principle and then to make conscious use of It.

In treating children we often have to treat the parents. We must not only say, "This child is perfect" (speaking the name of the child), but we must know that the parents also recognize its perfection. The child's perfection must be a part of their knowledge and we must heal their stream of consciousness about him; otherwise their fear might continue to pour itself into the receptive thought of the child. Generally speaking, in treating children we have to heal the thought of the parents as well as that of the child.

This same practice should be followed when one is treating people who are in a negative atmosphere, or an atmosphere of doubt, fear, or uncertainty.

If one is treating to heal an organic disease one must know there is no organic disease. Know that there is a Law of perfection, peace, and wholeness, and that there is no other law. Treatment must realize the perfection of the patient.

The practitioner must know when he makes his statements of truth for anyone that each statement definitely neutralizes the belief in its opposite. This not only clarifies thought but destroys every evidence of imperfection. To one who is just beginning this form of treatment there may come a reaction of doubt, a vague sense of uncertainty and a feeling that nothing is being done. This thought arises from the habitual belief that the subjective or physical universe is the only reality.

When you make your statements reassure yourself that what you are doing is real, genuine, and certain. Build up your faith. Say, "I know, and I know that I know. I am conscious of my ability to use this word." We all have this inner sense of certainty and we should use it. When you begin to use it as though it were really true you will be surprised at the remarkable results which follow. Your word must know that it is power, that there is nothing that can hinder it from operation, that there is no mind to oppose it, that it has no adversary, that it cannot be refused, that it is certain to work, and that it will do what it is supposed to do.

As told on page 212, healing is not creating a perfect idea; it is the revelation of a perfect idea. The text says that there is no process *in* healing but that there is one *of* healing. This means that while we teach a definite technique for giving a treatment, which of course is a process of thought, it is not the technique which does the work; the technique is the *way* through which we arrive at a mental conclusion which makes the work possible. In practical application you may shift your technique around from time to time, but always you will be dealing with the same Law.

The different metaphysical schools obtain results, not because of what they believe but sometimes in spite of what they believe, since it is always the belief and never the thing believed in that produces results. We should learn something from each method but be coerced by none. In this way we shall have the best the world has to offer without being caught in any particular web of prejudice. Every great religion and every system of thought will teach us something. We should gather the kernels from all, accepting the husks from none. The secret of the whole thing is the belief. In spiritual mind healing any statement that convinces the thought of the practitioner is a good statement to make.

Undoubtedly there is a psychic and a spiritual body within the physical, and it is our theory that the psychic body is the cause of the physical, or at least directly and dynamically influences it. The spiritual idea dominates our psychic or subjective side. The spiritual body cannot be congested; the spiritual mind is perfect; there is no inaction, overaction, or false action in Truth. The re-education of thought to these new ideas always tends toward spiritual uplift and physical healing. The one who has the most complete conviction of this idea and who directs his conviction in the most definite manner will make the most efficient practitioner.

We do not deny the fact of poverty or disease; neither should we confuse fact with the possibility of changing such fact. It may be a fact that we are unhappy but it does not necessarily follow that we must remain so. It may be a fact that we are suffering physical pain but it does not follow that we must continue to suffer it. We must not confuse fact with necessity, which is what Jesus meant when he said, *Judge not according to appearances.*

The spiritual mind healer treats disease as a fact but not as a verity; he treats discord as an experience but not as a necessity. He knows that while thoughts of lack produce lack, the Creative Principle is still one of abundance. He knows that even though all are more or less restricted, the real Law of Life is one of freedom.

His standard, then, or the basic principle upon which his treatment is built, is a standard of perfection in so far as he is able to perceive perfection. All of his statements tend to announce and accentuate this perfection. They must transcend the thought which produces the discord. Hence he covers fear with faith, evil with love, and discord with harmony, always declaring that one is true while the other is false. How can he find the proper spiritual equivalent for accomplishing this unless he first has an abiding faith in the Spiritual Universe in which he lives?

Summary

God, the Infinite Knower, and the Law of Mind in Action, the Infinite Doer, are the two great realities with which we deal. In treatment you use the Law definitely, specifically, and consciously, even as you commune with the Spirit personally and intimately.

Your treatment is a statement in the Law of Mind about some person, place, or thing. Therefore it is specific and definite. It must have a high spiritual content, while at the same time being the conscious use of a definite Law which is understood.

The Law of Mind is not selective; It has no definite purpose of Its own. You give It purpose. It is merely the medium through which some action takes place.

It is true that both ignorance and superstition confuse the Law of Mind in Action with the personalness of the Creative Spirit which is God. The Law of Mind in Action is like any other law in nature. It is impersonal but exact.

However, we must be careful not to confuse the idea of this subjective or subconscious Law with something that is nonintelligent, for the Law contains all intelligence even though It is not selective or personal. Just as the creative soil knows how to make an oak tree out of an acorn without knowing that it is doing that particular thing (without comparing what it is doing with something else), so the Law of Mind knows how to create any situation but does so in an impersonal way. It is infinite compared to our conscious thought, while at the same time It is a Doer and not a Knower. This is one of the most important things to understand about the Law of Mind in Action. It is Creative Intelligence acting as Law. It does not exercise volition, but It is directed by volition.

Be sure that you think these things through until they become reasonable and rational, because you are the thinker who has both consciousness and volition. You are the one who uses the Law.

Questions

Brief answers to these questions should be written out by the student after studying the lesson, and the answers compared with those which will be included in next week's lesson.

1. State the difference between Spirit and Law.
2. In spiritual treatment does it make any difference whether your patient is physically present or physically absent?
3. In mental treatment why must there be a sense of conscious direction as well as spiritual realization?
4. What is a scientific mental and spiritual practitioner?
5. Why are statements such as "God is," "God is good and perfect," "God is all there is," "God is ever-present," etc., effective in mental treatment?
6. Why is it that the Law can act for us only at the level of our own recognition?
7. What do we mean by saying that the Law of Mind is not selective?
8. Differentiate between the Law of Mind and the Personalness of Spirit.
9. What do we mean when we say that man is a center of God-consciousness?
10. What is a mental practitioner's sole responsibility in giving a treatment?
11. How can the Law, which makes us sick and impoverishes us, also heal and enrich us?
12. Should a mental and spiritual practitioner ever feel that he is dealing with two opposing powers?
13. In treating children why should we also treat the parents?

14. How would one build up faith in one's ability effectively to treat?
15. Why is it that the different metaphysical schools obtain largely the same results in mental practice?
16. How should we proceed in our search after Truth in order to arrive at the best that life has to offer?
17. How should we mentally treat the fact of inharmony, confusion, discord, and the like?

Answers to Questions on Lesson 29

1. Recognizing the physical as an effect of the mental, the spiritual practitioner treats to realize that back of both the physical and mental there is a Spiritual Man.
2. In mental and spiritual treatment the practitioner does not deny the physical body, poverty, and unhappiness. He does, however, affirm their opposite by announcing the presence of perfect life, perfect action, happiness and abundance.
3. By the higher realm of causation we mean an inner awareness which no longer contradicts unity, wholeness, and perfection.
4. The mental equivalent for right action is a spiritual realization that there is one Perfect Presence acting in accord with harmony, abundance, wholeness, etc.
5. By *the meat which perisheth* is meant that all created things and events are temporary, made to use, enjoy, and discard. The soul alone is permanent.
6. The real power of a mental treatment is a spiritual consciousness of wholeness.
7. The mental technique for spiritual treatment is the thought process through which one goes to arrive at a spiritual consciousness of wholeness.
8. In mental treatment we combat negative conditions to a certain degree. We do this with a recognition that they are experiences which give way before the light of Truth, but not that they are entities in themselves.
9. The secret of the ages, relative to unity and multiplicity, is that all creation comes from one Source, and all people are rooted in one Mind and Spirit.
10. By the mental practitioner lifting his thought about his patient is meant that he mentally rises above any thought or condition which is negatively affecting his patient.
11. By a practitioner mentally condemning his patient is meant that he might, either consciously or unconsciously, feel it necessary for his patient to continue to suffer because of previous mistakes.
12. A practitioner should never mentally condemn his patient. It is the practitioner's business to heal both the mistake and its consequence without passing judgment. He should bless and curse not.
13. *The engine of the subjective mind* is the creative but mechanical side of mind, which is controlled by conscious thought, the engineer.
14. We re-educate our mind by transmuting our old thought patterns into less limiting ones.
15. One would treat a fatalist by knowing for him that man has but one perfect source and destiny and that the only law is a law of good.

16. In treating a person who has a consciousness of loneliness we should declare that he is unified with life, surrounded by loving friends who appreciate his worth, and that he is inwardly conscious of this truth.
17. The general line of thought embodied in all treatments must either directly or by implication contradict the negation while affirming its opposite.
18. No one really knows whether, in treatment, our thought goes *out* or *in*. But this we do know—the practitioner never seeks to project his thought. He seeks only to become inwardly aware of the truth of the statements which he makes.

The Great Surrender

Every man's search is after something that will make him whole and happy, something that will cause him to feel safe and secure, and, we believe, something that will make him certain that he is going to live forever somewhere. We cannot believe that the Divine Intelligence which created everything, including ourselves, could possibly have done so without at the same time providing a way for us to live as happy and whole human and divine beings.

Jesus said that he was the way, the truth, and the life. He had discovered the secret which delivered to him all life, love, and power. This life, this love, and this power is what he taught. Since he so completely proved his power, it is wise for us to follow the rules he laid down for us. He stated one of these rules when he said... *and he that loseth his life for my sake, shall find it.*

At first this seems like a hard and strange thing to do. None of us wishes to lose his life. It cannot be possible that Jesus meant that we should literally lose our lives, but rather that there must be things in our lives that we should let go of. There must be something that is attached to us that does not belong to the real man. And so we should seek to find the fundamental truth that he taught.

If we do this we shall find that the thing Jesus laid the greatest emphasis on was the idea that we are spiritual beings living in a spiritual universe, right now; that God, the Supreme Spirit and Intelligence in the universe, and the Power that governs everything, is not some far-off Presence; it is something that is immediate, a Presence that is here with us now. He said that this Presence is not only with us but within us; we live in It and It moves through us.

When Jesus said that we must lose our lives he must have been referring to that part of us which denies this Supreme Presence, that part of us which lives contrary to It, that part of us which is out of harmony with It. He was telling us that there are certain things we have to surrender before we can find our true center, the real spirit or the perfect man which he always assumed to be there.

Jesus said, *Blessed are the meek: for they shall inherit the earth*. This sounds as though he were telling us that we cannot inherit the Kingdom of God until we renounce the kingdom of man. Yet we find him multiplying the loaves and fishes when the multitude was hungry. He turned water into wine at the wedding feast, and in every way seemed to meet human needs whenever they arose.

So even in teaching us that we must surrender something he was not telling us that we should live in poverty or limitation. What he was saying is that when we put our trust in external things alone we are certain to become disillusioned, for a person may have a fortune one day and lose it in the next; he may have a position of high power and suddenly lose all public acclaim.

Jesus was telling us about something more real than this, but something which contained everything necessary to living even in this world. For he knew that we need food and clothing and shelter. He was not saying that the Divine Will imposes suffering on us, but rather that when we fail to live in accord with the Divine we bring suffering on ourselves.

So we see that losing our lives, or making the great surrender to the Spirit, does not mean losing anything worthwhile, but getting rid of those things which deny the presence and the power of the Spirit right here on earth. It is the great negations of life that we have to surrender, the doubts and fears and uncertainties, the coldness and unkindness, the lack of love.

All of these negative things Jesus called sins. But the word sin has been misinterpreted and misconstrued, for the original meaning of sin was to miss the mark, to make a mistake, to err in judgment, or to do something that separates us from the conscious daily realization that we already are one with the Supreme Giver of life.

God is love and we cannot get close to the nature of love while we hate. It is the hate we have to surrender and not the love. When Jesus said you have to lose your life to find it he was saying: You have to lose your hate if you wish to find love; you have to let go of everything that is unkind if you wish to discover kindness; you even have to surrender fear if you wish to discover faith. Everything that denies faith and love and life and truth and beauty, Jesus called a sin, a mistake, missing the mark.

It is not easy to make this surrender because we are in the habit of thinking of ourselves as being such strong, self-reliant personalities that we can sweep everything before us. It is not easy to be meek.

But again we should examine the meaning of meekness. While we do not find any arrogance in the life of Jesus, we find a terrific strength of character, a will to accomplish what he set out to do, a determination to fulfill his mission. When he said that the meek shall inherit the earth he was not saying that we have to be wishy-washy or willy-nilly, but that in true meekness we should recognize that all power finally rests in the Spirit.

To be meek is to be humble before the truth. A person is truly meek or humble when he looks upon the grandeur of a mountain or the vastness of the ocean or thinks about the bigness of things. He does not become lost in this bigness or this grandeur, but he does stand in awe before it. When he does this, something deep within him responds, something within him embraces the ocean, something within him melts into the mountain, and he becomes one with them. This is true meekness.

Jesus said, *Blessed are they that do hunger and thirst after righteousness: for they shall be filled.* Everyone longs to be made whole; everyone hungers and thirsts after peace and joy. Jesus used the expression *hunger and thirst* because everyone knows how it feels to be hungry and thirsty. When we are hungry we go in search of food. When we are thirsty we look for water. There is a deep hunger in everyone, a deep thirst after another kind of food and another kind of drink which Jesus said is not only natural but necessary to man. For he said that man does not live by bread alone, but by every word that proceedeth from the mouth of God.

Consider how the scientific mind hungers after knowledge. The scientist feels incomplete until he has wrested the secrets of nature from the invisible and brought them forth into realities. But in his search he has to surrender all personal opinion, all arrogant attitudes of mind, and in true meekness follow the scientific pathway which leads to the discovery of a principle in nature that he inherits after he has first surrendered himself to it.

No one makes a greater surrender than the scientist, for he is always willing to be led by the truth no matter what path it seems to take. Truth and science in many ways mean the same thing, for all scientific research is a process of seeking out the laws of nature, discovering how they work, and then subjecting the individual will to the way they work. It is in this way alone that science makes progress. This is always the path that it follows.

We all hunger and thirst after love because we feel incomplete without it. But have we looked into the nature of love? Have we followed the method that science, which is a search after truth, finds necessary? We hunger and thirst after love but how often do we follow another thought of Jesus where he said, *Greater love hath no man than this, that a man lay down his life for his friends.*

We cannot suppose that Jesus meant that we should give up our lives, because this would serve no good purpose. He must have meant that we lay down everything that constitutes the great unreality, the great lie, the great separation. Love is kind, and we must lay down all unkindness before we can discover love.

We want peace of mind and an inward sense of security, but are we willing to follow another teaching of Jesus in which he said, *But I say unto you, that ye resist not evil . . .* We are full of resistance and combativeness and antagonism. And the reason we are over-aggressive is because we feel insecure. We put up a great big bluff and make a big noise and throw ourselves around because of this feeling of insecurity.

Resist not evil. We wonder if Jesus knew what he was talking about until we discover the secret which is simplicity itself. When we resist we make that thing real in our imagination which we are sincerely trying to get rid of. We become a house divided against itself, which Jesus said cannot stand. True nonresistance is the surrender of every arrogant attitude of mind to good, and good alone. Those who have made this surrender have found real peace of mind, happiness, and wholeness in the only place where it can be found, which is within themselves.

Perhaps Jesus was teaching the greatest surrender of all when he said, *Fear not, little flock, for it is your Father's good pleasure to give you the kingdom.* We have thought that we must work so hard to attain this Kingdom; there is so much we have to do about it. This has become such a burden on our minds that we have gotten our little human selves so completely in the way that the Kingdom which was given cannot be accepted. Life is the gift of God and not of man. That is why Jesus said that no man has the power to give it or to take it away. Are we willing to let go of this inflated ego of ours, this gigantic make-believe, this mask we wear, this camouflage, and in simplicity accept life?

Jesus taught another thing that has to do with the great surrender. He said we must become as little children. How difficult it is for us to become as a child. Yet every searcher after scientific truths knows that he must become as a little child if he wishes to unlock the secrets of nature and find the true cause of things.

The intellect is apt to get in the way of faith, for while the logic of faith may be of the intellect, its essence and meaning are in the childlike heart. We must be born into the Kingdom of God, in a certain sense, just as we were born into the human kingdom from the great mother heart of love and life.

Jesus taught that the great reality of life is love, but the way this reality works is through law, and every man must reap as he sows. So he put before us the two great possibilities of life and asked this question: Wilt thou be made whole? If so, follow the divine light that I have revealed to you and you will discover it within yourself. There in the Secret Place of the Most High you shall abide under the shadow of the Almighty.

Spiritual Mind Treatment Is Not Well-Wishing

When you give a spiritual mind treatment you are not wishing that someone will be healed. You are not hoping that someone will be healed. You are not asking that someone shall be healed. You are making definite statements in the Mind Principle about some person or situation, or you are entertaining a state of realization in your own consciousness for someone or something. You are not petitioning God to please do this or that, or something else.

Not that there is anything wrong with this, because any sincere petition to one's God will have a power equal to the conviction of the petitioner. The Principle of the Law of Mind in Action must act on the mental attitude entertained and the words used, because this is Its nature. In doing this It must correspond with the acceptance of the one making the petition.

When we say that spiritual mind treatment is not well-wishing, we are in no way criticizing the sincerity or the spiritual power of any form of petition. What we are doing is restating our own position by saying that we cannot believe in a Supreme Power which acts more favorably for one than for another. Such a belief would immediately take us out of the realm of law and order into the realm of chaos. We should never criticize any person's form of prayer, nor should we try to convince a person that our method of communion with the Invisible is superior to his.

But when it comes to a conscious use of the Principle of Mind we must not forget that we are dealing with such a Principle. Therefore our method of procedure is different. Instead of asking for something we are accepting something. Instead of hoping that something will happen we are endeavoring to know that it has happened or is happening. This is a fine point in the Science of Mind and it should not be overlooked.

We believe in spiritual communion, which is the drawing of the essence of Reality into our own minds through keeping the thought uplifted and in tune with the Ultimate Harmony. We believe that the Divine Presence is immanent in everything and in every person. This of course is the very basis of our assumption. It is the rock or the foundation upon which our edifice is built. Man not only can talk with God but he can receive a direct answer through intuition. Through such communion he enters into the realm of Reality and imbibes the Spirit of Truth.

In giving a treatment we proceed on the assumption that there is an intelligent Creative Principle in everything and in everyone which responds to our word exactly the way we speak it. There could be no Science of Mind unless this were true. Therefore a spiritual mind treatment in actual operation is a series of statements logically presented to the Principle of Mind, based on the assumption of Perfect God, Perfect Man, and Perfect Being.

Looking away from the appearance, no matter what the appearance may be, and turning to Reality, our statements are made to conform with the Realities felt. God is all there is; therefore this negative condition need not be and should not be and is not.

In the argumentative method of treatment the argument proceeds along this basis until the practitioner comes to the logical conclusion that since God is all there is, and since harmony constitutes the only Reality, this person or this condition does of necessity conform to Reality; this word is the law of elimination to everything that disputes or denies that which is perfect.

A combination of feeling the Divine Presence and making statements in the Law of Mind constitutes both inspirational and scientific spiritual mind treatment. Therefore it is plain that such treatment is not well-wishing, hoping, or longing. It is not a petition. It is a bold, flat, definite, predetermined statement, concise, clear, and dynamic.

But we hasten to add that it is not as though a large amount of good were now to be hurled at an equal amount of evil. It is not storming the gates of Heaven with an affirmative petition. It is more like the calm contemplation of the mind which says there is a light, and because there is, darkness disappears.

We do not question the physical diagnosis of the doctor or the mental diagnosis of the analyst, provided they are true. We do not deny either mind or body. We do affirm the Spirit as transcendent, having the ability to create new thoughts while new thoughts create new situations.

The practitioner should always know that his statements transcend not only physical or objective conditions, but subjective or unconscious causes as well. They are transcendent both of the cause and the effect of the negative condition, rising to a position in mind which starts new and clean and fresh.

This is what Jesus meant when he said in effect that there is a Truth which known will prove itself. *And ye shall know the truth, and the truth shall make you free*. He recognized a Truth transcendent of all negation.

BACK OF the visible is a permanence of Spirit and Law ever acting and reacting upon each other. A flow of consciousness into form, and a flow of form into consciousness. Creation is ever pushing out and being drawn back.

> *We can commune with the Eternal because the other side of our nature is the Eternal, and this side is the use we are making of the other side.*

WE ARRIVE at the essence of life through spiritual perception, at the practice of it through mental action, and at the experience of it through concrete demonstration.

Where the vision is set
there Reality will appear to us.

LOOKING THROUGH the objective and subjective into a universal height, depth and breadth, is penetrating not only the real nature of man but also the nature of God. We must start with a Divine incarnation if we hope to arrive at a real understanding of our true nature.

> *What we call the subjective impulsion to action is often greater than the conscious or objective or intellectual capacity to resist action.*

IT HAS BEEN written that the eye must be free from tears before we can see Reality and the ears free from confusion before we can hear It.

We must climb if we would view
the length and breadth of Reality.

UNIVERSAL LOVE to all people and to all things is but returning love to the source of all love, to Him who creates all in love and holds all in Divine care. The sun shines on all alike. Shall we separate and divide where God has so carefully united?

> *Anyone who in love unifies with Life will find that he has a universal language with which he can speak to prince or pauper.*

WE DO NOT have to heal ourselves of what the other fellow thinks; we have to heal ourselves of what we think.

When every man learns to speak the Truth,
complete salvation will come to the world.

What Is Spirituality?

We hear a great deal about certain people being spiritual, and there is nothing wrong with this provided it does not become a maudlin attitude.

Spirituality is rather an elusive thing. I cannot think of a better illustration to use than to compare it with the idea of beauty which a great artist must entertain if he is to create a worthwhile object of art. We do not say that such a one has great beauty but that he has great appreciation for beauty. We know that the artist feels beauty, senses its presence, and to a degree communes with it, indrawing it into his own soul that he may outbreathe it through his performance.

Perfect technique alone does not result in great art. We speak of the soul of an artist, that subtle and indefinable something which is the essence of all art. This is a definite feeling, a communion with Invisible Harmony, the Supreme Being, the Mind and Heart of God, or the Creative Essence.

It is the same with what we call spirituality, which is a word too often misused. From our viewpoint spirituality is one's recognition of the Universe as a Living Presence of Good, Truth, Beauty, Peace, Power, and Love. And to this should be added happiness, joy, enthusiasm, and Universal Harmony, which like the great rhythm of Life flows through everything.

There is a vast difference between this type of spiritual consciousness and theological dogma, or even logical arguments. It is an essence diffused, a consciousness transcendent, and a faith that has passed beyond the point of argument into conviction and union and complete acceptance.

Such spirituality we cannot divorce from the highest use of the Science of Mind. It is like the heat in fire, the colors in a prism, the invisible power flowing through a dynamo. It is like something that is caught from the invisible for the purpose of taking temporary form. It is the background of all spiritual mind treatment, and we should not separate it from our conscious use of the Law of Mind.

Spirituality is a constant, consistent attempt to feel the Presence of God in everything and in everyone. Such an attitude need not be put into words because words cannot express such a feeling. But out of the feeling, words will flow and when they do they will always be correct.

Spirituality cannot be taught but it can be felt, it can be practiced, it can be embodied. But each in his own consciousness must experience it in his own way, and his way will always be best for him. Indeed it will be the only way he could do it, because in the secret precinct of the mind which is alone with God nothing else can enter.

Listening daily to that which can only be felt, daily sensing and communing with that which is too intangible to put into words, one finds an essence flowing through one's thought which can be neither analyzed nor described.

Do not wonder whether or not you are spiritual; rather accept the fact that you must be. In a sense you had nothing to do with it. This is your nature. You are rooted in the Supreme Mind, in the Everlasting Spirit, in the Perfect Presence.

Spirituality is the consciousness that comes through communing with God, for treatment is a definite act and however spiritual, must still take a definite form. One should not study to be spiritual as much as one should contemplate in order to imbibe the essence of Spirit, to speak from Its center.

In this, as in everything else, practice will perfect your method, and consciousness will make your method effective.

Beatitudes of Today

ILLUMINED ... are they whose love includes both saint and sinner, for they shall know love.

BEAUTIFUL ... are all who think no evil and listen not to false report or unkind word. Their faces are good to look upon.

DEATHLESS ... are they who believe in eternal existence. Such need not die to become immortal.

AFFLUENT ... are they who contemplate substance, for supply shall be theirs.

BLESSED ... are they to whom goodness alone is true, for evil shall be to them as though it were not.

TRANQUIL ... are they whose minds are at peace. They shall reflect a universe of power.

GODLIKE ... are sympathy, compassion and understanding of the human, for thus is Divinity unveiled.

INDEPENDENT ... are they who shall mind their own affairs, for no virtue excelleth this.

STRONG ... are they who can stand in authority without arrogance, for they shall still stand.

... Ernest Holmes

Meditation

I know that there is a Presence that came with me when I entered this life, and that this same Presence will go with me when I leave this physical form, for It is the presence of Eternal Life, that Life that cannot die. And so I have no fear of the past, the present or the future, but I live this day as though God really were all in all, over all, and through all.

I invite the Divine Presence into my mind; I open all doorways of my consciousness in complete belief. I let that mind be in me which was also in Christ, the Mind of God, the Living Spirit Almighty.

I know that the invisible guest within me, the angel of God's presence, is counseling me wisely, leading me unerringly, directing my thoughts and actions in harmony, in peace, in love and cooperation.

Because God cannot fail, and because the Divine Presence within me is God as my real self, I know that there is a power flowing through my word of faith which makes straight the way before me.

I know that the great Giver of Life is giving, through me, that gift which is gladly made and which returns multiplied, only to go out again to increase its blessing and to multiply its own good as it blesses others.

Bibles of the World

Fragments from the spiritual history of the race
revealing fundamental UNITY of religious thought and experience

CHRISTIANITY—Ye shall know the truth, and the truth shall make you free.
The Spirit of truth will guide you into all truth.

To this end was I born, and for this cause came I into the world; that I should bear witness unto the truth.
God is light; and in him is no darkness at all.

CONFUCIANISM—He who knows the truth is not equal to him who loves it.

HINDUISM—Truth is the base that bears the earth.
Truth alone conquers, not falsehood.
Without anxious care, be ever fixed on truth.

ISLAM—The truth is from thy Lord.
Truth is come; and falsehood is vanished.
Verily, falsehood is a thing that vanisheth.

SIKHISM—Truth and falsehood stand to one another
In the relation of a stone to an earthen vessel.
If a stone be thrown at an earthen vessel,
It is the earthen vessel which will break,
It is the earthen vessel that suffereth.
Truth is immovable and on safe ground,
Falsehood standeth, and trembleth, on an insecure basis.
Falsehood, which is deceitful, ever aileth,
Truth is ever safe and whole.

What Can Be Healed

Office of the Dean

My Dear Friend,
With God all things are possible. Why, then, is it that everyone appears to be limited? Since God is perfect, why are we imperfect; God is good, so why should evil exist? I do not think there is any answer to these questions other than that we all are individuals with the right of choice.

We are all on the pathway of self-discovery. The thing we seem not to have realized is that when we discover the true self we shall also be finding God in the only place He is to be found, at the center of our own being.

And is it not wonderful that the discovery of God and the real self become one and the same thing, and are an intimate, personal something to each one of us? While your God and my God is the same God, each approaches the Divine Presence in his own way. Each in his own way makes the discovery for himself.

This is the meaning of our supplements, *The Individual and the Universal* and *How Does God Know What I Am Doing?* We want you to read these two short articles several times and devote some time to thinking about them.

Each individual, in a certain place in his consciousness, finds himself alone with the Great Reality, that Reality which knows neither big nor little but only the joy of Its own being coming into self-expression through us.

Sincerely,
Ernest Holmes

Lesson 31

Page 215 to top of page 218

When we ask the question "What can be healed through spiritual mental methods?" we should remember that with Spirit all things are possible. The mental practitioner holds no controversy with himself over what can or cannot be healed. He knows in every instance that his word is the Law unto the thing whereto it is spoken.

Since he is never treating the physical man, and since his entire field is one of thought, he can just as well rearrange his thinking about one type of disease as another. Hence there is no hard and no easy from his viewpoint. He is always seeking to bring about a recognition of the spiritual man who is already perfect, and declaring that this spiritual man who is already perfect is the only man there is.

The practitioner turns resolutely from all negative appearances and seeks in every way possible to enter a state of spiritual realization about his patient. Turn again to the definition of *Realization* on page 625, where the statement is made that we should turn to the Living Presence within us. We should endeavor to let the One Mind flow through us. We should seek to comprehend the unity of Good, the allness of God, and the ever-availability of the immutable Law.

The light does not inquire whether or not the darkness is dense or only partial, for *the light is shining in the darkness and the darkness has never put it out* (John 1:5—American Translation). So in our spiritual realization we should seek a consciousness of wholeness. If that consciousness is more complete than the discord which we seek to neutralize, then its very presence will dissipate that discord.

The definition of *Reason* on pages 625 and 626 points out that the Creative Medium reasons only deductively. Now if we have a Creative Medium which can reason only deductively and if It is infinite, then once It receives the impress of any idea there can be no argument within It as to whether or not It is able to bring this idea into form. If that which is Infinite does not inquire into the Truth since It already is the Truth, it follows that there can be no limit to Its ability to perform. This is something we should never lose sight of. When we speak of things which are hard to heal and things which are easy to heal we are referring to our human comprehension.

One might ask, for example, "How heavy a weight can you lift?" And the answer might be, "I can lift ten pounds" or "fifty pounds" or "one hundred pounds." But at some certain point, physical man is limited. We would never ask, "How great a weight can that which is infinite in its power hold up?" We should know that there can be no limit.

So it is with spiritual mind healing. If we think our isolated thought or will power must accomplish the healing, then of course we shall feel limited in our capacity to use such power. But if we realize that we are dealing with a creative Power which is infinite, there is no longer a question of what It can or what It cannot heal. The question would be, "What can we conceive of It as healing?" This is the only problem which confronts us.

Read the definition of *Receptivity* on page 626. The Spirit can give us only what we take. And because this taking is a mental act, the Spirit can give us only what we comprehend. Therefore we should continuously treat to know that we receive more and better things. There should be an ever-increasing consciousness of the power of our word.

Any statement which will strengthen our conviction of the power of our word will actually give us more power. The Power already exists and we use It. Since our use of It is a thing of thought, the more completely we are convinced of our ability to use It, the more perfectly we shall use It.

Turn again to the Meditation on page 545, *The Word of Power*, used in Lesson 11. Remind yourself of the real Power with which you are dealing. When we ask the question, "What should we try to heal in spiritual treatment?" there is only one answer: *Try to heal everything; work for all who ask for your help, and you will help all for whom you work.*

The Law knows nothing about disease any more than It knows about big and little. The Law knows only to do and does only what It knows. Remember, that in referring to the Law we are not talking about the Spirit. We are talking about the mechanical, not the spontaneous side of thought.

In the first paragraph on page 396 we have a more complete explanation of the Law as a mirror. As Law It does not know what It is doing but It knows how to do it, and while this seems one of the enigmas of the universe, it is really true.

On page 397, third paragraph, you will find it stated that the Law *obeys the orders that are given It whether we are conscious or unconscious that such orders are being given.* In other words, the subjective state of our thought is continuously recording impressions in Mind. These impressions are largely unconscious to us although they are part of our subjective thought processes. In this way continuously we are attracting conditions which are not in our conscious thought, but which come as a result of the operation of the Law of Cause and Effect.

Again remember that the Law of Cause and Effect is something we use. Hence a practitioner realizes his word as the activity of the Spirit in him and through him, the activity of God, which is not *some*-mighty but *all*-mighty.

We must be conscious that we are doing this by the power of the God within us, and the God within us is the same God who was within Jesus. The Law which we use is the same Law which controls everything. So never argue as to whether or not you have the power. The only question is how much of the Power which you have are you going to use in any particular case. Make your statements in Mind definitely, consciously, and concretely, and believe that they are the Truth. Your word *is* the Law unto any particular thing which you speak. In the great Creative Medium your word starts a particular chain of cause and effect and as this word unfolds it will produce a logical outpicturing of the realization you had when the word was spoken.

Instead of struggling over external conditions or situations, what we really work with are thoughts and ideas. We are ever seeking to convince our own minds of the supremacy of Good. Therefore we transfer the burden of responsibility from the personal self to the impersonal Law. Say something like this: *If God is all there is and this Word is the Word of God, then there is no limit to what it can do. The Omnipotent cannot be circumscribed. The Omniscient does not need to be told anything. The Omnipotent need not borrow power; It* is *power.*

On page 456, which describes the incident in which Jesus healed the lunatic (taken from Matthew 17: 14-19), you will see that he rebuked the idea of evil. Evil disappears where there is a consciousness of Reality, of Unity, and of Goodness.

When we consider the calm, undisturbed stand which Jesus took in the face of every type of lack, limitation, fear, or sickness, we must realize that he had an inner sense of absolute authority over negation. This same spiritual exaltation we seek to attain. There is nothing mysterious or weird about this. It is merely a persistent, ever-increasing sense of certainty, an ever-expanding consciousness of Reality, an ever-deepening atmosphere of Good. We must never forget that the power which Jesus used is the same Mind which we use. Mind is One, changeless, indestructible, eternal, and indivisible. It is from our consciousness of this unity with the Whole that we treat.

When we give mental spiritual treatments, as suggested at the bottom of page 216, we must be careful not to dwell on negation. This does not mean that we should never use denials, because very frequently denials have the effect of immediately neutralizing a wrong mental atmosphere. But in using such denials we should never feel that we are combating some adversary. The negation has only the power which has been given to it. The correct explanation is what dissipates it. Therefore it is proper to say that a negative condition is neither person, place, nor thing. It has no power to operate, no intelligence, is not a law, is neither cause, medium, nor effect, and cannot enter the experience of our patient.

One should use any statement which convinces his own mind that as a result of his word the undesirable condition will be dissipated. From this viewpoint an affirmation and a denial are practically the same thing. Denial is an affirmation placed in the form of denial. However, in using our denials we should be careful that they do not become monotonous negations.

It is possible for a person to deny evil so strenuously that his denial becomes an affirmation of it. This is what we mean when we say to avoid dwelling too much on the negative. From the standpoint of Reality evil is a myth, or at least a mistake; certainly never God-ordained and most assuredly not to be equated with good. We must feel that evil disappears before our word just as darkness disappears before light.

It is not that we will the disappearance of evil. It is not that we pray that it shall be overcome, nor that we long for the appearance of good. It is that we inwardly believe that evil is neither person, place, nor thing. The Universe cannot be divided against Itself, as we have so often repeated in these lessons. This is the true meaning of spiritual nonresistance, which you will find defined on page 614. We *resist not evil* by knowing that it is not. By negation, defined on the same page, we mean any belief in duality.

We start with the assumption that God is all there is beside Whom there is none other; that there is no law to support any form of evil; that all pain, want, lack, and limitation are negations of the Truth, that is, they are denials of something which is really true. Hence every denial of Truth is merely a belief that that particular Truth has an opposite. We uncover the belief and reveal the Truth. When this is done we discover that Truth revealed is demonstrated.

This was the method Jesus used, and is the method used in modern applied psychology, such as analytical psychology and psychiatry. All of these methods rest upon the assumption that the Truth known, seen, understood, declared, and believed in automatically dissipates its opposite; that the explanation is the cure; that the revelation of Reality to the mind is accompanied by an objective manifestation of that Reality. Thus the word becomes flesh and dwells among us.

The individual *I* is an incarnation of the Universal *I AM*. The eternal *I AM* is in the midst of each one of us, and the individualization of that eternal Reality is the real self. In treatment we seek to speak from this real self, which is forever one with the eternal *I AM*.

This is what is referred to in symbolic literature as the I Am Consciousness. It means the consciousness of God, the consciousness of Allness, the sense of Wholeness. The consciousness of the *I AM*, then, is that thought which believes in the supremacy of Good.

If we use the statement, "I Am in the midst of thee is mighty to heal," we mean that God incarnated in us is perfect Life. The realization of this perfect Life automatically dissipates shadows of dis-ease and fear. We put our conviction into words and declare that these words are the law unto the thing whereto they are spoken. It is a simple but effective process. The one using it must be certain that he does believe that his word is Law.

Always in treatment we realize that the Kingdom of God is at hand, That is, we live in the Kingdom of God right now. This has been referred to as the Kingdom Consciousness. There is nothing mysterious about this. It is merely a sense of the eternal harmony as being ever-present; God over all, in all, and through all. This Kingdom Consciousness is a mental acceptance of the Divine Presence immanent in all people, while at the same time being transcendent. Refer again to the definition of *Transcendent* on page 638, and *Immanent* on page 600.

In the consciousness of the *I AM* and in the consciousness of the Kingdom of God, Christ dwells. This has been called the Christ Consciousness. But the Christ Consciousness does not mean anything strange or unnatural. It means that we have the same mind which Jesus used, the mind which is conscious of its complete unity with God.

Turn again to our definition of *The Christ* on page 578 and of *Consciousness* on page 580. The consciousness of Christ or the mind which Jesus used is our awareness of the God within us, the *I AM That I Am, beside which there is none other*, operating through us. In mental treatments we should become increasingly aware of this Divine Presence for it is the power back of our word. In such degree as we do become aware of this Christ Consciousness, fear and limitation drop from us and there comes a new and an increasing conviction of the power of our own word.

You will find that your consciousness of the power of your word increases in exact proportion as you believe there is something back of that word bigger than you are. That is, bigger than you are as an isolated person. This is why prayer has had power throughout the ages. Through prayer people have risen to mental heights which only spiritual conviction can create. This is why so many psychologists and others are telling us today that we must get back to religion and to faith. They are quite right.

But do not forget that religion means a way of life, not merely a certain way of thinking. Faith is an attitude which no longer denies the good it would affirm. The spiritual mind practitioner must have this deep, abiding faith, this great conviction which has been called the Christ Consciousness, which Jesus called the Kingdom of Heaven.

Summary

We never ask what can be healed spiritually. We ask to what extent can we perceive that God is all there is, the only Presence, the only Power, and the final Reality. Since we personally do not heal or demonstrate, our whole endeavor is to arrive at a spiritual conclusion. And because this is accomplished by our thought processes, there is nothing to hinder us from pushing our consciousness away from our imperfect experiences and entertaining more and greater and better ones.

In order to do this we have to turn from the objective appearance to the Spiritual Presence. Whether we arrive at these things through reason or by intuition makes no difference; the goal is the same. We are dealing with a Power that is Infinite and a Presence that is Perfect. To what extent can we sense this Power of the Infinite and this sweet and intimate Perfection of the Divine Presence? The Law of Good knows only good, and it is our business to sense this good. We use this Law. It is a Law that executes our will and choice. In doing this we must entertain a calm and peaceful attitude in our own consciousness, and think through all confusion to the place of calm which already exists at the center of our being.

The Truth seen, known, and definitely spoken, is the Power of the mental treatment. The Kingdom of God is here and now. It is our business to see it. The Christ Consciousness is the realization that God is at the center of everything. Sensing this something which is bigger than you are gives power to your words. Therefore you take the power out. You do not put it in.

Religion is a way of life, of thinking, and of living. It is a continual communing with the Divine, an ever-increasing consciousness of Its Presence and Its Joy.

Questions

Brief answers to these questions should be written out by the student after studying the lesson, and the answers compared with those which will be included in next week's lesson.

1. What should a mental practitioner treat?
2. Should a mental practitioner consider one case more difficult than another?
3. What is the Living Presence within us?
4. What is a practitioner's spiritual realization about his patient?
5. In what way do we compare spiritual realization with the light shining in the darkness?
6. In what way is the Law of Mind limited in Its working for us?
7. What do we mean by the mechanical and spontaneous side of thought?
8. Explain the difference between mental Law and Spirit.
9. In what way is the mental Law like a mirror?
10. Is it possible to experience conditions which we have not consciously imaged in the Law?
11. How can we eliminate undesirable conditions which we have unconsciously imaged in the Law?
12. If the Law of Cause and Effect governs everything, how do we escape becoming fatalists?
13. How shall we transfer the burden of personal responsibility?
14. How is evil made to disappear?
15. What do we mean by spiritual exaltation, from a practical viewpoint?
16. What is spiritual nonresistance?
17. What is the Kingdom Consciousness?
18. What causes an expansion of our consciousness of power?
19. Why do many psychologists advocate a return to religion?

Answers to Questions on Lesson 30

1. The Spirit is the *knower*, the Law is a *mechanical force.*
2. In spiritual treatment it makes no difference whether your patient is physically present or physically absent, because the Law which you use is ever-present and always available. However, the physical presence of the patient makes it possible for the practitioner to explain the action of the Law.
3. In treatment there must be a sense of conscious direction as well as spiritual realization, because spiritual realization is a recognition of the Power, while conscious direction is a definite use of that Power.
4. A scientific mental and spiritual practitioner is one who believes in the Law, has faith in his ability to use It, and uses It both consciously and definitely.
5. Such statements as "God is all there is," etc., are effective in treatment because they stimulate faith and expectancy.
6. The Law can act for us only at the level of our recognition because our recognition gives direction to the Law, which of Itself is neutral.
7. When we say, "The Law of Mind is not selective," we mean that the Law of Mind has no definite intention for us. We decide what It is going to do, so far as we are concerned.
8. The Law of Mind means the mechanics of Spirit. It means the impersonal Law of the Universe. It is the Law of Cause and Effect. It is a mechanical force. The Personalness of Spirit means the Divine Essence or knowingness of God, personal to each because It is personified through each.
9. When we say man is a center of God Consciousness we mean that man individualizes the Infinite Spirit of God.
10. A mental practitioner's sole responsibility, in giving a treatment, is to arrive at a state of consciousness which affirms the desired result and which no longer denies such affirmation.
11. The Law which makes us sick and impoverishes us can also heal and enrich us because this Law, which is the Universal Law of Cause and Effect, automatically reproduces the images of our thought.
12. A practitioner should never feel that he is dealing with two opposing powers. He should know that he is dealing with One Divine Presence which ever responds to him with love and harmony, and with One Universal Law, which because of Its nature must bind or free according to the way in which he uses It.
13. In treating children we should also treat the parents because the thought and belief of the parents so completely surround the child and are more or less unconsciously accepted by him.
14. A person would build up faith in his ability to treat effectively by continuously reassuring himself that he is dealing with a spiritual Principle which operates independent of anyone's belief or of any existing circumstance.
15. Different metaphysical schools obtain largely the same results in mental practice because of their belief in some transcendent power.

16. In our search after Truth, in order to arrive at the best that life has to offer we should be willing to study different systems of thought, taking from each the best that it has to offer.
17. In mentally treating inharmony, confusion, discord, etc., we must know that the fact is but a passing experience, not an eternal verity; hence it can be changed. We accomplish this by supplying a spiritual equivalent such as harmony for inharmony, peace for confusion, etc.

The Individual and the Universal

Our Textbook states that we individualize the Universal and Universalize the individual.

This sounds like rather an abstract statement until we understand its simplicity. The ancients said that every man is a microcosm within a Macrocosm, a little world within a Big World, or an individual within the Universal. Jesus said, *Believest thou not that I am in the Father, and the Father in me? The words that I speak unto you I speak not of myself: but the Father that dwelleth in me, he doeth the works.*

What does this mean? The answer is simple, and yet it is that type of simplicity from which the most profound conclusions are reached.

There is no such thing as an individual anything in the Universe. For instance, we as individuals do not have an individual gravitational force that holds us in place. We do not possess an individual law of mathematics or principle of harmony. Rather we are immersed in all of these things, and they individualize through us in accord with the use that we make of them.

When Emerson said that there is one mind common to all individual men he reached one of the highest perceptions of the ages. Nor was he denying the reality of our own being. He was saying in substance, "You are because God is. You live because God lives in you." Each one of us individualizes the Universal Mind by our use of It. The sum total of our mental and emotional reactions surrounds us with a field of thought which is operated upon by a larger field of Mind, Law and Action.

This is why you do not send out thoughts or hold them or will or wish or concentrate when you give a treatment. You make a definite statement in this Universal field of Mind which individualizes for the person, place, or thing you identify your statement with. Your treatment is an individualization of the Universal Mind, but the moment it is given, it becomes a Universalization of the individual mind.

This sounds abstract, so we shall make it more understandable by way of an illustration. When a farmer sows grain he is individualizing the creative soil of a universal medium. The creativity was there before he used it. It would be there if he did not use it. It is, was, and will remain just what it was, nothing more and nothing less.

Without being consciously aware of the fact, the farmer has learned that he as an individual can sow the seed of his choice. The Universal is now individualizing for him at the point of decision in his personal life.

But the moment he sows the seed a Universal process is set in operation, and that which was individual passes from the point of his conscious volition, selectivity, and will, into a Universal field of creative reaction. He actually is individualizing the Universal, but the moment he does so his individualization is acted upon by the Universal, and thus it becomes a Universal operation.

This is true in everything we do. We are individual points in the Consciousness of God or the original Creative Spirit of the Universe. We are points where It thinks through us as us, or as we say, God as man in man is man.

But the God that is in man is the same God that is Universal. There is no wall of separation, no barrier, no place where one begins and the other leaves off. All is One and One is All. The creativity of thought is not dependent upon the thinker. Only the choice of thinking is dependent upon the thinker. The creative activity of thought belongs to the Universe.

This is one of the fine points in our philosophy, and one of the main points in the Science of Mind. Every advance in science is built on the simple proposition that nature obeys us when we obey it.

It is said by those who understand ancient symbology that this is why Jesus washed the disciples' feet. It was as though he were saying to them, "If I your master wash your feet, ought you not to wash one another's feet?" Everything that Jesus did was to demonstrate the Divine Reality and the laws which govern Its operation. The Lord or the Law serves us but first we must obey It. Therefore when one of the disciples protested and told Jesus he could not permit him to wash his feet, Jesus answered, *For I have given you an example, that ye should do as I have done to you.*

I hope you will think long and deeply upon this idea of the individualization of the Universal and the Universalization of the individual, always remembering that in no way does this contradict either the supremacy of God or the reality of man. Man as an individual does not disappear because God is incarnated in him or because his life is God, nor does the Universal Law dominate him in his personal choice. It is complete cooperation based on unity.

If we had to make things happen or push our thought out or influence or dominate and beat down opposition, we should be faced with an impossible task. We never try to coerce anything in dealing with the laws of nature.

One of the things we must come to understand in dealing with the Laws of Spirit is that we are still operating in a realm of law and order. We are operated upon by gravitational force. While it is true that we can change our individual position in it, it is also true that whatever position we take we are still operated upon by it.

So it is with our word, our treatment, our prayer, our affirmation. It operates in a larger field and is operated upon by a Supreme Law. This is why we can have faith in it and patiently, cheerfully, and expectantly await the outcome, knowing that as a man sows, so shall he also reap.

How Does God Know What I Am Doing?

Frequently people ask, "Why should God be interested in my little affairs?" I remember once speaking to one of our Trustees who had been ill for several weeks. I asked him why he had not requested treatment. He said, "I did not wish to bother God with such a small thing."

This is a natural enough reaction, and yet it is built on ignorance of cosmic laws. We might ask, "Is there more life in an elephant than in a flea?" Or from the standpoint of the Infinite, "Is a giant Sequoia of more importance than a rose blossoming by the wayside?" Of course not. There is no big and no little either to the Divine Presence or to the Law which governs everything. Is not the rose rooted in the same soil in which the tree is rooted? It is merely a different type of manifestation of life, taking a separate form but rooted in a common unity.

We should eliminate the idea of big and little or hard and easy because they do not exist in the Creative Mind of the Universe. Things exist there as ideas, while it is the nature of the Law of Mind to cause these ideas to take forms native to such ideas. All ideas are brought into form or fruition through the one medium. A person running a peanut stand on some street corner and affirming the presence of activity in his business is invoking the same Law as the builders of a railroad or an Empire State Building are invoking.

The Law always takes the form that we give It. We may call it big or little or important or unimportant, but the Law as such knows nothing about comparative degrees. The very nature of this Law is such that it cannot say "I am big" in one place and "I am little" in another. It can say only "I am and that also I am," including what we call big and little, as it automatically flows through everything, taking the form of all things.

In our treatments we entertain an idea and accept a form, because from the viewpoint of the Law one thing is as important as another. When we ask ourselves how is it that God knows who we are and that our little affairs are important, the answer is that God knows everything, not as big and little but only as action and reaction, only as contemplation which produces its own reaction.

All great spiritual teachers have told us this, and they were right. All thought of big and little, hard and easy, can and cannot, must be divorced from our treatment, remembering that the same ingenuity, the same Creative Power that flows into the largest form also creates the smallest form.

Comparatives do not belong to the Universe. They are merely differentiations in our own mind. Dropping them completely out of our thought we contemplate neither the big nor the little, but the thing itself taking particular form.

A great load will fall from our mind if we will stop thinking about big and little or hard and easy. If you set a spool of thread in front of a mirror it will be reflected, or if you stand in front of the mirror you yourself will be reflected. This larger form will be reflected as readily as the smaller form. The mirror knows nothing about size, but reflects automatically the form held in front of it.

We are told that there are many heavenly bodies millions of times larger than the earth; there are many that are smaller, but the same Cause created them, not as big or little but merely as expressions of Itself.

In a certain sense this makes the creation of a mud cake by a child as important as the building of an empire, not that it is fraught with as much significance to human experience, but that from the standpoint of the creative genius of the Universe they are just creations.

Is a sunset of less importance than an epic poem? And in reality would the healing of tuberculosis or cancer be of greater importance than the healing of an ordinary cold, or the removal of a wart?

We are told in psychosomatic medicine that warts are easily removed by suggestion, and yet a wart is a definite form rooted in the physical body. How do we know but that if our idea of cancer were as lightly held as our idea of a wart, a simple suggestion would dissolve it as quickly and as easily? We do not. From the standpoint of the ultimate Spirit of creativity there is no reason whatsoever to deny the liquidation of one as easily as another.

It must be, then, that the obstruction is in our own consciousness, or in our unconscious resistance to the thought of big and little or hard and easy. This is what we must overcome.

NOTHING in the manifest universe stays put, nothing is permanent. It is the lack of permanence in the objective world that makes it subject to the interior process of a Universal Will. Everything is will and representation. Mind is permanent, never changes; the activity of Mind forever changes. There is change in the midst of permanency.

> *When we free our minds from the thought that time is passing, we shall remain young. Time is not passing, we are passing through it.*

ANTIQUITY reveals what we might have done; current events portray our present states of thought; the possibility of the future is already inherent in our imagination.

In reality each is a guest of the Universal and Infinite Host.

THE INCARNATION of God is both universal and individual. Universally it is the pushing out of Spirit into Self-expression. Individually it is a personification of this Spirit. Thus each personifies that which at the center is a Unitary Wholeness.

> *Man is not something apart from or other than the Thing Itself. Man is that Universal Creativeness operating at the level of his own comprehension.*

IMAGINATION, will and volition, fused into one, is what we call a person. The creative center of man' s being is Spirit, that which makes him a conscious entity.

So close, so immediate is the Divine Presence that it is impossible to lift a hand without It.

OUR ENTIRE practice is built upon this Simple premise, that we are living in a Spiritual Universe now; that we are spiritual beings in this Universe; that we are as perfect now as we ever shall become; and that the realization of this perfection breaks down the barriers which appear to hide it from us, looses the chains of suggestion, and unbinds the victim of false belief.

> *We are hiding our Divinity behind a mask, but back of the mask is a unique individualization of God. When we unmask the mind we reveal the real person.*

MAN has always been potential in the Universal Matrix; he is now individualized, and must forever increase from where he is, eternally expanding.

No man has ever exhausted the possibilities of the self which he is.

How to Build Your Tomorrow Today

Life is an adventure in which we never know what is going to happen just beyond the turn of the road. But too often our today is filled with regrets over the past. If we could convince ourselves that the limitations of the past need not be carried into the future, what a happy outlook we should have.

One of the outstanding things that Jesus taught was that the mistakes of yesterday can be canceled, that God's creation is always taking place, and no matter what the experiences of yesterday may have been, they can be changed.

Jesus did not seem to think that this change required months and years of strenuous effort. Unlike those around him, he knew that God, or the Divine Spirit, wishes only good for everyone. He knew that we are all rooted in pure Spirit, in perfect Life, and that at any moment we can so unify ourselves with the Power of Good that evil will disappear from our experience.

Even as what we did yesterday set the Law of Life in motion to create what we are doing today, so what we are doing today sets this same Law in motion to create what will happen to us tomorrow. What we did yesterday is carried over into today only because we give our consent to it. What we are thinking and doing today can create the kind of tomorrow we wish to experience if we will change our outlook on life.

But since today is the only day in which we live and yesterday has forever passed, the change that we need to make within ourselves must be made today. And so we have to live each day as though it were complete and perfect within itself. We have to live each day as though all the joy there is in the universe were ours now. And we have to live each day as though all the joy we ever expect to experience were ours now.

If we would make every day a day of praise and thanksgiving, a day in which we recognize the Divine Bounty and the Eternal Goodness, and if we live today as though God were the only Presence and the only Power there is, we would not have to worry about tomorrow.

We are all human and we have all made mistakes. The starting point for creating a better future for ourselves is to deliberately free our minds from the mistakes of yesterday and feel that they need no longer be held against us; they need no longer be a liability.

Too often our minds are so burdened because of the mistakes we have made that we do not take time to forgive ourselves and others and start over again. And so it is wise to occasionally review the past and try to find out just what we have been thinking and doing to create this burden in our minds.

Suppose we have had a deep sense of animosity toward others and because of this find that we are not meeting people in the right spirit, and they, naturally, respond to us the way we meet them. Our whole set of human relations is out of harmony.

We cannot go back over the past and relive it. We cannot make adjustments in the past. We have to make them in the present. It is not going to do us any good to sit around and cry over the past and bemoan our fate, because in the very day in which we are living we are creating our tomorrows, which will become monotonous repetitions of our yesterdays.

So today is the time in which we should cut loose from the threads of previous experiences, wherever they were negative, and deliberately make up our minds that we shall no longer create our future out of the old past. If we have had antagonisms and resentments in the past, today is the only day in which we can change them.

How, then, shall we do this? We must arrive at some practical way, some definite and concrete method, and deliberately use the Law of Good just as we would any other law in nature. In doing this, the one who is suffering from his past mistakes of resentment and animosity merely turns quietly to himself and says:

> *I have decided to change all this. I want to like people and I want them to like me. I want to get along happily with others. I forgive myself for everything that has happened up until now. I loose it and let it go. I not only forgive myself, I forgive everyone who I feel has held anything against me. I forgive and I am forgiven.*

And back of this simple statement we should know that all the Power in the universe conspires to help us. We should feel that we live in an eternal presence of pure Spirit whose whole purpose is good, whose whole desire is constructive, and whose whole feeling toward us is one of love and compassion. Therefore we should say:

> *Knowing that God is the only Presence and the only Power in the universe, and knowing that God is love, I deliberately turn from everything that is unlike this love. I desire that this love and compassion and well-wishing for others shall be the whole theme of my life.*

It does not seem possible that so simple a method as this can produce such a dynamic result. But experience has definitely proved that it can. Anyone who tries this method will experience definite results. The most wonderful thing about it is we do not have to change anything but ourselves. For every man is the cause of his own experience, whether he knows it or not. We all are carrying the negative experiences of our past into the future merely because we have not disconnected them from our minds. If we are creating a negative future it is because we have not changed our thought about it.

We have seen the same thing happen to people who had failed in the past, as though nothing could ever work out right for them. We have seen them deliberately change their thought, disconnect their memory from failure, push it aside mentally as though it no longer belonged, as though it were no longer a part of them, and affirm that good alone accompanies them, that life is made to live successfully and happily. Accepting this and daily affirming it, we have seen failure and defeat turn into success and triumph.

We have not the slightest doubt that when we do this we are using an all-powerful Law, the Law of Good we talk so much about, the Law which controls everything. We are swinging into line with the great harmony of the Universe.

But before we can entirely disconnect ourselves from the negations of the past we have to learn to fill the mind with positive acceptances which are so much greater and deeper than the negations we have been entertaining that they consume them by their very presence, just as light dissipates darkness.

It is not going to do us any good just to make a lot of idle resolutions or to make up our minds that we are going to create such a dynamic personality that nothing can withstand it. This is too much like a person whistling in the dark because he is afraid. What we have to do is get back to some fundamental proposition which ties us directly into the Mind of God, and with the simple acknowledgment that there is a Law of Good in which we have complete confidence, reverse our whole mental outlook on life.

If we disconnect ourselves from the past and find ourselves firmly rooted in God today, in love, in hope, in joyful expectancy and in grateful acknowledgment, and if we learn to harmonize with everything that transpires today, tomorrow will blossom like a new flower in our experience.

Or we might think of it in another way. When we are weeding our gardens we often find certain plants that are choking out the growth of the things we wish to harvest. So we pull them up, throw them aside, cultivating only those plants that we want to mature. We do this today. Yesterday is past and tomorrow has not arrived. So the only time we can weed our garden is today.

And one other thing we have to realize is that we did not make the laws of life; we only use them. The Power that makes the garden is a Power greater than we are. All we do is use It. Of necessity the creative soil had to produce the weeds that hamper the growth of the desirable plants, and of necessity the same law has to stop creating them when we uproot them.

Now if we can shift this whole scene into the mind, into our thinking, then we shall have a key to the situation. This has to do with the moment in which we live. Are we permitting love to blossom in our lives? Of course we want it to, but are we deliberately uprooting everything that denies love, and trusting to the Lord of creation to produce the desired harvest?

What if we are confused and distraught and upset and all out of sorts? What if the pressure of the past has appeared to cloud the sunlight of the present? The past is gone and the sun is shining on the other side of the clouds. And so let us deliberately resolve to change our thinking today and make up our minds that we can have confidence in life.

No one can be hurt by doing this. We have everything to gain and nothing to lose. We can uproot all the unhappy thoughts of the past, all the thoughts of failure, all the doubts and fears, all the little petty animosities and disagreements if we really want to. And we can create our own future today just by carefully guarding our thoughts. But how can we do this unless our faith in life is greater than our fear, unless hope rises triumphant over despair, or until love cancels everything unlovable?

This takes us back to what is the great need of the world, the world that somewhere along the line has lost its vision of God. We have gone on our own too long. We have separated ourselves from the source of our being. We are like persons lost in a fog. The one great resolution we should make today as we turn from the mistakes of the past and look to the future with hope—the one great resolution we need to make, above and beyond all others and more important than all, is that we will find God.

And since we must deal with people and events, and since our lives must be spent with others and in doing things, how can we expect to find God outside His own creation? How can we expect to realize Him in the emptiness of space if we have refused to see Him in those we meet? And how can we find Him in those we meet and in the events that transpire around us unless we have first discovered Him at the center of our own being? We cannot.

The starting point is at the center of our own being. When we awaken the Divine within us it will reach out and embrace everything around us, and it will discover the same Presence in people and in events and in all nature. For God is not separate from what He is doing. The Divine Life is in everyone and in everything.

This is the secret that Jesus discovered. This is why he was able to speak as no other person ever spoke. This is why he was able to perform the miracles of love and healing and in so doing prove a fact so simple, so fundamental, but so powerful that people stand in awe before it—the simple fact that God is right where you are.

Meditation

Forgetting everything that was wrong in the past, and looking toward that which is right in the future, I turn my thought to that which is good, to that which is lovely, to that which is true.

Forgiving myself for the mistakes of the past, I loose them and let them go, and in my imagination turn with hope and joy to the future.

I press forward to the goal. I am letting all the fears and failures and mistakes of the past fall backward and eliminate themselves from my experience. Knowing that there is nothing in the Universe that wishes me other than good, I loose myself from everything that has seemed evil.

It is my desire that only that which is right, that which is constructive, that which is life-giving, shall remain in my thought. It is my desire that only that which is good shall go from me to others.

Believing absolutely in the Law of Good, and accepting the Divine guidance in love and in peace and in joy, I press forward to the goal of happiness and fulfillment.

Blessing everything that I do, I know that I am blessed. Loving all whom I meet, I know that I am loved.

Today is my day. Tomorrow belongs to God.

Bibles of the World

Fragments from the spiritual history of the race
revealing fundamental UNITY of religious thought and experience

BUDDHISM—He who strives to grasp the teaching lights up the world, as the moon released from a cloud lights up the night.

JUDAISM and CHRISTIANITY—Brethren! Ye have been called unto liberty. Only use not liberty for an occasion to the flesh.
By love serve one another.
Be hospitable to one another, without grudging. Whatever the gifts which each has received, use them for one another as good stewards of the manifold grace of God. Let it be with the strength which God supplies.
A good man obtaineth favor of the Lord.

ISLAM—God will increase the guidance of the already guided.

TAOISM—The want of placidity and the want of contentment are contrary to the character (nature); and where this obtains, it is impossible that any man or state should anywhere long abide.

CONFUCIANISM—The superior man has neither anxiety nor fear. When internal examination discovers nothing wrong, what is there to be anxious about? What is there to fear?
If a man put himself aright, what difficulty will he have in the public service? But if he cannot put himself aright, how is he going to put others aright?

HINDUISM—Everything here on earth is overcome by those whose mind remains balanced. The Eternal is incorruptible and balanced. Therefore men are established in the Eternal.

Depend On Principle

Office of the Dean

My Dear Friend,

You will find three supplements to this lesson, to which we hope you will give considerable attention. It is important to realize that Principle is never bound by precedent. What has transpired in our experience up until now need have nothing to do with what may happen tomorrow.

This was the great realization of Jesus and the one which placed his teaching beyond and above those who preceded him. They had believed that every individual was bound by the events in his life, and that each must suffer because of previous mistakes. As far as we know, Jesus was the first one to repudiate this theory and to say that each day is a new beginning if we recognize it as such.

This is one of the most important things for us to remember, because being human we have all made mistakes, and being Divine we can transcend them through introducing a new and a higher order of causation. We must, then, deliberately turn from every negative experience, and begin to change our whole mental outlook until it more nearly fits the Divine Pattern. Each individual must do this for himself. It is good that this is true, and that no one can live for us but ourselves.

Keeping our vision steadfastly fixed on the Divine, we remold the human into a pattern that is less limited and less circumscribed. There should be a joy in doing this, an exaltation, an enthusiastic approach, for if Life is for us who can be against us? One with God is a majority.

Sincerely,
Ernest Holmes

Lesson 32

Top of page 218 to *How Habits Are Acquired,* page 222

The first thing to do in beginning a series of treatments for any person is to work for the removal of all fear and doubt. In the first paragraph at the top of page 218 is the suggestion that we should conform our arguments so that they will measure up to the spiritual ideal.

Just what does it mean to conform an argument to an ideal? You start with the thought that the person whom you are seeking to help, being Divine, has perfect circulation; that there is a circulation of Divine Ideas flowing through him. But if according to his experience you discover that he has poor physical circulation you must conform your belief about his physical circulation to the statement which you have made about the circulation of the Divine Ideas within him.

Your statement in such a case might be "This man, being Pure Spirit and having the Divine Ideas of harmony, peace, and joy circulating through him, must have perfect circulation in his physical being. Circulation is a spiritual idea flowing through this man. His circulation is always complete and perfect. It is never retarded, never over-active, never inactive. Its action is always in harmonious accord with

Reality. It is always perfect. Perfect God, Perfect Man, perfect relationship or unity between God and man."

Your argument is now conformed to your premise, that is, to the spiritual Principle upon which the treatment is based. This is what is meant by conforming one's statements to the idea upon which a treatment should be based.

We begin all treatments by removing the sense of fear. This is done by knowing that there is no fear. Perfect Love casts out fear. The idea of fear is dissipated when the mental conviction of faith dawns upon the consciousness. Fear cannot abide where faith is. Therefore our statements must conform to a sense of peace.

Turn to the Meditation, *I Fear No Evil*, page 533, for an example of this. It is not necessary that you use these exact words, but it is necessary that you use some statements which will heal the thought of fear about your patient. You will find another treatment on page 521, *I Shall Not Doubt Nor Fear*. Statements similar to these are convincing; indeed any statement is effective which reassures the mind that there is nothing of which to be afraid.

It is easy to believe that God is perfect, but we must continue this belief by stating that man, being the spiritual manifestation of God, also is perfect. Jesus said, *Be ye therefore perfect, even as your Father in heaven is perfect.* I do not think any of us will find difficulty in declaring for the perfection of the spiritual man. The statements which we make are made about the spiritual man. Our whole treatment is for the purpose of arriving at a mental conviction of the spiritual man.

As we inwardly perceive and embody ideas about this spiritual man the outward form changes to correspond with the inward conviction. We must have a complete conviction that the statements which we make are true. Turn to page 436, under the heading, *Entering the Kingdom of Reality*. Read again the story of the healing of the Centurion's servant on page 437 discussed in Lesson 5. Jesus healed by his inner knowingness, and we must do the same.

We do not say that the outward man is perfect. The patient comes to us because he suffers from pain or from some physical imperfection. It is the spiritual man whom we believe to be perfect and all our statements are made about him. At the same time we declare that this is the Truth about the *whole* man; that this spiritual Truth about him is made manifest in the flesh.

Our text states that if our realization becomes a subjective embodiment, a healing will take place. Turn again to our definitions of *Subjective* on page 634 and you will realize anew that subjective embodiment means an inner subconscious idea. When you say that your patient is perfect, and there is no longer anything in you that denies this statement, you have embodied the belief of his perfection.

When this embodiment is lacking continue to treat. This is possible because statements in mind have a definite reaction, and one type of thought neutralizes another. Continuous affirmations of Truth must destroy opposite beliefs. This will happen gradually, if not immediately. Always the practitioner is working with the idea that God is all there is and that he has the supreme right on his side.

Let us again consider the idea that the will of God and the nature of God are one and the same. This means that if the nature of God is perfect, peaceful, and harmonious, then since God cannot have any will opposed to His nature (for such a supposition would be self-destructive), it follows that we are not only obeying the will of God when we think harmony but we are using the Law in the highest way when we declare for harmony.

A declaration of harmony must always take precedence over a belief in discord. If this were not true we would have no Principle to demonstrate. Our universe would be resolved into an eternal combat, with evil victorious one time and good the next. This is not only unthinkable; it is impossible. Hence you may know that a statement of Truth does take precedence over that which is not so. Make your declarations with absolute conviction. This is what is meant by *lighting our torch with fire from heaven*.

How can the practitioner realize that all power is given unto him (as Jesus affirmed when he said that all power was given unto him in heaven and on earth) unless his thought is in harmony with the Infinite Will or the Infinite Nature? In such decree as his thought is in harmony with peace, all peace is given unto him because peace already is. It is the nature of God. You will find a definition of *Peace* on page 617. Turn also to page 478 under the heading, *Let Not Your Heart Be Troubled*, and you will find that Jesus spoke with that calm certainty which has been the inheritance of all who have believed in the ever-available presence of Spirit.

The practitioner must believe that man is spiritual, that he himself is spiritual, that his patient is spiritual, that the Law of Good is available and takes precedence over every experience of evil, lack, want, and limitation. He does not treat the physical man but he works to arrive at a recognition and realization of the spiritual man, stating that this is the Truth about the whole man and is now made manifest in the experience of the person whom he is helping. He supplies the mental equivalent of life for his patient and leaves the Law to do the rest.

You will find an example of the methods of treatment starting at the bottom of page 611 and a definition of *Mental Equivalent* on page 610. If you have any doubt as to what is meant by the expression, *Let the Law do the work*, turn again to the definition of *Law* on page 605. We must always refresh our memories with the meaning of words until their meaning is so clear to us that we need no longer inquire about them.

The best we know is the best we can do today. We may not be able to walk on the water or turn water into wine or multiply the loaves and fishes, but it is amazing what we are able to do. We should not deny ourselves the privilege of using what understanding we have today, hoping and expecting for more tomorrow. As our text states on page 219, *Principle is Infinite, but we shall demonstrate Its power only at the level of our concept of It*. This again is the Law of Cause and Effect, of balance, of equilibrium, of polarity, of reflection at work.

Permit nothing to hinder you from using this Law to the fullest of your understanding today. Be not at all dismayed if you do not use It as perfectly as you think you should, for each must begin right where he is. How could he begin anywhere else? As suggested at the top of page 220, if we need a crutch we must use one. The only way that we shall know that we do not need one is by demonstrating that we can walk without it. We do not dishonor God when we use the crutch; we need have no superstition about our use of it. If we would do away with our need for it we must first heal ourselves. In short, each demonstrates at the level of his present knowledge and goes on from there. We must be content with this while always striving for something greater.

As stated many times in this series of lessons, we must cooperate with all forms of healing, for anything which helps humanity is good. But because our field is one of mind, the practitioner of this science works in mind alone. If a person is not able to convince himself of the truth of his statements he keeps on repeating them. Gradually this repetition induces a state of belief. The scientific practitioner is one who is willing to work until he gets results. He never depends upon any weird performance, any psychic impression, or any strange sensation, but if in working with his Principle he makes right use of his technique he is certain to produce good results.

One of the difficulties we have to combat is ignorance and superstition. All superstition is ignorance. We must come to understand definitely what we are doing and have faith in ourselves because we understand the Law which is operating. Therefore we should never say that we lack the power to heal, since it is not a question of personal power. The electrician would never say he lacked the power to provide the conditions for lighting a building. It has nothing to do with *his* power, from a personal viewpoint. It has to do only with the law which responds to his correct use of it. So it is in our field. Our Law is Mind in action; our Principle is the Unity, the Omnipresence, and therefore the ever-availability of Good. Our technique consists of a series of statements claiming this Good, affirming Its presence and Its action in us and in those whom we seek to help.

If a person feels any doubt about his own ability to heal, he must first heal himself of this negative thought and then he will be able to proceed in a scientific manner. No doubt the time will come when arguments of this type will no longer be necessary, but while they are necessary do not refuse to use them; they will be effective. This is what distinguishes a scientific practitioner from one who works by the law of chance—he may or may not arrive at a proper conclusion, but the scientific practitioner works until he does arrive.

You are depending upon Principle (analyzed on page 221). Principle is power and It is absolute. Turn again to our definition of *Power* on page 620 and the definition of *Absolute* on page 575. Principle is absolute and unconditioned by any present fact. It is never bound by anything that is already done, but remains free and unlimited. To Principle all things are possible.

The one thing that can deny the Power of this Principle is our own belief. This belief is as much subjective as it is objective. Before a person can change his belief he often has to change his inward thought, because the subjective belief often denies and neutralizes the affirmation of the objective beliefs. Faith, to be complete, must be embodied in the subconscious thought. There must be nothing within us that denies what we affirm. The Absolute is. The Absolute is God. The Absolute, the God-power, the Unconditioned, the Unlimited, exists around us and within us. This Absolute appears to each one in the form of his belief.

Turn again to the definition of *Relativity and Absoluteness* on page 627. Even the Absolute must appear to us as relative because It appears to us in the form of our own belief. This does not limit the Absolute, but does confine our use of It to our concept of It at any particular time.

To make this point more understandable, the fact of our individuality makes it necessary that the law of liberty bind us until we understand that such bondage is not real, but suppositional. Then, seeing through the bondage to the Principle of Liberty, we outline our experience in the Absolute in a less limited way. Thus we are gradually freed. This is the meaning of the external upward spiral. We shall never cease expanding. Jesus said, *In my Father's house are many mansions*. So we shall never stop progressing.

If we think of disease as an entity rather than as thought force we shall have to concede that such an entity would have a mind of its own. Then any combat with it would be with a person rather than with a belief. Do not forget that belief can be experienced with as great a *seeming* reality as Truth. The suffering of a man who labors under a hallucination is real enough to him. But if the hallucination were an entity of itself neither prayer, treatment, nor medical assistance could in any way disrupt it, because being a person it would do as it chose to do. So our thought must always be clear about this.

Disease is not an entity, but it is a definite experience from which we all suffer more or less. But knowing that it is not an entity, and theoretically resolving it into a state of consciousness, belief, thought, or subjective reaction, we know that we have the weapons at hand with which to combat it. This is what spiritual mind healing is and does. Therefore when you give a treatment you are setting a vibration in motion in Law which must not only accept what you say but the way in which you say it.

A treatment should be free from struggle. There should be a great sense of calm and peace accompanying it, a great conviction of the allness of God, a deep realization of the indwelling Principle of Christ in you. From this Principle you speak. The Father in you is perfect. Read the third paragraph on page 417, the definition of *I AM*.

Remember again that there is no personal responsibility in this, only a definite obligation to work in your own mind until you bring your consciousness to an acceptance of the Truth about your patient. If you are treating yourself, as the text suggests on page 222, call your own name, or say, "I am thus and so." If you are working for someone else speak his name, say, "This treatment is for him." Then forget all about him and give the treatment, never trying to send out a thought.

In some way which we do not clearly understand and cannot definitely follow, this word does become the Law unto that person and does operate through him, and you will always find a reaction as a result of your work.

Summary

All treatment begins with removing the sense of fear as far as possible. Treatment is clearing away the obstructions that deny the Divine Presence, and revealing the Spirit of Perfection at the center of everything. Perfect Love alone casts out fear. Not only must we declare that God is perfect; we must finish this declaration by saying that spiritual man is perfect because he is one with the Father of all.

Our statements are made about the spiritual man not about the objective man. It is the physical and the mental man that suffers. Spirit is never troubled. It is always perfect.

When our conscious statements of Reality become a subjective embodiment they automatically cause the Law to react in a new way.

The nature of God and the will of the Divine Being are the same thing. All power is given unto us in such degree as we harmonize with the fundamental Reality. We must believe that man is spiritual, that God is right where man is, and that the Divine Will is the only good there is.

Using the Law to the best of our understanding today will enable us to better use It tomorrow. We have to begin right where we are.

We seek to cooperate with every method of healing and with all people who seek to benefit the human race. We must claim that we have the power to heal, since a denial of this claim is an affirmation of its opposite. If we feel that we lack the ability to heal we must reassure ourselves of what really does the healing. In this way we shall gain confidence because we are in league with the greater Reality.

Questions

Brief answers to these questions should be written out by the student after studying the lesson, and the answers compared with those which will be included in next week's lesson.

1. What is the first thing a mental and spiritual practitioner should do in beginning a series of treatments?
2. What do we mean by removing an idea from consciousness?
3. How shall we remove fear from consciousness?
4. What mental perception furnishes the correct spiritual equivalent for physical circulation?
5. In spiritual mind healing is it necessary to use exact words or set formulas?
6. What is the mental practitioner's concept of the physical body?
7. Why must a declaration of harmony take precedence over discord?
8. What is meant by letting the Law do the work?
9. Why should we never say we lack the power to heal?
10. If each has the ability to use the Power which heals, why do we ever fail to demonstrate?
11. What should we do on failing to demonstrate according to our desires?
12. What distinguishes a scientific mental practitioner from one who works by the law of chance?
13. Why is the mental Principle unconditioned by any present fact?
14. What appears to limit the power of the mental Principle in our lives?
15. When is faith complete?
16. Is disease an entity of itself?
17. If disease is not an entity, is it a hallucination?
18. How does our treatment reach our patient?

Answers to Questions on Lesson 31

1. A mental practitioner should treat any condition which needs to be changed.
2. Since a spiritual practitioner never treats the physical being but seeks to embody a realization of the Spiritual Being, he should not think of one case as being more difficult to handle than another.
3. The Living Presence within us is the incarnation of Spirit, the Word of God, the voice of authority, and the light which dispels darkness.
4. A practitioner's spiritual realization about his patient is his consciousness of his patient's innate perfection and wholeness.
5. We compare spiritual realization with the light shining in the darkness, because the light is not affected by the darkness but dissipates the darkness by its very presence.
6. In working for us the Law of Mind, which of Itself is limitless, is of necessity limited to our spiritual vision, mental acceptance, and subjective embodiment of ideas. (*Spiritual vision* means an inner awareness of our unity with Perfect Life. *Mental acceptance* means a state of awareness which no longer denies this spiritual recognition. *Subjective embodiment* means that our habitual thought patterns completely accept and become a perfect replica of this spiritual realization.)
7. The mechanical side of thought is the mental Law of Cause and Effect. The spontaneous side of thought means the conscious thought.
8. Mental Law like all law is a mechanical force, while Spirit is Self-knowingness.
9. The mental Law is like a mirror because It reflects that which is imaged in It, without argument or decision of Its own.
10. It is possible to experience conditions which we have not consciously imaged in the Law, because we subjectively receive many impressions of which we are not consciously aware. These subjective impressions are always imaged in the Law.
11. We can eliminate undesirable conditions which we have unconsciously accepted by the law of reversal, which means consciously changing the subjective images of thought by dwelling upon more desirable thought patterns, i.e., using the Law of Cause and Effect in a different way.
12. Even though the Law of Cause and Effect governs everything, we escape becoming fatalists because the Law of Itself does nothing unless It is first set in motion by the activity of Spirit. Man being spiritual can both use and reverse any human sequence in the effects of the Law of Cause and Effect.
13. We transfer the burden of personal responsibility by realizing *first*, Divine Guidance governing our thought; *second*, having implicit confidence in the fact that the Law of Cause and Effect must respond to our thought.
14. Evil is made to disappear by a conscious recognition of good and a subjective reaction to it.
15. From a practical viewpoint spiritual exaltation means an ever-increasing awareness of good, an increased sense of certainty and security, built upon the realization of our unity with all the Power there is.

16. Spiritual nonresistance is not so much a denial of our contention against evil, as it is a realization that evil has no power, is not a thing of itself, and becomes dissipated by a recognition of its unreality.
17. The Kingdom Consciousness is the realization that the Kingdom of Good, Harmony, etc., is at hand, and in all people.
18. An expansion of our consciousness of power is brought about through realizing that the Power which we use is infinite and may always be relied upon.
19. Many psychologists advocate a return to religion because only through the mystical sense do we come in contact with transcendent power.

What Goes Out Must Return

After the newcomer to this field has learned of the creative power of thought, he is intrigued by the wonder of it. He is fascinated by the fact that thought is creative; that what he thinks takes form in his experience. What could be more natural than that he should begin to use this Law for every purpose possible for the benefit of himself, as well as for others? There is nothing wrong with this, for salvation does begin at home, and only the one who has proved this Law for himself is in a position to use It for others with any hope of success.

At first we are prone to treat everything and everyone around us in an attempt to influence our environment and people, and exercise control over things to our own liking. Most of us pass through this phase, but it is only a phase. As we progress in this science we come to realize that the aim in scientific treatment is not upon people and things. We treat ourself, our own mind, our own consciousness, no matter what the desired end may be, and gradually we learn that, as Emerson said, *we must stay at home with the cause*.

Our thought does not go out to influence persons or things. What it does is readjust our own consciousness, our thinking, to include a larger and a more harmonious field of action. We learn that when we get our own consciousness straightened out, things in our external world adjust themselves to meet our new and better inward awareness.

Now there is a reason for all this, and like everything else the process is governed by an exact law. When Einstein announced that everything bends back upon itself, even time, space, and light, he was scientifically and mathematically approving what the Divine Intuition of the ages had always taught, that everything which goes out will come back again. This is why Jesus said, *For all they that take the sword, shall perish with the sword.* And why Emerson said, *If the red slayer think he slays, Or if the slain think he is slain, they know not well the subtle ways, I keep, and pass, and turn again.*

That which goes out will again return. Why? Because everything travels in circles. This Einstein has proved; this the great teachers have taught us. Everything moves in circles. Therefore the outflowing or the beginning of any sequence of action and reaction will have to be equal to the in-moving or the back-flowing or the return of that sequence.

In a certain sense we can say that since what we push out must move in a circle, it must move back to its original position, and in completing the circle reunites with itself. What we push out from this one point will return to the same point from which it was pushed.

For an illustration let us take a person who has learned that he can use the Law. If he has been more or less lonely and without friends, it is quite natural for him to start treating people to get them to like him. He might say, "Wherever I go I shall be met by love and friendship. I shall be received with joy, and I shall be appreciated." He feels that his thought is going out to influence those whom he contacts.

Now he is right as far as he has gone, and he will get definite results, but sooner or later he will discover the real secret, which is that if he is friendly he will attract friends; if he is happy he will attract happiness. He will no longer expect to influence people. His consciousness of Love will have so expanded that out of the fullness of his heart he will exclaim, "I love everyone, I am love; I am a friend to everyone; nothing that is good is excluded from my consciousness." He has set up a center within himself that automatically radiates to every circumference in his experience, and because everything moves in circles it will again return to him.

The burden has been removed from his mind, and he knows that he can stay at home with a cause which operates upon nothing but himself to produce the desired result. This is one of the greatest secrets of this science.

Of course this same principle can be applied to everything we are doing. "I am success; I am happiness; I am joy. I am one with all the good there is. I understand everyone and everyone understands me."

The real secret is that everything moves in circles. Everything bends back upon itself. What goes out must return. What is embodied within will complete its own circle, and if we wish to enlarge our experience we must increase our capacity to understand, to feel, to embody, and to know.

Again we are brought back to the saying of Jesus: *Ye shall know the truth, and the truth shall make you free*. In other words, if we really know the Truth, the Truth will make us free, because the Truth Itself is freedom; It is wholeness. The Truth is God.

Meditation

Realizing that God is love, I open my whole consciousness to this Divine Love, knowing that It flows through me and animates everything I am and everything I do.

Realizing that God is the Great Giver, I open my whole consciousness to receive every gift of heaven. And realizing that God is the Great Forgiver, I joyously forgive myself and everyone else; I absolve myself and all others from any previous mistakes.

Because I know that I live in a universe of law and order, I carefully refrain from all unjust judgment or unkind criticism or condemnation, and open my whole consciousness to the influx of the Love which forever more blesses everyone and everything.

As I feel the Divine Presence all around me, so do I feel It around others. All the yesterdays, with their mistakes, depart from me and from my thought of others. And this moment in which I live brings to me, and to everyone upon whom my thought rests, a deep sense of a new hope, a greater power, a higher good.

As I turn to the Eternal Heart of Love I feel the enveloping presence of infinite peace and joy. And feeling this Divine glory around and within me, I turn to the whole world—to those whom I know and those who are unknown to me—and bless and love and give, because I know that the Eternal Heart beats in all creation, in every person, and the Eternal Goodness flows through all.

The Law of Mental Equivalents

In our field we hear a great deal about what is called the Law of Mental Equivalents. We sometimes wonder what this means, and we shall keep on wondering until we have reduced it to its greatest simplicity.

The Law of Mental Equivalents means that everything that is consciously and subjectively embodied in our thinking tends to radiate an atmosphere, a vibration, a current of thought, an inward acceptance which automatically attracts to itself that which is like itself.

We are getting back again to the idea of everything moving in circles. The Law of Mental Equivalents means that there shall be within the body of our thinking not only an acceptance of the good we desire, but an inward experience of the meaning of that good, a real sense and a real feeling that we now possess it.

It is easy enough, then, to see that the Law of Mental Equivalents means a subjective embodiment even more than it does a conscious statement. It means that when we do make a conscious statement there shall no longer be anything in us that denies or repudiates it.

But this subjective embodiment of ideas is something that consciously can be generated. We can not only change our objective thinking by a process of careful treatment, but we can change the whole subjective field of our thought, because most of our thinking is unconscious. Therefore the mental embodiment of an idea or the true mental equivalent of something is not so much the word we speak as it is something we feel in the heart.

We all have a definite content of unconscious thinking, of unconscious expectation, of unconscious frustration and desire, and this is just as much a part of the process of our thinking as the words we use consciously, and it is just as certain to be operated upon by the Law of Life. This we sometimes overlook. But if these things are true, then the first thing we must change is ourselves.

This is sometimes a long and arduous process, for a person does not change all of the patterns of his thought in a moment. Rather it is little by little, until gradually the old thought patterns become transformed into new ones by some inner alchemy of the mind, the operation of which we do not see but the manifestation of which we do experience.

For instance, an individual who has not met with as much good and happiness in life as he should have, should select a definite time each day to treat himself. The treatment should be something like this:

> *I know that all the good there is belongs to me. God is good, good is God. I am surrounded by good, I am enveloped in it; I feel its presence.*
>
> *There is nothing in me that can reject that good. My whole inner feeling entertains it and experiences it. My whole expectation is one of joy and pleasurable anticipation. All the old thoughts of fear and doubt and uncertainty have vanished. Within me is the Secret Place of the Most High; within me is the Presence and the Power and the Will to know and to do and to be.*
>
> *There is nothing in me that can deny this statement or refuse to accept it. There is nothing in me that can limit me. My memory is one of happiness; my anticipation is one of joy; my experience is one of pleasure.*

This would be a broad gauge treatment, and practiced over a period of many days would be very effectual.

This would be true of any idea we wish to embody. We should think about it and feel it, envision it, and try to think of the meaning of each word. Accepting it consciously, we should let it sink deeply into the unconscious, until the subjectivity of our thought shall have accepted its meaning; then we shall have arrived at the mental equivalent of the idea.

Principle and Precedent

All mankind is more or less following the patterns of thought in which it is immersed. Whether we choose to call this the collective unconscious, the carnal mind, or the influence of race suggestion makes no difference. Most of us follow the patterns of thought as they have been laid down through the ages. We say things must happen today and tomorrow because they happened yesterday and the day before. Psychologists contend that a neurotic thought pattern will repeat itself with monotonous regularity until the pattern is changed.

Advances in science and civilization come through breaking down the belief that things have to be the way they are because they have always been that way.

But the laws of nature or the principles that govern life know nothing about precedents. At one time we used tallow candles; now we have electric lights. There was nothing in nature that prohibited the world from having had electric lights ten thousand years ago, but no one knew anything about them. But when the day arrived that somebody discovered the new possibility, the laws of nature complied and delivered the secret which made the new possible.

The world has always said wars must continue to be because they always have been. People have always believed that the different countries could not settle their difficulties by peaceful methods. This precedent is of such long standing that it is a difficult thing to overcome. Yet sooner or later it will have to be overcome if the world is to survive.

The same thing has happened throughout the history of spiritual evolution, or the unfoldment of man's thought about his relationship with God. People have prayed to a Power higher than themselves and occasionally their prayers have been answered affirmatively. Perhaps they have always been answered in accordance with the way they have prayed. However it has always been accepted that some prayers are answered while others are not. Because of this a precedent was established which made the answer to prayer an unpredictable thing.

This is one of the precedents which needs to be broken, for we must allow spiritual activity a larger scope. When we realize that all the spiritual power there is, is at our disposal, and that no matter how limited a viewpoint we may have had yesterday (with the limitations that follow that viewpoint), today we can increase our field of inward awareness, then we make possible a greater influx of the Divine through the human, that is, through our own thinking.

But we can never do this unless we believe that we can, for the belief that we cannot binds us back to the old precedents and compels us to accept only as much good as has been experienced in the past. If we can get it firmly fixed in mind that Principle is never bound by precedent, that the doing of new things in science through new discoveries always existed as a possibility, and that there was nothing in nature which prohibited the larger experiences, we shall no longer be hypnotized by the past.

It is probable that most of us go through life more or less hypnotized by what everyone has believed. We say that the good we desire cannot come to us because we have never experienced it. Or we say the good we desire is too much to expect, or there is not enough good to go around, or that God does not hear our prayer. Too often we turn over the possibilities of the individual life to the acceptance of the collective group.

We should do the exact opposite. We should break down the hypnotic suggestions that bind us, and create new avenues in the mind for a fresh approach and a new outlook to the Spirit. This is something that every person must do for himself. But there must be a method or a way to begin.

We should start with the firm conviction that we are dealing with a Power which is not bound. It is not limited. It is not only some power; It is all Power. It is not difficult to convince the mind of this, since plain reasoning compels one to accept such a viewpoint.

Next we must assure ourselves that we have access to this Power. We could never do this if we felt that the Power were external to us, if It were something apart from or different from our own being. We discover that God is immediate and personal, a possibility latent within the self but ready to be called upon and used.

Our next step is to identify the self with this Power. *I Am that which thou art, thou art that which I am.* We are one with this Power, in It, with It, and some part of It.

Having identified ourselves with the Power which is the Law, and the Presence which is the Spirit, we must consciously increase our expectation and deepen our realization. This is done by meditation, communing with the Divine, until gradually we so extend our concepts of life and the possibilities of living that we are no longer bound by our old thought patterns.

There are simple techniques which help us to do this. As an example, we might say:

> *I am one with all the Power there is; I am one with all the Presence there is. There is One Life, that Life is God, that Life is my life now. This power, this Presence, and this Life are perfect, complete, whole, happy.*

We identify the mind with this wholeness, with this happiness, with this perfection, affirming its presence and embodying a certain feeling about it, an inward awareness. This practice must continue until the idea becomes real to us, not as though we were something apart from or approaching the Reality, but as though we were operating from the very center of It, which of course we are.

Then we can continue by saying:

> *There are new thoughts, new ideas coming to me. I open my whole consciousness to the influx of that which is larger and better. I identify my mind with inward peace and joy.*

At times we may be confronted with negative arguments of set mental patterns which circumscribe, limit and depress the mind. Our senses may try to insist that we follow the old established precedents as our true guide, since they have been adhered to by mankind from time immemorial.

Right here a certain amount of adventure, of imagination must be brought into play to create a feeling of acceptance which will break down these old thought patterns. We must understand that they are not the truth of God's Being but merely monotonous repetitions of all of the negative thought of the ages. We must know that our new declarations of Truth have the power within themselves to completely destroy the old thought patterns.

An argument similar to the following is a good one to use in such cases:

> *I am no longer hypnotized by the old thought patterns; I am no longer bound by these precedents; I am no longer limited to what everyone has believed, because I now know it has no truth, no reality, and no law to support it. It is but a phantom.*

Such an argument in mind will tend to destroy old beliefs, and give us the leeway that is necessary if we are to initiate new, larger, better, and less limited ideas. Imagination and feeling will play a great part in overcoming the old limitations, and our newly acquired inward awareness will proclaim to us that we are and always have been a part of God's Universe. The words which we speak will connect us with that which is greater than our previous experiences.

We must come to know that no past experiences need bind the possibility of new and better ones, until finally we think more and more completely from the standpoint not only that God is all there is and that all things are possible to God, but that through our knowledge of this, the greater possibility is ours today.

Identifying ourselves with this more complete life, we begin to specialize this universal concept by identifying the things we are doing with the greater possibility. In a certain sense this is letting fire down from heaven, or bringing light into a darkened room.

In actual practice it is a consistent process of identifying the personal self with the impersonal, man with God, life with living, prayer with performance, the Universal Spirit with our own spiritual being which is part of that Universal Spirit, and then bringing these larger thought patterns to bear upon the things we are doing in everyday life.

Principle is not bound by precedent. There is no law in the Universe that seeks to perpetuate old limitations, but there is a law which responds to our greater vision at the exact level of that vision. The mind should be kept in a buoyant, expectant, enthusiastic attitude; all weightiness and confusion must be eliminated, and we must think back to that which is boundless and free.

This is a secret we hold with ourselves and with Life, or God. Do not ask that someone else justify you in your belief, for this is confusion. Do not ask by what authority we do these things, for this would be to limit our activities to the way other people have done them. Here is where the mind must work alone, increasing its own sphere, reaffirming its own position, awakening itself to the greater influx.

Just as surely as we do this we shall find that the prison walls of the lesser self begin to crumble, the horizon of experiences begins to push itself farther away and because more spiritual territory is taken in, greater experiences are bound to follow.

The Lord Is My Shepherd: An Interpretation of the Twenty-third Psalm

Centuries ago the Psalmist caught a Divine inspiration and began to think about God as the Good Shepherd. And as he did so, a great wave of peace flowed through his whole being, a feeling of trust and confidence, and his soul began to sing within him.

Of all the inspired writings of the ages none is more beautiful than the Twenty-third Psalm, none more filled with quiet contentment and complete assurance, none more replete with the comfort and consolation of the thought that we are not left alone to buffet our way through life, here or hereafter.

THE LORD IS MY SHEPHERD; I SHALL NOT WANT . . .

A shepherd cares for his sheep lovingly and kindly; feeds and shelters them and tends them if they are ill. Throughout the Bible we find references to the shepherd as a loving Presence, guiding, guarding, and keeping. The sheep do not worry; they are not afraid, for they have a sense of being cared for, a feeling of security. When we let the Lord of all creation take care of us we are following the Good Shepherd, who knows his sheep and loves them.

HE MAKETH ME TO LIE DOWN IN GREEN PASTURES . . .

To lie down in a pasture suggests relaxation in the midst of abundance, an abundance which is already provided, a good which is Divinely given. Green pastures refers to a place of rest. Green is the most restful and comforting color in nature. It brings to our minds the picture of finding a shady nook where we can rest in the middle of the day.

HE LEADETH ME BESIDE THE STILL WATERS . . .

To complete the picture the Psalmist tells us that this pasture is beside still waters, which refers to the River of Life in which there Is no conflict, no turmoil.

HE RESTORETH MY SOUL . . .

Just let all the cares of yesterday flow out and all the burdens go with them, for the soul cannot be restored by the River of Life unless it lets go of the past and discovers that a new future is forever flowing around it—something fresh and clean and new and wonderful.

HE LEADETH ME IN THE PATHS OF RIGHTEOUSNESS FOR HIS NAME'S SAKE . . .

When we follow the pathway of righteousness, which means right-use-ness, and when we take the name of God with us, then we are in line with the great harmony of the Universe and we are restored in body, mind, and soul because the Spirit makes everything new.

YEA, THOUGH I WALK THROUGH THE VALLEY OF THE SHADOW OF DEATH, I WILL FEAR NO EVIL: FOR THOU ART WITH ME . . .

Death is but a shadow cast by life. The Divine Spirit brought us into this world; It has never deserted us, and It will remain with us forever. We cannot wander away from God. It is destined by the Divine Will that good shall come at last alike to all.

THY ROD AND THY STAFF THEY COMFORT ME . . .

A rod or staff was used by the shepherd to protect himself and his sheep. Like many other symbols in the Bible it refers to the staff of Truth or our complete reliance on the Law of Good.

THOU PREPAREST A TABLE BEFORE ME IN THE PRESENCE OF MINE ENEMIES . . .

The table of the Lord is forever spread and on It are the gifts of Life, including health, happiness, joy, and success in living. Good can be found anywhere, if we look for it. Abundance can spring from want, peace from confusion, and joy from unhappiness, right where we are. The table of God is eternally spread, but if we are too busy to come and eat, then we cannot expect to partake of the Divine Bounty.

THOU ANOINTEST MY HEAD WITH OIL . . .

The Eastern custom of the host anointing the heads of his guests with oil was a symbol of complete hospitality, of perfect welcome.

MY CUP RUNNETH OVER . . .

God's abundance is an extravagant abundance; It is limitless. Our cup could be filled and running over if we would only hold it right side up. Too often we reverse this process because we do not realize that the Divine Spirit wishes us to have everything that is good and withholds nothing from us.

SURELY GOODNESS AND MERCY SHALL FOLLOW ME ALL THE DAYS OF MY LIFE;
AND I WILL DWELL IN THE HOUSE OF THE LORD FOREVER.

Goodness will always be available to us and there will always be mercy for our mistakes. This goodness and this mercy will never forsake us, because there is a Presence and a Power that goes with us and is within us—the loving Presence of the Divine Spirit and the all-conquering Power of the Law of Good.

Treating Specific Conditions

Office of the Dean

My Dear Friend,

It is necessary to understand that there is a real ego or spiritual entity at the center of our being. While the psychological (mental) ego is acquired, the spiritual ego is Divine; it is the gift of Heaven. Each man is an individualized center in the consciousness of God, not by will or choice but because of the nature of his being.

Back of the human personality is the Divine, the person who is one with God, shaped after the pattern of perfection, and living, moving, and having his being in the Creative Spirit. As we gradually re-form our ideas and relationships to life to meet this new pattern, the mind becomes clarified and the mental ego becomes poised and balanced, because it is drawing directly upon the spiritual ego.

As a result of this, the mental ego is animated by a new and happier outlook, finds itself sustained by a new strength, and guided by a greater intelligence. In this way the human personality gradually takes on and embodies the essence of Life Itself. It becomes more dynamic.

Everything we need for the development of personality is latent within us, whether it be power, peace, joy, or wholeness. Our objective and subjective ego or personality usually wears a mask that conceals the true identity, the spiritual ego, which is as eternal as God.

Our whole endeavor should be to uncover this Divinity and unite it with everything we are doing.

Sincerely,
Ernest Holmes

Lesson 33

How Habits Are Acquired, page 222, to *Treating Lung Trouble,* page 228

In the first paragraph under the heading, *How Habits Are Acquired*, are the words, *At the root of all habit is one basic thing: the desire to express life.* If you will turn to page 596 for a definition of *Habit* you will learn that habit is subjective. By subjective we do not mean inactive. In one sense a habit is a subjective activity, the impulse of which is often greater than is one's will or intellectual capacity to control. That is why habits control us. Back of all habit there is a desire for self-expression.

Desire is really a Divine thing, as we state on page 584. It is an urge which, operating as law, produces psychic energy. This energy must find an outlet. Back of all false desire there is a legitimate necessity for self-expression, a Divine Urge impelling one into self-realization. There is nothing wrong about this Urge. It is fundamental to the evolution of human life and has its basis in that Divinity which impels all action.

On page 642 you will find a definition of *Urge*. It is a push, a drive, an impulsion. This impulsion takes place on two planes—the human and the Divine. The Cosmic Urge is a result of a cosmic necessity, or the Mind of God working through us. There is also a psychic urge and a desire urge, which may arise from more external impulsions. The human urge may or may not lead to that which is constructive. The Divine Urge would of necessity be constructive.

Any urge one has which tends to destroy the unity of the whole necessarily arises from a false source, while any urge that expresses the true nature of Spirit must be Divine. If you will read again the section on *Repression*, pages 627 to 629, you will refresh your memory as to just how this fundamental urge toward self-expression operates.

One thing is certain; we must control the emotions or they will control us. We must control the desires or they will control us. Now habit may be either the result of an emotional desire toward self-expression or merely the result of automatic and mechanical repetition, such as learning to drive an automobile. But always habit is something which has passed from the conscious into the subconscious field of automatic action; from a spontaneous to a mechanical basis.

Back of many vicious habits there is an unconscious desire to escape the realities of everyday life. People who feel unable to cope with situations as they arise have an unconscious longing to escape meeting such situations; therefore their thought turning in upon itself rather than outward creates all types of morbid reactions, and in many instances actually controls the entire habit life of the individual. The article on *Alcoholism* in Lesson 24 explained and illustrated this point more fully.

A realization that Spirit is not bound by any destructive desire or necessity will generally loosen the hold wrong habits have on the individual. To declare for one's freedom from undesirable habits, to declare that the Truth within is supreme and that we desire nothing which can harm us, is the pathway to freedom from these habits. See page 553, discussed in Lesson 23, for an example of this form of treatment.

As suggested in the textbook at the top of page 223, you do not treat the habit. You treat, rather, to free your patient from the sense of bondage to such a habit. You treat to know that he is conscious of a full and complete expression of Spirit within him. He knows that the Spirit within him is happy and satisfied; It is already expressed.

Always treat to remove any sense of inferiority on the part of your patient. Know that he is not trying to escape from anything, to run away from anything, to avoid anything. He meets each and every issue of the day with complete composure, with calm trust, and with an abiding faith in the Divine within him. He knows that he is greater than any circumstance or situation which he can possibly meet. He is consciously aware of the Supreme Spirit dominating his soul, controlling his destiny, governing his every action. His physical body cannot cry out demanding any form of drug, or pleasure to be derived from alcohol.

His memory cannot hold any image of the belief that he ever derived pleasure from any false habit; neither can his imagination and expectation hold out any promise of deriving benefit from any such habit. His thought, imagination, feeling, will, and consciousness are free. *You* are conscious of this and *he* is conscious of it; the Truth is conscious of it. The habit is neither person, place, nor thing; has no location; cannot function; is neither cause, medium, nor effect; is neither law, process, nor order. Being nothing, and being seen to be nothing, there is nothing left to react. Therefore it no longer has any power over this man.

This is not a process of the will. You do not tell the man to will anything; neither do you will anything for him. It is a process of clearing up the thought, the belief, both conscious and subjective, that there is anything which can control the Spirit, for the Spirit is *above all, and through all, and in (you) all.* In a certain sense you heal yourself of the belief that the patient has an objectionable habit. Therefore you must believe that he is greater than the habit and that what you know is greater than the habit.

There must be a sense of calm trust, an absolute denial that the habit is person, place or thing, a realization that it was merely a passing fancy which no longer has any root in the man's consciousness. It was never an entity, never can be one. It cannot argue. It has no life apart from the imagination which gives it life. In your imagination, in your feeling, in your thought, and in your treatment, you deny that it has any right to exist. Work until you receive a sense of freedom for him, then declare that freedom is the only law unto him and that he is now free forever.

We pass now to the method of treating pain. We must treat pain with that sense of peace defined in Lesson 32. Pain is handled from the standpoint that it is discord, disharmony, disunion, separation from good. We are to know that there is no irritation, no agitation, no inflammation in Spirit, and since man is Pure Spirit, what is true about Spirit is true about him.

Treat to remove every sense of fear. The Spirit is not afraid of anything. Man is not afraid of anything. Your patient is not afraid of anything. He has perfect faith, confidence, and trust in himself and in life. Infinite Peace pervades every atom of his being, fills him with a sense of calm. All confusion and all congestion are removed and perfect circulation is restored through your realization of the Divine Life flowing through him. *Be still and know that I am God* is a good thought in treating to heal pain. As our text says, in Spirit there is no struggle, no fear, no tension, and no sense of conflict.

The practitioner neutralizes the belief in the necessity of pain and declares that it is neutralized in the consciousness of his patient. He does not address the patient mentally. He heals his own thought about his patient, and this being accomplished, a new subjective law is set in motion for him.

Turn to the bottom of page 510 for an example of treating to know that there is no pain. Claim for your patient whatever you believe to be true about Spirit. God does not suffer; therefore your patient does not suffer. Remember your work takes place in Mind. Through your right thought you are attempting to heal physical suffering; therefore in your own thought and imagination you must rise above pain to that place where peace alone exists—a peace so complete that it cannot have pain. In such degree as you rise to this elevated consciousness about your patient he will be relieved.

Our text states that every treatment must cover the entire case and have within itself that which would neutralize anything wrong. Every treatment, then, is complete within itself. In other words, when you give a mental treatment, that treatment is not complete until you have brought your own mind to a clear perception of the spiritual nature of your patient and his immunity from suffering.

Turn again to page 638 for a definition of *Treatment*, discussed in Lessons 10 and 23, and to the definition of *Methods of Treatment*, pages 611 and 612, discussed in the previous lesson. Treatment, you see, is a mental thing. It is something one does within one's own thought. It is a process of thinking, arguing, realizing. It is a method of mental procedure whereby a person builds up a state of consciousness in his own mind about someone else whom he calls his patient.

It necessarily follows that since this is true, the treatment cannot have an effect transcending the state of realization or recognition which the practitioner creates at any particular time in his own consciousness about his patient. Therefore, in any particular treatment be sure that you build up a complete consciousness, a complete realization of your patient's perfection, of his spiritual nature and his Divine Being.

Remove the sense of confusion or doubt, fear or uncertainty. Declare that the one you are treating is a spiritual and a perfect being, and as such is immune to disease, pain, and suffering. Know that disease has no power, and have an abiding sense of your own unity with Good. Feel that your word is supreme, that it is absolute, that it is the Law.

Let there be no question in your own mind about this because the word can reach a plane of power equal only to your recognition. Therefore be certain that your own spiritual comprehension is clear and definite. Be sure that your word *is* Law. Know that it neutralizes every false thought about your patient and completely frees him. Never complete a treatment without arriving at this conclusion of perfection, of peace, of spiritual immunity—spiritual man transcends every limitation of the flesh; man is God incarnated as a human being.

Whether it takes five minutes or five hours to arrive at this conclusion, it must be arrived at; this state of realization and recognition must be achieved. Turn to page 554 for an example of treatment for the healing of confusion and discord, and again turn to the definition of *Realization* on page 625, discussed in Lessons 10 and 31. Try to realize what these words at the end of the treatment to heal confusion mean: *This consciousness of Wholeness, this recognition of the Self, obliterates every belief of confusion and discord from my life* (page 555).

As a practitioner you must recognize that your own life is Pure Spirit and feel that the life of your patient is also Pure Spirit. You must know that your word actually obliterates all discord and confusion from his life. You could not do this if you were treating him merely as a physical being. You could not do it if you were treating him merely as a physical, psychological, or mental being. You can arrive at this conclusion only through *spiritual* realization. That is why it is impossible to separate the most effective psychological treatment from some adequate spiritual interpretation of the universe. You must treat until you arrive at this conclusion.

Let us next consider treating to heal headaches. Treat not only to remove the sense of confusion, but treat to know that there is no congestion. The Spirit is not congested. It is not inhibited in Its action; It is always self-expressed. Treat to know that the chemistry of the physical body is balanced in the divine and perfect poise of the Universe. Whatever that physical body needs it has, and if there is any apparent lack it is instantly supplied. The Spirit in the person knows what he has need of, and compels him to understand and use whatever he needs. Know that all ideas are assimilated; that there is perfect circulation through every part of the body.

The ideas of your patient never become congested, confused, nor inhibited. These ideas always flow with perfect freedom and they flow in perfect joy. There is no habit of headache. The head represents the capacity of man to think straight, to know the Truth, and he is conscious that his nature is spiritual and perfect right now. The head being an avenue for the outlet of this spiritual life is entirely an effect controlled by the supreme consciousness behind it, a consciousness of unity, of harmony, of love, of reason, of truth, and of beauty.

There is no inaction and no overaction, there is no congestion and no confusion. Thought flows through this person with calm, enthusiastic peace and your word removes any sense of congestion and any belief in pain. You know that that wrong belief cannot repeat itself. It is not a law; it has no history; it has no past; it has no future; it has no present; therefore it is wiped out in your own thought for the other person. This is the way to give a treatment. This form of treatment is bound to be effective. Be sure that you clear up your own consciousness, leaving the Law to do the rest.

As suggested in the second paragraph of page 227, if thought, whether in a conscious or a subjective state, were a thing apart from us, we could not change it. The whole art and science of mental healing rests upon the basic principle that thought can be changed. Therefore the Law reacts in a new way.

As before discussed, the Law Itself cannot be changed but our position in the Law can be. The practitioner creates a new mental tendency for his patient by declaring the Truth. Treat until you get results. Apparently there is no other way. When the results are obtained the treatment is complete. This method should be pursued in all cases.

We come now to the application of our Principle to the treatment of insanity. We do this by realizing that there is but One Mind which is God. This Mind being the only Mind there is, is the mind of your patient right now. As there is no other mind there is no individual mind to be deranged; there is no confusion. The Mind of God is this man's mind and is functioning through his intellect, through his conscious perception at this very moment.

Use any argument which will convince yourself that the Mind of God has never been disturbed, upset, or separated from Itself or divided against Itself. Whatever statement you make about the Mind of God, declare it to be true about your patient because his mind is God. His mind is God because there is no other mind. There is only One; the One Mind is perfect. This One is all there is and this One includes your patient.

It is certain that there would be no insanity if conscious intelligence flowed always to the point of self-knowing perception. Hence your treatment must cover all of these beliefs, all of these manifestations. And you must work until you know that there is nothing left to be deranged.

Be sure to realize that this is done in your own consciousness. The whole treatment takes place there and nowhere else. There is no other place where it could take place. Be certain that you arrive at the conclusion that there is One Mind, and stay with it. This Mind is manifest in your patient now.

If you are working with a physical diagnosis, make your treatment cover whatever is held to be physically wrong about your patient. Cause your treatment to cover his case. For instance, if physical examination shows that he has suffered severe emotional shock, deny any effect of emotional shock. If physical diagnosis shows that there is lack of chemical balance in the man's body, declare that there is correct chemical balance. If your patient needs a different diet, the result of your treatment will cause him to seek and find a correct one.

In every case make your argument cover the need in that particular instance. Always complete your treatment with a realization, if possible, of the One Perfect Being manifest everywhere, and particularly in your patient.

Summary

There is nothing wrong with desire, since it is at the very root of everything. Man is created to express Life and to come into complete fulfillment. There is a Cosmic Urge back of everything. Life seeks expression through everything.

We must control our emotions or they will control us. Most wrong habits are the result of misusing a creative urge which properly used would result in the fulfillment of our desires.

Will is not a creative force; it is a directive force. Yet we need the will even as we need the intellect, because without them we could not come to points of decision or self-expression.

Always in treating pain we seek to embody the idea of peace and the removal of fear and confusion.

Every treatment is complete within itself and should be given as though it were the only treatment ever necessary.

Treatment is always a method whereby one builds up a state of consciousness that is consistent with the fundamental harmony of the Universe.

The time necessary to give a proper treatment depends on the time it takes to clear up your own consciousness. Whether this takes five minutes or five hours, it is always necessary to get a clearance.

When you are working with a physical diagnosis your statements must cover whatever is held to be physically wrong with the patient.

Questions

Brief answers to these questions should be written out by the student after studying the lesson, and the answers compared with those which will be included in next week's lesson.

1. What is the root of all habit?
2. When does a habit become fixed?

3. Are habits necessarily destructive?
4. What do we mean by psychic energy?
5. What is back of the urge toward self-expression?
6. What seems to be back of many vicious habits?
7. How do we mentally treat to remove vicious habits?
8. What do we mean by mentally working until we receive a sense of freedom for our patient?
9. How do we mentally treat to remove pain?
10. What do we mean when we say, *Every treatment should be complete within itself*?
11. What is a mental treatment?
12. Does mental treatment deal with the physical, mental or spiritual man?
13. What do we mean by our word being law?
14. Can our word as law ever fail to produce the desired result?
15. How long does it take to give an effective mental treatment?
16. Why is it impossible to separate the most effective mental treatment from spiritual realization?
17. How shall we treat to heal headaches?
18. How do we mentally treat cases of insanity or mental derangement?
19. In working from a physical diagnosis, how shall we proceed with our mental treatment?
20. When physical diagnosis shows the need of a change of diet, how should we treat?

Answers to Questions on Lesson 32

1. The first thing a mental and spiritual practitioner should do in beginning a series of treatments is to treat for the removal of fear from his own consciousness and the consciousness of his patient.
2. Consciousness, from the viewpoint of mental healing, means one's perception of existence. It means one's entire mental life, both conscious and subjective. To remove an idea from consciousness means to replace that idea by substituting a more desirable one.
3. We remove fear from consciousness by substituting faith.
4. The mental perception which furnishes a correct spiritual equivalent for physical circulation is a sincere belief in and recognition of the Divine Life Stream ever-circulating through one as perfect harmony and balance.
5. In spiritual mind healing a person does not necessarily use exact words or set formulas. He uses any words or thoughts that will convince his own mind.
6. The mental practitioner's concept of the physical body is that it is a body of spiritual ideas held in form by the Life Principle which animates them. Each idea represents a Divine Activity.
7. A declaration of harmony must take precedence over discord because harmony is the true nature of Reality, while discord is a misinterpretation of Reality.

8. By letting the Law do the work is meant that our words are executed by the Principle of Mind, which is the Law.
9. We should never say we lack the power to heal, because the power to heal lies in the Principle of Life which is ever-present and which is the creative agency. Hence each has the ability to use this Power.
10. While each has the ability to heal, we may fail to demonstrate because we frequently lack the mental equivalent of our desire.
11. When we fail to demonstrate according to our desire we should continue to work until our inner conviction becomes a mental embodiment of our desire; then we shall demonstrate.
12. The difference between a scientific mental practitioner and one who works by the law of chance is that the scientific practitioner has a definite mental Principle which he consciously uses for definite purposes. The unscientific, having no such principle, works only by chance.
13. The mental Principle is unconditioned by any present or existing fact because the Power which creates facts can remold, disintegrate, or change them.
14. In reality, nothing can limit the Power of the mental Principle, but our belief does limit Its activity in us to the level of such belief.
15. Faith is complete when the subjective state of our thought no longer denies that which we affirm.
16. If disease were an entity of itself, i.e., had consciousness and direction, it could not be successfully treated, either mentally or physically.
17. While disease is not an entity it is more than an illusion. It is an actual personal experience from which one suffers.
18. We do not know exactly how our treatment reaches our patient. We do not hold thoughts for him; neither do we send our thought out to him. We do, however, arrive at a definite mental conclusion about him, leaving the result to the Law.

The Discovery of God Is Personal

No one can find God for us; each individual must do this for himself. We cannot find God outside the self because we cannot go outside the self. There is no place where we begin and God leaves off. We can find God only within ourselves.

At first this seems almost blasphemous, as though one were setting oneself up as God, but such is not the case. One is merely setting oneself up as a center in the consciousness of God, forever one with God, an Incarnation of the Universal. The gift is not of man's endeavor, but of Life Itself. This is the gift made from the foundation of the world, and is self-evidently true.

It does not look as though we could discover God within the self because we look at ourselves and say, "Well, look at me! I am poor, weak, miserable, unhappy, disconsolate and forlorn, and you tell me that I shall find God in the midst of this chaotic mass which I call myself." It does look discouraging, and like a forlorn hope.

But still we must consider this the starting point, for there can be no other place to begin on the road to self-discovery, the discovery that leads back to the original force. Gradually, as we shear the belief in separation from our consciousness, the chaos produced by it, the inhibitions and inner turmoil, we emerge on the other side of this chaotic mass and find that Heaven was waiting there all the time. Nothing had happened to It; as in the experience of the Prodigal of old, the Father's house was still where it always had been.

But just wishing, hoping, or longing will not bring about this self-discovery. There must be a persistent and painstaking attempt to separate everything from us that does not belong to the spiritual man.

It might be well to use an illustration here. Suppose we have no peace of mind, are confused, have no contentment, no security, and are consequently beset with anxiety and uncertainty and the feeling that the times are out of joint, how shall we proceed?

First of all we should have at least a sound mental equivalent and psychological basis for a new conviction. How did we get here anyway? We know very well we did not put ourselves here. Nothing is more certain than that man never created himself. He merely awakes to self-discovery.

Therefore we detach all confusion from the mind by identifying ourselves with the Spirit. God is not poor; not weak, not unhappy; God is not frustrated; God is not in lack; and what is true about God is true about us; therefore there is no unhappiness to the real self. There is no insecurity in the spiritual ego. There is no frustration in the Mind of God within us.

Logic and reason both conspire to show us that this must be true, and no matter what the appearance may be to the contrary, there is still a Spiritual Center. *Standeth God within the shadows, keeping watch upon His own.* We, too, must keep watch, uprooting a false thought here and another one there, until finally both in intellect and in feeling we reach back to the center, the Divine Presence within us.

Others may show us how they did this, may even suggest how we can proceed, but there is a path that every man must walk alone. Yet not alone, because forevermore there is a Spirit that beckons, a Presence that feels out toward us as we feel toward It. Some day we shall all rest in Its warm embrace.

Yes, the discovery of the self is to the self and by the self. There is no use delaying, no use waiting for something to come along or someone who can do this for us, for no such person exists. This is why Jesus told his followers that it was expedient that he go away in order that the Spirit of Truth might reveal to them the meaning of everything he had taught them.

We should not wish it otherwise, for if someone else held the key to our Palace, how should we enter? If someone else had to live for us we could never live for ourselves. The great and long and meaningful secret of Life is bound up in this self-discovery, and the most fortunate moment in our lives will be that moment when we come to realize that we must take ourselves for better or for worse. Starting right where we are and disregarding time or effort, counting as gain only that which conspires to awaken us to the ultimate Reality, we shall travel back to the Center and the Source.

But there should be no morbid outlook on this, for why need we encounter more unhappiness? Why not think of the opportunity as one filled with peace and fraught with opportunities? Once we are sure there is a goal to reach and the Spirit is directing us, we can be certain that we shall one day arrive, perhaps today, perhaps tomorrow, but is not each step on the road one step closer to reaching it?

Let us all, then, accept the simple fact that the road to God is through the self, and that the pathway to an ever-increasing experience can be filled with joy. We can sing as we go along, and why need we deny ourselves the privilege of immediate union, for all the long tomorrows will be but continuations of the short todays. Why not find Life here and now?

Practical Suggestion for Mental Treatment

Do Not Deny Your Understanding

Your consciousness of good is the law of elimination to every discord. Your treatment enforces the Law and is the activity of Its power. Be sure you do not deny your own understanding.

The inertia of human thought, rising as it does from the morbidity of race consciousness and the mesmeric grip of race suggestion, seeks to claim that you do not have the power to heal, the consciousness to heal, or the spiritual capacity to heal. Recognize this false argument for what it is. It is nothing claiming to be something. It is a lie claiming to be the truth. It is a habit of thought unwilling to surrender itself.

You must know that the thought of truth dispels this mental inertia, and frees the consciousness. Heal the thought and the Law of Perfection will establish harmony.

Know that It does this immediately. Every treatment must incorporate within it the consciousness of completion, of perfection, of fulfillment, in the here and in the now.

Use positive statements to declare that the Divine Power which you use frees you from the hypnotic belief that would deny you the privilege of helping all who come to you. A practitioner must continuously be conscious that all the good there is, is his; not *some* part of it but *all* of it. It is not only available; it is workable. It is not only ever-present; it always responds to him.

The Fruit of Good and Evil

Evil as a thing of itself never originated unless God created it, for as our Scripture says, *All things were made by him, and without him was not anything made that was made.*

And yet evil is an experience of the human being, if by evil we mean sickness, want, lack and impoverishment, unhappiness, physical deterioration or physical death. Here we are confronted by the problem of something that is and is not at the same time. How can a thing be and not be? To understand how it could be and yet not be really is a problem.

It seems to us that this problem is solved only in such degree as we realize that evil is never a thing in itself or of itself. It is merely a limited use or perhaps a misuse of a Creative Power which is complete and perfect within Itself.

We do not deny that people experience what we call evil, for such a denial would be absurd and would place us in a position of saying that everything we do not like is unreal. This is far from an intelligent position, for everything is as real as it is supposed to be and people actually do suffer physical and mental pains. But if this suffering were designed by the All-Creative Wisdom, then we could not possibly escape it. Moreover, God Himself would be evil. We read in Habakkuk 1:13: *Thou art of purer eyes than to behold evil, and canst not look on iniquity.*

The experience of evil is more than imagination. It is actual experience, and it would be useless for us to deny it. If we can feel that it is something the human being has created through ignorance rather than something that is ordained and predetermined, we shall be in a better position to combat it. We must come to know and sense that certain something which is perfect and complete, and which being Omnipresent must be at the center of everything, including ourselves.

The origin of evil is in the human mind, and the belief in devil, hell, purgatory, and limbo has its origin in the human mind, and nowhere else. This must be erased from the mind. We must come to know that there can be no ultimate evil. We must have the assurance that evil will disappear from our experience in such degree as we no longer feed it with our imagination, or through our acts create situations that encourage it.

You will remember that according to the story of the Garden of Eden, God created man and woman and set them in the Garden, which was an earthly paradise. The River of Life flowed through the garden, watering it, and it contained every kind of fruit and plant necessary to man's physical well-being.

Adam and Eve were told to enjoy this garden, to live in it and be happy. But they were warned that while they could eat of all the fruits that grew in the garden, there was one tree from which they should not eat. This was called the Tree of the Knowledge of Good and Evil.

At once we see the meaning of this. We can eat from the tree which bears the fruit of love, and the more we eat from it the better off we shall be. But if we begin to mix love with hate we come into confusion. The fruit does not digest because hate is contrary to the nature of love.

It is natural that we should ask, Why did a God who is all-wise, all-powerful, and all-good, create a tree that could bear the fruit of hate? The answer is simple: Man has self-choice or he would not be a person, and having self-choice there must be more than one thing from which to choose. The very freedom with which he is endowed makes it possible for him to use that freedom, at least temporarily, in a way that will restrict him; otherwise he would not be free. Therefore man is given the right to choose, but with the right to choose must come the liability as well as the reward of his choice.

Well, man is a curious creature. He is born with an innate desire to explore everything. He has a great curiosity, and sometimes he wants to know why he cannot do exactly as he pleases and get away with it, and this is what he was forbidden to do. He was told he had freedom to do what he wanted to, provided he never used his freedom to destroy himself. And who can doubt the wisdom of this?

And now another symbol appears, the serpent. It is well to look into the original meaning of the word serpent. It was used in antiquity to designate the Life Principle and the way It works. The serpent meant the Life Principle, and while it was the serpent that tempted Eve, it was also the serpent that Moses lifted up in the wilderness, upon which the Children of Israel looked and were healed of their physical infirmities. And Jesus referred to this when he said, *As Moses lifted up the serpent in the wilderness, even so must the Son of man be lifted up.*

The great principles of nature exist to be used, and the laws of nature become our servants when we use them rightly. But these same laws, wrongly used, impose suffering upon us. We can use our minds to be happy or unhappy; we can think peace or confusion; we can be loving and kind, or disagreeable, because we are free.

If we were so created that we did not have this freedom we should be eternally bound. Life would have no meaning. Everywhere we look in our own lives and the lives of others we see the use and the abuse of this power. For instance, the atom bomb, they tell us, could destroy civilization and yet the same scientists who tell us this also inform us that the energy used in the atom bomb might run all the machinery in the world. The very power that can be used so destructively could, and should, be converted into an instrument that would help to bring freedom to everyone on earth.

We are finally discovering that the very power that makes us sick can heal us, the very things that bind us can free us, and that the imagination we use to destroy our happiness, rightly used, could create situations that would make everyone happy. Well, this is the meaning of the serpent and the savior and that great symbol which runs throughout the Bible depicting the right and the wrong way to use the power which is within us, the power that is greater than we are.

But again we must stop and ask ourselves a very important question, and one we find to be in most everyone's mind: Is evil, then, equal to good? The answer is *No*, for we have already found out that while we can love to any extent without being hurt, hate finally destroys itself and destroys us with it. But love harms no one. Good protects itself because God is good.

We are given the freedom to misuse the power of life, but only to a certain point. This is why the symbol goes on to show that when Adam and Eve finally decided to eat from the fruit of the Tree of the Knowledge of Good and Evil, and after they had done so, they were expelled from the Garden of Eden and compelled to earn their living by the sweat of their brow.

Looking into the story more carefully we discover that it was Eve who first ate the fruit, after which she gave it to Adam. Remembering that the Bible is the story of man and his relationship to life, we must expect to find in the symbol of Adam and Eve a great psychological truth common to all human beings. For Adam and Eve were not really a man and a woman, but represented two sides of our nature. We can liken Adam to the intellect, to our conscious self-choice, and we can liken Eve to our subconscious reaction, for this is what the story originally meant. And it is only in the last fifty years that we have discovered its importance.

We are all Adam and Eve, and when our intellects become coerced or misdirected they still find a subconscious reaction. And when the subconscious reaction becomes powerful enough it controls the intellect because of the unconscious thought patterns that are laid down in the mind. Finally, when these thought patterns become dominant they control even the intellect. This is what produces most insanity, and the psychosomatic relationships between the body and the mind.

Our present knowledge of the mind tells us exactly how these laws of mind work, and we now know that our mental and emotional reactions to life decide what is going to happen to us. Because of man's misuse of the power within him he is led on the pathway which produces bondage, weakness, and finally death.

And so we come to the other side of this great story which says, *For as in Adam all die, even so in Christ shall all be made alive*. So the symbol of the savior is presented—the man of God, the Christ within each one of us. And we are told to look unto this Christ, because he is one with God, if we wish salvation.

Of course we all wish salvation. We all want to be happy; we should like to be well. We have never yet met anyone who did not wish to be successful. We want people to like us. We greatly desire to love and be loved. And above everything else, we want and need an inward sense of security and peace of mind.

It is true that we all long for the Kingdom of God on earth, whether or not we know it. And the great struggle of man is toward freedom, emancipation from want and fear and disease, and from everything that can hurt. We all long to return to our lost paradise. Man is put on earth to enjoy life and he is given the freedom to decide how he is to live, and always there is placed before him the possibility of two things: to be, or not to be.

Finally all real power must rest on the side of good, and finally evil will be vanquished by good. This is the whole meaning of the story of the savior, the lifting up of the Life Principle on the Tree of Life—the coming to realize that we are one with God forever.

Just as the Old Testament tells us of the fall of man through his misuse of the laws of life, so the New Testament tells us of the redemption of man, the triumph of the Spirit, and the return to that heavenly home from which we all came. This is why Jesus said, *I am the way, the truth and the life*, by which he meant that God in me and God in you is the way, the truth, and the life.

The story of the Garden of Eden is completed through the triumph of the cross, by a man who knew that every man is Divine and that God intends good to come to everyone. So Jesus exalted the Life Principle rather than debasing It. He discovered the meaning of life at the center of his own being, and showed humanity for all time what can happen when someone lives as though God were real to him, as though love were the final power, and good the final arbiter of fate.

What are we going to do with this greatest of all truths—the relationship that we as individuals have to the Divine Spirit which is already perfect, and which desires only our good. We have come to the crossroads of time and the decision is ours. But like everything else, this decision has to start with the individual life. And if we are weary of our troubles there is something we can do about it. We can begin to exalt the Life Principle within us. We can lift up the serpent until we behold the face of the savior.

Meditation

A thought for meditation is suggested by Paul's words: KNOW YE NOT THAT YE ARE THE TEMPLE OF GOD, AND THAT THE SPIRIT OF GOD DWELLETH IN YOU? (I Corinthians 3:16)

We wish to come better to understand and inwardly to feel the meaning of that Divine Body which is perfect. We seek now to identify our physical body with this complete and perfect Spirit of Life within us.

I am conscious that I am in the midst of Perfect Life. I am aware that the Divine Spirit is around me and within me. I know that there is a Perfect Presence at the center of everything. This Presence is real to me.

I am one with the Infinite Spirit of wholeness. This indwelling Presence now manifests Itself in and through every cell of my being. This body of mine is a temple of the Living God.

I know that every action, every cell, every atom of my being is at this instant being brought into perfect harmony and perfect health; that every shadow of doubt or worry or fear is instantly dispelled from the radiance of His glory which indwells me.

I am quickened with the Life of God. I am blessed in the Love of God. I am secure in His divine keeping.

I give thanks for the spiritual awakening at the center of my being, and I listen to the Still Small Voice of God proclaim Its own glory in my life as It says to me, *Thou art my beloved Son, in whom I am well pleased.*

Self-Awareness Is Not Enough

We have been talking about regression and the need for meeting situations as they come along, without fear and without in any way trying to avoid them. For every issue of life must be met right where it is, and what is wrong must be made right.

This coming to understand our psychological difficulties, and how to clear the passageway in order that the original Source of Life may flow through us unobstructed, in its broadest sense is called self-awareness. It means a clearing up in the mind of the unconscious repressions and conflicts which are so deeply buried that we are aware of them only because these conflicts re-echo in everything we do, say, and think. Coming to one's self, coming to awareness, coming to understand why and how we started on the wrong path emotionally, explaining this to the self, is what is meant by self-awareness.

But just self-awareness is not enough, for this reason: There is an incessant urge back of everything to create, to express life, to come to the gratification of happiness, peace, joy, and self-expression. Self-awareness is not enough. It is merely clearing the track for right action. Something has to be done with self-awareness. We are not seeking a way to escape from Life or living, for this would be the exact opposite of the whole purpose of existence, which is to express the self.

We have hands and feet as well as a mind, and unless the hands and feet are employed, together with all other faculties, we shall not come into complete self-expression. This is why physical therapeutics is used. People are told to do something with their hands and feet, to paint pictures or write poems or songs, to learn to dance, to have a hobby, to play golf, to enjoy life; all of which means entering into the spirit of living and being some part of it.

Self-awareness without self-expression can almost as readily produce emotional disturbances as can the lack of self-awareness. It can easily become another frustration, causing the mind continually to revert to itself and become self-centered. Life must be expansive and expressive. One is not happy unless one has a purpose in living.

Too frequently older people become frustrated because there is no longer anything to engage their attention. They must find something to take up their time, whether it be gardening or calling on the sick or helping to take care of someone's children. Any activity that engages the attention and produces the gratification of outward self-expression is not only good, but necessary.

We do not teach people to sit still and monotonously repeat "God is all there is," for while it is true that God is all there is, it is also true that God is everything that is. The Creative Genius of the universe goes forth into action everywhere. There is no monotony in nature. The individual life must avoid monotony and self-centeredness through self-expression.

Consequently, after we have come to self-awareness we must start expressing again, no matter what our age. Engage in the joy of living, and do it with others. The well-integrated person gets along with other people, not by tolerance but through cooperation. This is the game of life and it must be played.

Bibles of the World

Fragments from the spiritual history of the race
revealing fundamental UNITY of religious thought and experience

CHRISTIANITY—God is a Spirit; and they that worship him must worship him in spirit and in truth.
No man hath seen God at any time.

JUDAISM—Our God is a living God.
His power fills the universe. He was before the world saw light. He will be when the world exists no more. He formed thee; with His spirit thou breathest.

HINDUISM—But verily thou art not able to behold me with these eyes; the divine eye I give unto thee.
Not in the sight abides his form, none beholds him by the eye. Those who know him dwelling in the heart (in the ether of the heart) by the heart (pure intellect) and mind, become immortal.
That particle which is the Soul of all this Truth; it is the Universal Soul.
The Supreme Soul hath another name, viz., Pure Knowledge.

TAOISM—Immovable is God alone, and rightly He alone; for He Himself is in Himself and by Himself, completely full and perfect.

GNOSTICISM—Primal Origin of my origination; Thou Primal Substance of my substance; First Breath of breath, the breath that is in me.

ISLAM—God is as a soul and the world as a body.

There is no private conversation between three people
But He is a fourth among them.
He is in their midst wherever they are.

Treating Specific Conditions

Office of the Dean

My Dear Friend,

Everyone wishes to be prosperous. God cannot be limited, and the Principle of Mind contains all possibility. This is the basis for our article, *Pray and Prosper*. If you practice the ideas set down in this article you cannot fail to get results. Our philosophy and our religion are practical because they contain a science that works like a law. This law is the Law of Mind in Action and can be definitely and consciously used for specific purposes.

To learn to pray aright is to learn how to demonstrate happiness and abundance and everything that makes life worthwhile. There is nothing selfish about this since you never wish anything for yourself that you would not wish for another, but the starting point must begin at home. Unless a person is able to better himself, how can he hope to help others, or what object lesson would he provide to demonstrate to them that there is a Power greater than they are that can be used?

But as our article, *Let Us Not Fool Ourselves*, states, this practice is not a method whereby one deludes oneself, saying peace when there is no peace, or that everything is all right when it is all wrong. This would be the blind leading the blind. Rather our practice is making over our lives to conform to the Divine Reality, and we must start right where we are, and little by little, no matter what time it takes, change our consciousness until its automatic reaction in the Law of Mind changes our conditions.

This I am sure you are doing.

Sincerely,
Ernest Holmes

Lesson 34

Treating Lung Trouble, page 228 through page 233

In treating lung trouble we work to realize that there is One Body; it is the Body of God, and it is perfect. The body is the objective manifestation of the invisible Spirit manifesting Itself through man.

Body is a Divine Idea. It is a combination of Divine Ideas. Each idea is harmoniously related to every other idea; no idea of Spirit is consumed, wasted away, or destroyed. There is no unconscious motivation toward self-destruction. Your patient is not trying to escape life, either consciously or unconsciously. He faces life serenely, calmly, and with perfect confidence. He has complete trust in the Infinite Goodness. He is one with Truth and Beauty.

The Substance of Pure Spirit fills every atom of his being. He is an incarnation of God. Substance being eternal, changeless, and perfect, cannot be destroyed or impaired. Your patient is a spiritual entity composed of perfect ideas. All sense of fear is removed from his consciousness. All belief in separation from love, life, self-expression, and fulfillment is removed. He has an abiding consciousness of love; he has a sense of fulfillment and of self-expression. Love is in him, around him, and through him. Love fills every atom of his being with its pure Substance and perfect Life.

So you work until there is no sense of wasted substance. Fear is removed, together with doubt, uncertainty, the sense of loneliness, or of a lack of affection and love. The man stands forth a glorified being. Such work cannot fail to have good results.

In spiritual mind healing, never forget that substance is spiritual. This spiritual substance takes temporary form in the flesh. In line with our last lesson, we think of the body as a manifestation of this spiritual substance. We think of each organ and function of the body as a definite outlet for some quality of Spirit. For instance, if eyesight or vision represents the ability of Spirit to perceive Its own ideas, it is certain that the Spirit never loses this ability.

In any ordinary case of faulty vision some strain has entered. This is being recognized more and more by oculists, and the relief of strain is the basic principle of some modern methods of treating the eyes. Use is made of a combination of mental relaxation and relaxation through eye exercises.

Where the thought becomes too set or strained it may produce a physical correspondent in the eyes. In treating for perfect vision always treat for mental relaxation. Work to know that the eyes represent the ability of the Spirit to perceive Its own ideas. Vision is spiritual and not material.

In every case when you treat a patient for physical healing you should substitute the spiritual sense for the physical object. The spiritual mind practitioner converts the physical object into a thing of thought, into the expression of a Divine Idea. Instead of thinking of the eyes as being organs which of themselves can see, he thinks of them as having the spiritual capacity to see. Vision is a spiritual quality of the soul. He does not treat the eyes as though they were separate organs; rather he is seeking to realize vision as a spiritual idea. In such degree as this spiritual idea is understood and its meaning embodied, the physical representation of this spiritual idea must correspond.

When Jesus told the blind man to look up and see, he undoubtedly had a consciousness of this spiritual vision, the Divine Seeing, the All-seeing Eye. It was his faith in this vision that enabled him to tell the man to look up and see. That faith must have been attained after much contemplation and a deep inner recognition and realization of his at-one-ment with Good.

It should not seem strange that the Power which makes the physical organ of sight is able to remold it. It should not seem at all strange that that which creates can re-create. The question is not, "Can the Creative Power re-create?" It is, "How shall we arrive at the spiritual realization that there is nothing which can destroy this creation?"

When Jesus told the man to look up it may have symbolized the fact that vision is from On High, and that if the man's imagination could return to its Source and Center he would instantly see. This faith of Jesus was justified through the restoration of the man's vision. Of course his spiritual vision had never been impaired.

In our mental work we must always base our arguments on the assumption that there is a Perfect Man, a Perfect God, and a Spiritual Universe. The spiritual mind healer cannot do effective work unless he is willing to submit his thought to the fundamental Principle that we are living in a Spiritual Universe right now. The practitioner transposes all apparently material or physical objects into their spiritual equivalents, realizing that wherever the spiritual equivalent is gained the physical reaction to it must be equal.

The real man has never lost his vision. The real man has never been strained over anything. The spiritual man has never lost any faculty. We wish to bring this out in our argument for the purpose of convincing our own consciousness, converting our own thought to the understanding that God is all there is, that God is in us now, and that the only real man is God manifesting as man.

Therefore the practitioner seeks to realize the omnipresence and availability of the idea of vision. There is no loss of vision, no change in vision, no farsightedness, no nearsightedness. The vision of God is immediately accessible, always operative, and exists where we appear to lack vision. It is as though we had true vision all the time, but true vision being a mental quality or a spiritual quality, has been covered up by confusion of thought. It is as though we removed the confusion and discovered that the true vision remains.

It is entirely possible for people to lose their vision because there are so many things in life at which they do not wish to look. It would be impossible to say how much loss of vision is due to this psychic cause. The action of the mind in shutting out or attempting to shut out the things one does not wish to see, closes the avenue of objective vision. The effect is the same as would occur were we looking down the road and someone held something in front of our eyes. The vision would still be perfect but it would be hindered by something which blocks it.

This is fundamental to the whole theory of analytical psychology which assumes that nature is perfect, but repression may adversely affect certain bodily functions. The spiritual practitioner, like the analyst, seeks to uncover the idea of vision. His method of procedure is more direct than the analyst, since he need not know what first started to obliterate the patient's vision. He starts out with the bold assumption that *vision is* and nothing has obstructed it. There is not now and never has been anything in this man's life which he is afraid to look at. There is no sense of strain.

Of course the spiritual practitioner is referring to the spiritual man, and we all can believe that the spiritual man is forever perfect. Remember the admonition of Jesus: *Be ye therefore perfect, even as your Father which is in heaven is perfect.*

We come now to the consideration of constipation as a form of mental congestion. It may seem rather strange to speak of mental congestion in this way, but nevertheless in your practice you will soon learn that a sick person is not one who merely has a sick body. Bodies of themselves do not move; they are moved from within. There is a psychic body which is just as real as the physical, and it undoubtedly controls the physical. The mental practitioner releases the tension of the psyche, which in its turn reacts on the physical plane. Bondage, from this viewpoint, is subjective and not objective. Congestion is subjective and not objective.

As heretofore stated, we treat man as a threefold being: *first*, Pure Spirit, spontaneous and volitional, self-conscious; *second*, subjective Law or creative medium, soul or psyche—creative, plastic, neutral, impersonal, receiving the impress of thought and acting upon it, not the Knower but always the Doer; *third*, the lower principle of man as body. Possibly we should say the outward manifestation of man as body, since we can hardly think of low or high in reality. Everything must have its place and we cannot say that the place of the body is less important than the place of thought.

The spiritual practitioner knows Spirit as the active Principle, the conscious Principle. Read again the definition of *Conscious Idea* and *Conscious Mind* on page 580. This Conscious Principle has either consciously or unconsciously impressed the Law of its being, which is entirely neutral, with certain ideas. These ideas may or may not have been true, but they have been received by the inner consciousness as though they were true, and being creative it has attempted to create them as though they were true. Therefore this subjective Principle within us may have received a false idea, but in attempting to interpret it, or bring it into fruition, it may have limited the physical man. It may have congested or produced some underaction or overaction in the functioning of the physical man.

The spiritual mind practitioner seeks to release this tension; He does this by carrying the thought back to the originating Principle, Pure Spirit. He conceives of this Pure Spirit as being ever active, never burdened, never limited in action; It contains neither bondage nor fear. This truth the practitioner is declaring about the Spirit, and this same truth he affirms to be the Law of Mind operating through his patient's physical being. He treats for complete relaxation, for the release from every sense of inactivity. There is no inaction, no inhibited action, no restricted action. All action is free, normal, natural, and harmonious.

As the action of Spirit takes place in this man it removes every belief in, or manifestation of, constipation. It is the action which purifies and clarifies. Elimination is perfect, neither overactive nor underactive. It is always harmonious. There is perfect spiritual assimilation, spiritual circulation, and spiritual elimination.

The practitioner must know that there is no resistance to Truth (top of page 233). Whatever the negative condition is, he must array his argument against it. It is self-evident that if the Truth is all there is, then there is nothing unlike It. There is nothing opposed to It that can hinder It. Its action must therefore be free, harmonious, and perfect. Whatever appears to inhibit It is false, even though it is an actual experience.

To repeat an illustration, people once believed the world to be flat, but the truth was that their belief did not flatten the world; it merely limited their experience of a round world. *Their* world *was* flat, but the real world was round.

So the spiritual practitioner must be on guard to separate the false from the true. He returns again and again to his fundamental proposition of Perfect God, Perfect Man, and Perfect Spiritual Universe. Over and over again he seeks to bring his thought about his patient into the silent recognition of the omnipresence of Good; of God as being all in all, over all, through all, and in all.

The practitioner argues against whatever appears to contradict this. He is an attorney pleading his case before the subjective Law which is ever plastic to his conviction. He must demonstrate that beliefs may change, but Truth cannot. Therefore he is sensible of the supremacy of spiritual thought force over apparent material resistance. He turns his thought over and over until finally he hits upon the Truth.

Sometimes he appears to do this more through good luck than good methods, but let him work until he does it, never doubting, never becoming discouraged, never denying himself the privilege of realizing the Truth. He must be thoroughly convinced that what he says is so.

Anyone who can do this will make a good practitioner. Anyone who can convince himself can perform apparent wonders. Anyone who can heal his own belief of what is wrong with his patient will have a patient who will come to him and say, "I am healed."

Summary

The substance of Spirit fills all space and animates every form. This substance is never more nor less; it is always complete and perfect. In spiritual mind treatment we translate physical things into their spiritual and mental correspondents. Man is spiritual as well as physical. He has no organs of sense separate from their spiritual equivalents. These spiritual equivalents are perfect because the Divine Pattern of man is perfect. Coming from God it could not be otherwise.

The Power that made these organs knows how to remake them, because the pattern back of and in them is never changed. What we do is to remove everything that denies this pattern, everything that obstructs it. The pattern then remolds its physical equivalent. This is the method we use, no matter what situation we wish to change.

There is a Spiritual Perfection at the center of everything, whether it be a physical organ or the whole Cosmos. The Spirit is always the active Principle in everything, and when we think back to this Spirit and affirm Its presence and Its perfection, It always tends to appear, because It was there all the time.

There is no real resistance to Spiritual Truth. The resistance is in our own minds, not in the Truth Itself. The spiritual mind practitioner never gets away from the idea that he is living in a Spiritual Universe right now.

In a certain sense the practitioner appears as an attorney pleading his case before the Law of Eternal Justice and Right. In such degree as he wins his mental plea, a change in physical or external conditions will take place.

Questions

Brief answers to these questions should be written out by the student after studying the lesson, and the answers compared with those which will be included in next week's lesson.

1. How do we mentally treat lung trouble?
2. What do we mean by Spiritual Substance relative to the physical body?
3. How do we mentally treat eye trouble?

4. What do we mean by substituting spiritual sense for the physical object?
5. Upon what general assumption should our work be based?
6. Why is it that the spiritual man has never lost any of his faculties?
7. In what way is spiritual mind healing more direct than psychological mind healing?
8. What is the course of procedure in mentally treating constipation?
9. What do we mean by our psychic body?
10. What is psychic tension?
11. In spiritual mind healing how do we treat to remove psychic tension?
12. What do we mean by arraying our mental argument against a negative condition?
13. What is the difference between a belief and a truth?
14. Can a false belief appear to be and act as though it were a truth?
15. What must a spiritual practitioner sense at all times?

Answers to Questions on Lesson 33

1. The root of all habit is the desire for self-expression.
2. A habit becomes fixed when it so completely enters into our subjective thought that it controls us, that is, we act without apparent conscious thought.
3. Habits are not necessarily destructive, for we learn to do many things automatically which are constructive and necessary.
4. By psychic energy we mean the dynamic power of mind, both conscious and subjective.
5. The urge toward self-expression is both cosmic and individual. The Cosmic Urge is the necessity the Life Principle is under of expressing Itself in creation. This is manifest throughout all nature. By individual urge we mean the personification of the Cosmic Urge, sometimes referred to as the evolutionary push.
6. Many vicious habits are escape mechanisms. They are results of one's inability to cope with the realities of life.
7. In treating for the removal of vicious habits we declare that our patient is free from any sense of separation from life or people. He is whole and complete within himself and is filled with a sense of well-being.
8. By mentally working until we receive a sense of freedom for our patient, we mean treating until our own thought accepts and believes that which we have stated to be true about him, and relaxes into a realization of his freedom and perfection.
9. We treat to remove pain by removing any sense of fear, and by declaring the presence of peace. We treat to realize perfect circulation and to know that confusion and congestion are removed.
10. When we say, *Every treatment should be complete within itself*, we mean that the practitioner should come to a full and complete realization of the spiritual nature and perfection of his patient when he treats him.
11. A mental treatment is a process of thought and spiritual realization which a person builds up within his own consciousness about himself, someone else, or some condition.
12. Mental treatment deals with the whole man, i.e., it does not separate body from consciousness, nor consciousness from the spiritual realization of man's unity with Life. The mental and spiritual

practitioner seeks to arrive at a spiritual realization of unity and wholeness, knowing that the mental and physical will automatically respond according to an exact Law of Cause and Effect.

13. By our word being Law we mean that the mental mechanism of a spiritual treatment sets a vibration of thought in motion in the medium of Mind, which causes this mental medium to respond in an exact manner.
14. Our word as law can fail to produce the desired result if we fail to arrive at a complete realization.
15. It takes as much time to give an effective mental treatment as it takes to arrive at a correct spiritual realization.
16. It is impossible to separate the most effective mental treatment from spiritual realization because only through spiritual realization do we arrive at a consciousness of our union with God, which is the highest mental concept which we can entertain.
17. In treating to heal headaches we seek to realize that the head is a channel through which Divine Intelligence operates. There is neither inaction, overaction nor congested action in this channel. There is no pressure, tension, nor confusion in the perfect flow of Life.
18. We treat mental cases or derangement by knowing there is only One Mind. This Mind is both Universal and individualized. This Mind is perfect and is the mind of our patient.
19. In working from a physical diagnosis we should mentally treat to neutralize the wrong physical condition which such diagnosis reveals.
20. When physical diagnosis shows the need of a change of diet, treat to know that Intelligence within your patient will lead him to the discovery of the diet which is best for him.

Let Us Not Fool Ourselves

In the Science of Mind we do not say everything is all right when it is all wrong. We do not say peace when there is no peace, but rather we try to discover what is wrong and why we do not have peace. We do not say that people are not poor, sick, or unhappy. We ask why these things should be if the original cause of all things is harmonious, perfect, radiant, and happy.

In the practice of spiritual mind healing we do not deny that people are ill, nor do we minimize the need of sanitation or of medical or surgical help. We seek to aid these other agencies by uniting with them in their efforts, by being grateful for their help, and by cooperating in every way possible with what they are doing. Some day when these things are better understood there will be complete cooperation between all these agencies, for man is spirit, mind, and body.

The body must be properly cared for, and we should come to understand body-mind relationships. In addition to this we must never forget that man is primarily a spiritual being with a mind and a body. It is only when these three are brought together that we can hope to have health, happiness, and success.

A person in our field would be deceiving himself if he refused to recognize that something could be wrong with the body and the mind even though nothing could be wrong with the spirit. This would be saying peace when there is no peace, and we must avoid such an assertion.

The spiritual mind healer recognizes the need of physical care. If he is intelligent he will never deny or seek to minimize the splendid work being done in the field of medicine, surgery, and psychiatry. But he does have something to add to these: he has the assurance that man is one with the Living Spirit.

If many of our physical troubles come from an inward sense of uncertainty and insecurity, it follows that we must find a security greater than that which comes from a sense of being isolated from the Universe, separated from the Cause of our being, or apart from God.

One of the chief offices of spiritual mind healing is to relieve the mind of fear, to compose the thought and permit it to reflect the deep inner feeling that comes from conscious union with the Spirit. Science and religion should walk hand in hand in the accomplishment of this purpose.

We have no one to denounce and nothing to antagonize. Seeking cooperation with all, we should endeavor to relieve the mind of the burden of fear, doubt, and uncertainty. All of these attitudes could be wrapped in one package and labeled a lack of faith in ourselves, in each other, and in Life.

Let us not fool ourselves by thinking that a few idle statements will do this. This calls for a calm, insistent determination to reorganize the whole body of our thinking until at last the little irritations and vexations at life, the too harsh differences of belief, and the disagreements with everything and everyone are redeemed. This redemption can come only through a conscious sense of our union with something greater than we are.

And in doing this we shall discover that love is the loadstone of Life. There is nothing cold or unfeeling about the philosophy of Religious Science and the practice of the Science of Mind. To be effective it must pulsate with deep feeling. As it reaches back to the Original Source it must bring some knowledge of the Kingdom of Heaven into the consciousness of man. Coldness, criticism, unkindness have no place in this philosophy or in this science.

The spiritual mind healer is always humble before the Great Whole, even though he speaks with the authority of faith in that Wholeness. He must be willing to place himself in the other person's position, and with true compassion enter into the thoughts and feelings of others, not as one caught in them or distraught by them, but as one who comes as a redeemer, a savior, to bring the Light of Truth to those who have lost the way.

If we think we can approach others in their need and help them without this deep inward feeling and desire, we are fooling ourselves. We shall find ourselves mumbling a lot of empty words which can find no corresponding chord in the heart of suffering humanity. Those who engage in this practice must have a deep desire and willingness to sympathize with the person who suffers.

There is no place in this practice for arrogance or the holier than thou attitude. The great have always been humble, the great have always been kind. The great have always been lovers of humanity.

Pray and Prosper

Prayer is communion with the Universal. It reaches its highest possibility when it rises above the limitations of any existing circumstance.

A belief in the Invisible is the very essence of faith. Prayer, or spiritual communion, demands a complete surrender. It knows that because the Creative Power of God is at hand, all things are possible.

We cannot doubt that the Spirit has already made the gift of Life—since we live. Ours is the privilege of acceptance.

God is not poor, weak, sick, nor unhappy. God is not impoverished, limited, nor in bondage. It is this Spirit to which we pray, the Reality which we approach at the center of our own being.

The purpose of prayer, or spiritual communion, is to seek conscious union with this indwelling Presence. Sometimes we arrive at a partial unity with Spirit. At other times we more completely enter into the contemplation of Reality. Always our prayer will be as effective as is the realization generated in the act of communion. Thus our words become *clothed upon* with the living Presence of an invisible Power ever projecting Itself into form through our meditation.

We must continue in faith until our Whole mental life, both conscious and subjective, responds. If we would pray and prosper we must believe that the Spirit is both willing and able to make the gift. But since the Spirit can give us only what we take, and since the taking is a mental act, we must train the mind to believe and accept. This is the secret of the power of prayer.

Jesus gave specific instructions for prayer. He likened the Divine Spirit to a Heavenly Father, and he placed the Kingdom of this Spirit at the center of man's being.

Our Father which art in heaven. The God Principle within us; the eternal Truth within us; the everlasting Presence within us.

Hallowed be thy name. Thy name is perfect; It is the all-inclusive name of the *I AM* beside which there is none other. It is the One, Only, and All, which includes everything that was, is, or is to be—the same yesterday, today, and forever.

Thy kingdom come. Thy will be done in earth, as it is in heaven. When the Kingdom of God is perceived and the Will and Nature of God understood, then shall the Power within us re-create and control our environment after the pattern of wholeness and abundance. When that which is without shall be controlled by that which is within; when the Kingdom of God comes on earth among men, It will heal all nations of sickness, war, and poverty, for the Kingdom of God is Wholeness, Unity, and Peace.

Give us this day our daily bread. This is an acknowledgment that Substance forever takes form in our affairs as manna from heaven. It is meant to include everything we shall ever need, whether it be a house to live in, an automobile to ride in, a suit of clothes to wear, bread to eat, and butter to put on our bread. It includes, according to the words of Jesus, *what things soever ye desire*. We must, however, be certain that the desire is consistent with the nature of Reality; and we may be certain that if our desire is toward a greater degree of livingness for ourselves and others, and harms no one, then it is the Divine Will. *Give us this day our daily bread* includes friendship, love, beauty, peace, poise, and power—for God is not only All, He is All-in-all and through all.

And forgive us our debts, as we forgive our debtors. We might say with Shakespeare, *There's the rub*, for it is a bold statement and mere protestations do not suffice. We must actually partake of the Divine Nature if we are to portray It. We must forgive if we are to be forgiven; we must love if we would be loved. *Give, and it shall be given unto you; good measure, pressed down, and shaken together, and running over, shall men give into your bosom.* And we must not overlook another statement of Jesus: *Judge not, that ye be not judged. For with what judgment ye judge, ye shall be judged; and with what measure ye mete, it shall be measured to you again.* Do we forsake all animosity in our desire to surrender our entire being to Love? Jesus plainly tells us that it is useless to lay our gifts upon the altar while our own mind is diseased with animosity and strife. *Forgive us our debts, as we forgive our debtors.* This is the Law of Cause and Effect. There is no escape from it.

And lead us not into temptation, but deliver us from evil. The All-creative Truth can never lead us into temptation, but an acknowledgment of Its presence and a desire to embody Its essence delivers us from every form of evil. *He shall give his angels charge over thee to keep thee in all thy ways.*

For thine is the kingdom, and the power, and the glory, for ever. The Kingdom, the Power, and the Glory of Reality never change. They are always the same, ever available, unwavering, consistent. The glory of Truth, the kingdom of Reality, and the power of Law are ever with us.

Jesus left explicit instructions relative to prayer. First of all he said, *Judge not according to appearances*. That is, do not be confused by the conditions around you. The waves may be turbulent and the boat storm-tossed. This appearance is real enough, but do not be confused over it. *Be still, and know that I am God.*

Judge not according to appearances. This is the first great instruction of Jesus—to have such faith and confidence in the Invisible that appearances no longer disturb you. When there were five thousand persons to be fed, and the only food in sight was a basket of bread and fish brought by a little boy for his lunch, Jesus accepted the small offering, and said in substance, "Let them be seated; make them comfortable; remove their fear; break down the barriers; let us bless the bread and the fish; and let the Lord of the harvest increase the supply and feed the famished." Jesus was not afraid when they brought the insane boy to him. Calmly he spoke to his troubled thought and stilled the strife that was raging in the mind of the demented. This, then, is the first great lesson: *Judge not according to appearances.*

Next we come to the preparation for prayer. Having shut out all appearances to the contrary, enter the closet. Jesus was not referring to any physical room or hiding place. To enter the closet means to withdraw into one's own thought, to shut out all confusion and discord. Here in the silence of the soul look to the All-creative Wisdom and Power, to the ever-present Substance. When we have entered the closet and shut the door to outward appearances, we are to make known our requests—*what things soever ye desire.*

Next Jesus tells us that we are to *believe that we actually possess* the objects of our desire, disregarding all appearances to the contrary. We are to enter into this invisible inheritance, acting as though it were true. *Thy Father which seeth in secret himself shall reward thee openly.*

Prayer is a thing of thought and feeling; therefore it is Mind in action. Prayer is a movement through our consciousness upon the Universe. Whenever our acceptance makes it possible, there will be an answer to our prayer which will mathematically correspond to the use we have been making of this Law of Mind.

Since prayer is Mind in action, we must be certain that the thoughts running through our prayers are those of exalted acceptance, of complete fulfillment here and now.

Even in divine communion we are dealing with the Law of Cause and Effect. Our prayer invokes this Divine Law and causes It to manifest in our external world at the level of our inner perception of Its working. Because this is true, prayer should always be definite, conscious, and active. When we plant a garden we invoke the creative fertility of the soil for definite purposes; we specialize its creative action that it may fulfill specific desires. And in the greater garden of the soul, the garden of the Life Principle Itself where we deal with thoughts and ideas as seeds, we should follow the same pattern.

Communion is not petition; it is an inward sense of Reality; it is something we sense, feel, and respond to. Communion is entering into conscious union with the essence of things. We must learn to commune with the indwelling Spirit, to feel Its presence, to sense Its power, and respond to Its influence.

We all know that it is impossible for one to become successful unless he first identifies himself with success. The great identification is with the *I AM* in the midst of our being. *The Lord thy God in the midst of thee, is mighty* to heal and to prosper. This act of spiritual identification, through conscious communion, is one of the supreme accomplishments of the soul.

Spiritual communion has this effect upon us. As consciousness ascends in realization, burdens gradually loosen themselves and roll backward, disappearing into oblivion. Thus prayer shifts the burden by entering into partnership with the Divine. This shifting of the burden is important, for when we feel isolated and struggling against odds we are not equal to the task before us. Life becomes a drudgery rather than a *Jubilant beholding*. But if we know the burden is lifted and set upon the shoulders of the Law, then power and speed come to hands and feet; joy floods the imagination with anticipation.

The Secret Place of the Most High is at the center of our own being, where in silence we wait on Spirit and permit the Perfect Law to fulfill our desire. This is waiting upon the Lord. We permit the Divine images of perfection to flow through our consciousness, reflecting themselves through the Law of Cause and Effect into our objective conditions.

There is no confusion in this Secret Place; none can enter It for us; none can prohibit Its entrance to us. The door is always open, the gate ever ajar. The Secret Place of the Most High is a place of light, of illumination, of poise and assurance. It is a place of rest.

Prayer can convert disease into health, poverty into wealth, misery into happiness. It can transmute our beliefs in the devil, or evil, into a picture of an Angel of Light, a guardian angel ever protecting us, forever going before and preparing the way; forever making perfect, plain and immediate the way; forever announcing, *I am the way, the truth and the life*

. This transforming power of silent communion is manifest as our spiritual vision looks up and not down.

Prayer not only receives the Divine Power, it projects It into manifestation. Prayer directs the Invisible Power for definite purposes. It does this by acknowledging the Power and by accepting that It has no opposites. Nothing hinders Spirit; nothing limits the Infinite; there are no obstructions to It. We are told that this Power breaks down the iron doors and the gates of brass. Such is the dynamic power of this silent communion with Reality.

The reflection of an image in a mirror is an exact likeness of the image which is held before the mirror. So the Law of Cause and Effect reflects back to us a likeness of the images of our thought. Prayer is a mirror reflecting the images of our thought through the Law of Good into our outward experiences. What are we reflecting, the glory of God or the confusion of man?

Prayer does not concentrate Substance; it merely focalizes our attention upon It. The Spirit is already omnipresent. We do not gather the principle of mathematics together and pile it up or concentrate it for our use; we merely draw upon it. So it is in the act of prayer. It is attention and not concentration; willingness and not will.

The very idea that we must concentrate something suggests coercion. It suggests a reluctance on the part of the Law or the Spirit in Its response to us. It suggests laborious effort. The Spirit never exerts effort; It merely remolds Itself in the form of Its own desire and immediately experiences that form, because It reflects Its own glory in the law of Its own Being. There is nothing to concentrate, nothing to force, nothing to argue with, nothing to oppose.

Spiritual communion is relaxing. There is neither stress nor strain in it. All the yesterdays of fear and failure are dropped from consciousness; today everything is filled with peace and joy. All of our tomorrows are still unborn; every day should view a new creation, a world more blessed than yesterday. We are to take no anxious thought for tomorrow. This does not mean that we are to act in an irresponsible or chaotic manner. It means that we are to live this day in calm confidence of the future. All of our memories of the past will be healed and all the pent-up energies of unexpressed desires will flow out from us in joyful expression if our communion with nature and with the Spirit becomes complete.

If we would pray and prosper we should realize that we are surrounded by a spiritual Substance which is forever taking form. Wherever we look we should see right action. Spiritual communion enables us to do this. It lifts our thought above the solid fact of a situation or circumstance. It resolves the fact into a fluid and remolds it into a new form.

Our lives should swing between prayer, meditation, and action. We used to pray, *Now I lay me down to sleep, I pray the Lord my soul to keep; if I should die before I wake, I pray the Lord my soul to take*. Someone has suggested that we add to this beautiful evening prayer one for the new day: *Now I get me up to work, I pray the Lord I shall not shirk; if I should die before the night, I pray the Lord my work's done right.*

It is not intended that we should spend all of our time in inaction, for the very law of our being is Mind acting. An active thought will always find itself surrounded with intelligent objective activities. God is in all events. We should go forth gladly to meet them. Not only in the stillness of the evening, or the quiet of midnight, but also in the rising tide of human endeavor when the spiritual sun climbs high, flooding the earth with its effulgent glory, is the presence of God revealed.

Joy infuses the commonplace with a creative activity. There is a song at the center of everything. The music of the spheres is no illusion. We must uncover this song and permit it to saturate our souls with joy. We cannot associate the Spirit with sadness or depression. The very thought of the *Fountain of Life* suggests something gushing forth, bubbling up from a subterranean passage whose flow is irresistible. The wind whispers, the leaves clap their hands, and the morning stars sing together.

Spiritual communion is not a droll affair. It is not a wailing wall, but the triumphant procession of the soul into the Secret Place of the Most High, where the scroll of Life is taken from the Ark of the Covenant on which are inscribed the joyous words, *I am the Lord thy God in the midst of thee.*

Enter into his gates with thanksgiving . . . make a joyful noise unto the Lord . . . Bless the Lord, O my soul, and all that is within me, bless his holy name. We are told to make known our requests with thanksgiving, and why should we not be grateful when we realize that the Divine gift is forever made? Why should our spirits not rise in joyful praise to the Life Principle which has delivered Its entire nature to us, withholding nothing? We know that when we praise animals they respond to us. We know that when we praise children they cooperate with us. Since the intelligence operating through animal and child responds to praise and thanksgiving, why should not everything respond in like manner? There is but one Spirit in all things.

When we condemn any physical organ we retard the circulation of the life forces through it. We should praise every organ of the body—*Bless the Lord, O my soul; and all that is within me, bless his holy name.* We should bless the action and the reaction of the life forces that flow through the body. We should bless everything that we do, everyone we meet, every letter we write, every person we think of, every incident that comes into our imagination. The desert shall rejoice and blossom as the rose by blessing it with the presence of seed, water, personal attention and cultivation. The music of the spheres is heard only by those who listen—not with an ear dulled by condemnation and censure, but with praise and thanksgiving.

Faith lays hold of a Power which is not only creative, but which creates out of Its own being. It is self-energizing. The creative energy of Spirit must be limitless. Therefore we can set no limit to the possibility of what It can do for us. Undoubtedly It is able to give us infinitely more than we have expected, understood, or accepted. We must believe that it will not only make the gift; It will also, out of Its own energy, out of Its own power, out of Its own Being, create the way, the method, and the means through which the gift is to come to us.

Wherever people meet together for prayer and spiritual communion, a field of faith is created which reacts upon everyone who enters it. An atmosphere of Reality has been recognized; a new vibratory law has been set in motion. It is easy to break one twig, but if we bind many twigs together they become unbreakable. In group consciousness the individual faith of each member is strengthened through union with all the others. *In union there is strength* is just as true in our mental life as it is in the body of our affairs.

Always we should seek the companionship of those whose faith may be added to ours. Thought atmospheres are real enough. We sense them in the quiet of the cathedral or at shrines where countless thousands have gathered with uplifted faith, seeking communion with the Eternal Reality. Thus the power of one is multiplied through combining it with the power of others. This is not because the Spirit listens more attentively to a group than to just one, but because often a group creates a larger hope and a greater expectancy. They develop a real dynamic field of faith.

True prayer always says, *Thy will be done*. An intelligent perspective of Truth recognizes that the Will of God and the Nature of the Divine Being are identical. God cannot will anything other than perfection; God cannot will anything other than abundance; God cannot will anything other than goodness, truth, and beauty.

Submission is to a superior Intelligence, not to an opposing power. Our request is made as to a friend who we know is both able and willing to respond. The recognition of the Spirit as a Friend, and the acceptance that this Friend acts in our behalf immediately and with power, brings the answer. Do we not pray for a harvest when we plant the seed? Are not seed time and harvest two ends of one law of cause and effect? Petition and acceptance are two ways of recognizing the Divine Giving which says, *Son, thou art ever with me, and all that I have is thine.*

We should not think it strange to speak of prayer as scientific. Science is a knowledge of laws and causes. The principle of any science has always existed. The discovery of such a principle and the gradual accumulation of facts relative to it prepare the way for a technique for its use. This is also true of prayer. We know that throughout the ages, at all times and under all situations, prayers have been answered by some invisible Agency which apparently is no respecter of persons, times, races, creeds, or cultures, but which forevermore proclaims, *Whosoever will, may come*.

The Agency which answers prayer is not concerned over particular religious convictions; never does It ask if we are intellectual, cultured, or ignorant; It responds alike to all. But since some prayers have not been answered, it is evident that the Power which answers must do so only under certain conditions. It is reasonable to assume that the one praying must consciously or unconsciously supply the conditions which make possible the granting of his request; that there is a science of prayer; that prayer deals not only with a Divine Beneficence but also with a Law of Cause and Effect.

Prayer is more than intellectual. It is a thing of feeling; a creative act. Just as an artist feels beauty rather than sees it, so we feel the Divine Presence as warmth, color, and life ever responding to us. There is an artistry in spiritual communion; a combination of mental attitudes, states of consciousness, thoughts, words, and feelings, which combined produce a subjective pattern of unity, harmony, and beauty.

Prayer is both an art and a science. Scientifically it has form; artistically it has color, feeling, conviction. Perhaps it is the finest of all arts. The approach to Spirit is entirely a thing of feeling. This feeling rises out of conviction, an intuitional sense, an inner witness. There is something within us which knew Reality long before the conscious intelligence was born. We feel our way back to the original Creative Genius of the Universe, the Infinite Artist whose creations are spread throughout all time and space.

Whatever apparent evil besets us can be neutralized through conscious communion with the indwelling Spirit. This is done by resolutely turning from thinking about evil, to the contemplation of its opposite which is good. All evil becomes suppositional; good alone is real. No matter what the negative experience appears to be, the real Truth about it is its exact opposite. If apparent evil says that we are sick, then the Truth declares that we are perfect; if the apparent evil says that we are unhappy, then the Truth declares that joy belongs to us; if the apparent evil says that we are alone and friendless, then the Truth declares that we are never alone. We are always one with the great Reality in which is included everything that is.

Evil is not overcome by fighting it or by recognizing it, but by nonresistance to it; by looking through the evil into the good. Thus evil becomes transmuted. Spiritual communion dissolves evil as light dissipates darkness.

It is not because of much speaking that our prayers are answered, but rather because of true acceptance. In this divine communion we should not try to think out beforehand what words we are going to use. Instead of listening to what we are saying we should say what we are listening to; there is a vast difference between these two mental attitudes. Our words should be the outcome of a deep inner conviction which goes beyond words, but which at the same time gives birth to them.

When we address the Divine Presence within and around us we should not do so with empty phrases but with thoughts filled with the deepest sense of Reality. When we use the words *all power* there should be a reaction in our consciousness that All Power is actually loosed through these words. Words spoken in silence with this deep conviction have more power than volumes merely repeated.

How can we anticipate unless we realize? How can we realize unless we recognize? And how can we recognize unless we believe? Spiritual communion anticipates the answer to its prayer, recognizes the presence of the answer, and rejoices in a complete acceptance that the request is granted. It sees the invisible take shape and form.

Spiritual communion places its bowl of acceptance under the ever-outpouring horn of plenty, and it places its bowl right side up rather than upside down. The Spirit can give us only what we take, and since the taking is an act of consciousness we must be actively aware of the presence of our desire. We must know that the gift is made even before we see it.

The Prayer of Love and Friendship

That they may be one, even as we are one. I perceive the Spirit of Wholeness, the Union of all life. Deep within my being I know that I am one with all people, all ages, all events. I am one with the Infinite and the Eternal. I am one with all the Goodness there is; one with all Power, and one with the only Presence... the Presence of God in me.

In everyone I meet I perceive this union. I meet it with joy; I am accepted by it even as I accept it. I cannot reject myself nor can I be rejected by myself. There is only One Self, which is God the Eternal Self. I am one with this Self; one with Love; one with Joy; one with Friendship.

This Oneness peoples my world with the loving attention of innumerable friends, with every human manifestation of the Divine Reality. I appreciate this Friend of mine Whom I meet in innumerable forms. Everywhere I go I shall meet Him; everywhere I look I shall see Him.

I am held in the embrace of the Eternal Presence. Every thought of disunion, separation, or unhappiness is forever gone from my mind. Love, Joy, and Companionship are permanently established in my experience.

The Prayer of the Perfect Heart

I am a center of Divine Perfection within me. I am free from every sense of burden, strain, or tension. My pulsation is in harmony with the Infinite Rhythm of the Universe. I am not troubled nor concerned over the future, worried over the past, nor afraid of the present. Perfect Love casts out all fear. The rhythm of my action is in perfect relaxation; its vitality is complete. The walls of my being are whole.

Joyfully the Spirit circulates through me, reaching every atom of my being with the message of perfect life and happiness. All tension, fear, and strain are removed. I rest in calm assurance that Eternal Goodness is forever around me.

There is One Heart; that is the Heart of Pure Spirit. That is my heart; that is at the center of my being. I sing the song of the Perfect Heart.

The Prayer for a Successful Business

No matter what others may say, think, or do, I know that I am a success now. I radiate joy and am filled with faith, hope, and expectancy. I refuse to think of failure or to doubt my own power, because I am depending on the Principle of Life Itself for all that I shall ever need.

I know that there comes to my attention everything that I need in order to project my business in every direction with the certainty of success. I see this expansion and pray that it may bless everyone who contacts it; that I may serve all who come near me; that all who know me shall feel my love and friendship and shall sense a warmth and color within me. I pray that everyone who touches my business in any way shall be uplifted and satisfied.

I bless and praise everyone who is in any way connected with my business. I draw them to me with the irresistible charm of Divine Union. I serve them and am served by them.

The reciprocal action of Love prospers those I serve as well as me. I am success, happiness, and fulfillment.

Group Prayer

The One Supreme Spirit is within, around, and through every member of this group. Each is a center of God-conscious Life, Truth, and Action. Infinite Intelligence governs, sustains, and animates every member of this body. Good alone goes from them and good alone, returns to them.

Infinite Mind establishes harmony and right adjustment of all personal, family, business, and social affairs or conditions in the life at each member. Each is supplied with every good thing. Each is happy, radiant, and complete. The Spirit of God manifests in each one as Peace, Harmony, and Wholeness.

Everything that any one of this group does, says, or thinks is governed by Infinite Intelligence and inspired by Divine Wisdom. Each is guided by Divine Intelligence into right action. Each is surrounded by friendship, love, and beauty.

Each person in this group is the manifestation of the Divine Spirit which never tires, which is birthless, deathless, and limitless. Each is receptive to the inexhaustible energy of the Universe and to Divine Guidance. Each is conscious of complete happiness, abundant health, and increasing prosperity. Each is aware of his partnership with the Infinite. Each knows that everything he does shall prosper. Each is conscious of inner peace and poise, and of a more abundant life.

Treating In the Consciousness of Love

Office of the Dean

My Dear Friend,

It is necessary in our philosophy that we include everything we know about the Laws of Mind and the way they work, and in no way do we ever wish to depart from common sense and resort to superstition in order to make our claims good.

The Universe is a vast system of law and order, peopled with a Divine Person and an Infinite Presence. In this vast Whole we live as both human and Divine beings. One part of us exists in the clouds of spiritual realization, and the other part is firmly planted on the ground. We must bring Heaven and earth together.

The superstitions and dogmas of theology, together with the fears and phobias of psychology, must be eliminated in so far as possible, and we must come to understand that man is on the pathway of an eternal evolution. No matter how much he has learned in the past he will learn more in the future, for Life is an eternal progression.

We want you to pay particular attention to the short article, *Regression*, because we are all more or less prone to seek escape through getting away from the responsibilities of life. In psychology they now know it is not enough merely to clear a passageway through the mind; something new and dynamic and creative must happen to the person who has been healed of his mental confusion.

So in our field we know it is not enough to say that God is all there is. But because God is all there is, that part of us which is Divine must come through the human into self-expression. Heaven and earth must blend.

Sincerely,
Ernest Holmes

Lesson 35

Page 234 to *Heart Trouble,* page 238

In giving mental and spiritual treatment for affections of the skin the practitioner works to know that the *outward* manifestation of the *inward* Principle of Life is harmonious. Since the inward Principle which is God must be perfect, the practitioner seeks to realize that the outward manifestation, the subjective covering of this Perfect Idea is never subject to any form of irritation, agitation, or inflammation. There is no nerve strain, no psychic strain, no mental strain. The blood stream flows in perfect purity. There is no poison in the spiritual system for Spirit cannot contain poison.

Remember that the spiritual mind healer is mentally practicing the presence of Perfection, and is therefore always speaking about the spiritual ideal. He never treats the disease as though it were a thing of itself. He has resolved things into thoughts and proceeds upon the basis that the thought is the thing.

The skin represents the objective covering of the physical body, uncontaminated by any inner turmoil and free from agitation. As a deep inner sense of calm, peace, and poise permeates the consciousness of the practitioner it will also permeate the consciousness of the patient. This consciousness, as it objectifies, will remove the manifestation of discord from the physical body. You will find a splendid meditation for this purpose on page 540, *Subtle Essence of Spirit Within Me*, and also *The Mantle of Love*, at the top of page 541.

In case you are treating the arms and hands read the meditation, *The Everlasting Arms*, page 540. The arms and hands represent man's ability to grasp ideas; to reach out and take hold of Reality. When in the process of evolution, which you will find defined on page 590 as *the passing of Spirit into form*, man's thought demanded an instrument with which to reach out and grasp, the Principle of Spirit unfolding from within him caused arms, hands, and fingers to become projected. They were formed as a definite result of this inner desire for self-expression, which we have defined as the Divine Urge, referred to in Lesson 25.

A definition of *Divine Urge* will be found on page 586. It is the inner craving for self-expression. The arms and hands are an outpicturing of this inward desire to express the Universal Self, which is God the Living Spirit Almighty.

Each of us is Universal, subjectively and spiritually. Read again the definition of *Spirit* at the bottom of page 633 to the middle of page 634, ending with *Spiritual Realization*, and recognize that the Spirit of God and the spirit of man is the same Spirit. Fundamentally there is only One Spirit, which is God. Our spiritual nature is God; therefore our spiritual nature is Universal. It could not be otherwise. When we function from pure intuition we instantly know without having to go through any process of reasoning, because there is some place within us which is forever one with the All.

The urge of the One to express Itself through us is what we call the Divine Urge, and what the psychologist calls the Libido, that emotional urge within life which causes all expression. The Libido of psychology and the Divine Urge of metaphysics have identical meaning, except that in metaphysics we deal with this not only from an individual but also from a Universal viewpoint. There is, then, a limitless urge back of self-expression. This limitless urge is occasioned by the necessity of the Spirit to come to expression.

The Spirit must not only have the desire *toward* self expression but It must *have* self-expression, else this desire would remain a dream. God's world is not a dream world but a world of intense reality. It is this desire to reach out and grasp that is made manifest through the arms and hands. The circulation of the Life Principle is complete in the spiritual arm and the spiritual hand, and this must be realized by the spiritual mind practitioner.

The expression, *itching palm*, is based on reality, for if the urge for self-expression were also compensated by an adequate realization of such urge there would be no itching palms. You will notice in your experience that when people come to you who have small water blisters on the back of their hands and wrists, almost invariably they will receive relief if you treat that the craving of their emotional nature for love receives satisfaction.

Just as the arms and hands represent man's ability to satisfy his desire to reach out and grasp things, so the feet and legs represent his ability to walk upright, or as Emerson suggested, to stand and run. We must realize that life cannot be broken down or burdened.

According to psychology, many a man has lost his ability to properly navigate, because his will and his emotions do not agree. This seems rather a fanciful notion, but nevertheless it is quite true and has been clearly demonstrated through analytical psychology, which seems to bear out the thought that the feet are an expression of the idea of propulsion.

If a person finds it necessary to go to certain places which he emotionally wishes to keep away from but where his will compels him to go, his emotion, being more creative than the will and working on the subjective side of life, may bring about some physical condition which would make it impossible for his feet to carry him. This would be what in psychology is called an unconscious compromise, and it would be interesting indeed to know to what extent foot trouble is influenced by this psychic split; that is, this subjective propulsion to move in two directions at the same time.

From the standpoint of spiritual treatment we must work to know that the feet and legs represent the idea of traveling about freely and that there is no confusion in this expression. Wherever we should go we are willing to go. Wherever we should not go we have no desire to go. We must work to know that the fullness of joy is ours, or the fullness of joy belongs to the one for whom we are working. Take the Meditation at the bottom of page 528, *My Feet Shall Not Falter*, and the following Meditation on page 529, *No Harm Shall Befall You.* Combining these two you will have a good illustration of a method of procedure in dealing with this particular idea.

Let us next take up the thought at false growths—tumors, cancers, gallstones, etc. The first paragraph (page 234) says, *Disease without thought could not manifest, no matter what the disease may be.* This is a self-evident proposition since it is certain that no one could be sick unless there were someone to know or experience disease.

In making this claim we do not deny that people have physical growths or manifestations of disharmony. What we are affirming is that the physical is an effect and not a cause, and if it is an effect it stands to reason that when the cause is reversed the effect will cease to function.

It is self-evident that the Principle within us which creates can re-create; that the Substance with which this creative Principle deals is fluidic. Just as water can be reduced to a certain temperature which will cause it to become solid, or take form, and when again subjected to a higher temperature this form will flow away, so we believe that many forms of disease are an effect of some subtle mental cause, and that by changing the cause the resultant form can be made to disappear.

The spiritual practitioner does all of his work in the field of mental causation. He resolves things into thoughts and proceeds to dissolve the thought rather than the thing. He seeks to change the consciousness back of the thought. Hence any statement similar to the one used in our lesson—*Every plant which my heavenly Father hath not planted shall be rooted up*—will tend to have a dissolving effect; actually will reduce a wrong state of consciousness.

The inner Principle is Pure Spirit unconfronted by any opposite. Therefore, from the standpoint of Spirit, disease is neither person, place, nor thing, has no law to support it, no one to believe it, no one through whom to function. It is neither cause, medium, nor effect; it has no history, no actuality, and no duration.

Turn to the Meditation, *The Healing of the Flesh*, page 510, where reference is made to the thought that *my flesh is one with the Body of God*. Every man's flesh is some part of the Body of God, some part of the Eternal Perfection, and we all know that God has no false growths.

The Spirit within, then, removes this false form and in its place restores harmony. The purifying, cleansing, vitalizing power of Pure Spirit animates your patient with perfect Life, dissolving everything unlike Itself, leaving nothing to be sick, sin, suffer, or die. Nothing false is ever framed in the Mind of God. The Mind of God is the mind of the man you are treating, and that is the only Mind which manifests. The only body is an aggregate of spiritual ideas, harmonious with the Principle operating through it, reflected by it, or manifest in it, whichever way you choose to state it.

The One Substance forever takes form, and any discordant form, from this standpoint, is an illusion. This does not mean that we actually deny the physical form. It does mean that in making our affirmations about the *spiritual* there is no false form, and since we are healing the mind through spiritual realization it is intelligent to state that the Spirit has no false growth, for in just such degree as we can perceive that our patient has none he will have none.

This is one of the great mysteries of the appearance and disappearance of what we call physical form, the mystery of creation. It takes us right back to the original point, that in the beginning of any creative series there is nothing but God. Refer again to Lesson 1 of this course. *In the beginning God*—Pure Spirit, Absolute Causation.

Now this beginning does not refer to any particular time but to all times; that is, the beginning is forever going on. Hence as a spiritual mind healer you have a right to know you are dealing with the beginning. In the beginning of your treatment your patient is spiritual and perfect and his physical body is made of Pure Spirit-Substance.

We know that in Spirit there is no malformation, no discordant formation. Every plant which God has not planted is rooted up. The axe of Truth strikes at the root at error. We must learn to speak with spiritual authority if we hope to be successful. We must know that the thought of the patient cannot consciously or unconsciously sustain any false growth. There is One Life, that Life is God, that Life is perfect, that Life is his life now. Work until in your own imagination the entire manifestation of discord disappears.

In considering the idea on page 236 of removing complexes, *Complex* is defined on page 579 as *an involved or twisted way of thinking*. From our viewpoint complex means a subjective discord, a subconscious or an unconscious denial of good. Some form of psychological complex, that is, some form of psychic disturbance, is behind most diseases. If one were successful in removing the complex, one would be successful in helping one's patient physically. If it were absolutely removed and the consciousness completely straightened out, a healing would take place. We must remember that the spirit of man is never sick. It is the physical and psychological man who suffers.

The psyche or soul or subjective life is the creator of human body and human destiny. It is a subconscious but not unconscious field of creative power and intelligence, having no intention or will of its own. It is Law. Refer again to page 605 for our definition of *Law*, discussed in Lessons 7, 24, 27 and 32.

The psyche or subjective part of us, having no intention of its own, receives the impress of our intention and attempts to interpret it. It asks no question as to whether or not this intention will work out harmoniously for us. It is merely a creative medium. It does not create any tendency for us; we create a tendency in it. It is a doer and not a knower, while at the same time it knows to do. It is conscious of only what is implanted in it.

The psyche or mental man appears to take its impressions from both the upper avenues of consciousness which is Pure Spirit, and from the lower avenues, or the subjective environment. By pure intuition it knows that Life is; by the implication of external discord it does not appear to know what Life is. By taking the direction which is given to it, it attempts to interpret that direction as though it were a truth.

The possibility of all mental and spiritual mind healing depends upon the suggestion of the existence of such a Principle. This is true regardless of whether we are dealing with psychology in the fields of psychiatry or psychoanalysis, or with metaphysics in our own field.

Nothing is more certain than that such a Principle does exist, and that the body is not self-created but is projected into form through a Law which has no intention of Its own other than to obey. Over and over we have discussed this Law both from Its individual and universal viewpoint, and we would do well continuously to remind ourselves that we deal with such a Law and that we may deal with It consciously.

The psyche, if it always received its impressions from On High, that is, through intuition or right reasoning, correct thinking, would never be sick, and if the psyche were never disturbed the physical being would be more harmonious. Hence it is not the physical body which we treat but the soul body. That is what is meant by our statement on page 236: *Treatment straightens out consciousness by clear thinking*, and when our inner consciousness agrees with the Truth a demonstration takes place.

The *defense mechanism* referred to in the fourth paragraph on page 236 means the unconscious attempt to escape the situations which we meet in life, causing us to do many strange things. We may unconsciously run away from situations which we should face. One person may get drunk rather than face reality. Another one may take dope rather than meet a dreaded situation. It is a well-known fact that many people have become blind because they were living close to things they did not wish to look at, or deaf because there were sounds or voices in their environment which they did not wish to hear, or as already covered in this lesson, they develop trouble with their feet because their emotions refuse to take them where the will directs.

Any subjective or psychic state of confusion is a mental inhibition, and in spiritual mind healing we must reverse this psychic position which the mind has taken. This is done by judging not from the external appearance but from an inner state of righteous or correct judgment, as Jesus suggested. We must know the Truth and the Truth is that we are born of eternal day. Turn to the Meditation, *Born of Eternal Day* on page 531.

We are some part of the Spirit and we are perfect beings now. There is such a thing as spiritual Truth and it is true that the knowledge of spiritual Truth frees us from bondage. Turn also to page 518 to the Meditations, *No Bondage, No Condemnation*, and *No False Habit*; and the Meditations on page 519, *No Hypnotism nor False Suggestion, No Mistakes*, and *No Responsibilities*. There are thoughts enough in these six meditations to remove any complex, provided one gains enough spiritual realization to see through the complex to the ultimate Reality, the Truth, which known, automatically produces freedom.

The spiritual mind healer must believe that there is a Truth, which understood, produces freedom, and he must know that it is possible for him to use It. He must realize that that which he knows will be effective in the direction which he designates. He gives conscious direction to a Law which of Itself has no conscious direction.

This is what is meant by knowing the Truth, and the Truth which he knows is that man is a *spiritual being right now, perfect right now, complete and whole right now*. In this consciousness Jesus forgave people their sins, told them to be happy, assured them that they were immortal, healed their superstitions and fears, declared that the Kingdom of Heaven was at hand, promised them a greater and a more abundant life, released them from condemnation.

Jesus freed men's souls from the effects of human conflict. He assured them that they were eternal beings on an endless pathway of self-expression and expansion. It is no wonder that people followed him gladly and through his consciousness caught a vision of that Divine Reality which we call God. The spiritual mind healer must do this, reflecting into the minds of his patients the clear images of perfection, declaring with absolute calm and poised conviction that the Law of Harmony is omnipotent, and knowing that nothing moves but Mind.

The practitioner learns to have sympathy with his patient but not with his ailments. He has already separated the belief from the believer. He harmonizes with the believer but disavows the belief. Through his mental right-seeing, through the spiritual vision in his consciousness, he proclaims the Truth about his patient, knowing that his word is the Law unto him and in that Law he has implicit faith.

Summary

This summary of the lesson, which deals mostly with specific cases, is to remind ourselves that in spiritual mind healing we automatically resolve the conditions into thoughts or mental states, knowing that the change in consciousness will produce a change in form.

The entire work of a practitioner is to straighten out his own consciousness for his patient. In doing this he carries his patient in thought back to pure and absolute Spirit which is the cause of all being. In his own mind he carries the patient to the Secret Place of the Most High, realizing that every physical organ, action, and function represents a spiritual idea and a perfect one. That which makes can remake; that which molds can remold.

The practitioner senses and states that everything that does not belong to the patient must be eliminated. Working patiently, carefully, and persistently in his own consciousness, he gets back to the realization of the Divine Spirit present in all things and in all people, and manifested in the life of the one he is working for. There is nothing wrong with God and there is nothing wrong with the spiritual man.

It is the business of the practitioner to so completely feel the presence of this Perfect Spirit that without hesitation he may affirm that everything unlike the Spirit is eliminated, and that there is nothing left but Pure Spirit. It would be impossible to do this unless he believed that Spirit is not only the one and only final Cause, but the one and only present, active Cause.

These things the practitioner explains to the patient in teaching him, and in the treatment which is confined to his own thinking about the patient he clears up everything that denies the inward perfect Spirit and Its actual manifestation. There is One Life, One Law, One Presence, One Power, and only One. In his own thought and will and imagination the practitioner makes everything subject to this unity.

Questions

Brief answers to these questions should be written out by the student after studying the lesson, and the answers compared with those which will be included in next week's lesson.

1. What spiritual realizations should be used in mentally treating affections of the skin?
2. What does it mean mentally to practice the presence of Perfection?
3. Why does a practitioner never treat disease as though it were a thing of itself?
4. What spiritual ideas do arms and hands represent?
5. How would we define: *first*, the metaphysical expression, the Divine Urge; *9*, the psychological term, Libido?
6. Why must Spirit have self-expression as well as desire toward self-expression?
7. What happens when the craving for self-expression is repressed or inhibited?
8. What might happen if a person by force of will compelled himself to go somewhere, while his emotion strongly desired him to remain where he was?
9. What is an unconscious compromise from the psychological viewpoint?
10. What spiritual capacity do the feet and legs represent?
11. In mentally treating feet and legs, what spiritual realization should we seek to embody?
12. Do we deny physical manifestations of disharmony?
13. How do we mentally treat to remove false growths?
14. What is a psychological complex?
15. Explain why the subconscious can have no will or intention of its own.
16. Is the subconscious individual or Universal?
17. What happens when we consciously impress subjectivity with a definite desire?

18. From what sources does the psyche or mental man receive its impressions?
19. Upon what principle is spiritual mind healing based?
20. What is that truth, which known, automatically produces freedom?
21. What do we mean by separating the belief from the believer in mental treatment?

Answers to Questions on Lesson 34

1. In mentally treating lung trouble work to realize that your patient's body is pure Spiritual Substance. Work to remove any sense of fear and frustration, and to know that he has a consciousness of love and fulfillment. Also work to know that he has no reason to escape the obligations and responsibilities of living.
2. By Spiritual Substance, relative to the physical body, we mean that the physical body is a manifestation of Divine Ideas harmoniously arranged and held in place by the Creative Intelligence which conceives them. (The body is not separate from Spirit but is Spirit in form.)
3. In mentally treating eye trouble, work to remove any sense of strain, and to realize that physical vision always perceives Divine Ideas.
4. In substituting spiritual sense for physical object we mean that we should endeavor to discover and recognize the spiritual equivalent which the organ represents. For example, the stomach represents the capacity to spiritually assimilate ideas; the blood stream represents the circulation of Life; the lower extremities represent the ability to progress, etc.
5. Our work should be based upon the general assumption that an invisible cause dominates everything, that the real man is spiritual and perfect, and the conscious realization of this truth is the power that heals.
6. The spiritual man has never lost any of his faculties because the real man is God manifesting as man.
7. Spiritual mind healing is more direct than psychological mind healing because it is not necessary for the spiritual practitioner to know the specific cause of his patient's trouble. The spiritual practitioner deals directly with the spiritual man.
8. In treating constipation we transpose the idea of physical congestion to mental congestion and know that Mind removes everything smoothly, harmoniously, and cannot be inhibited in Its action.
9. By our psychic body we mean the subjective or mental body.
10. Psychic tension is mental and emotional strain, both conscious and subjective.
11. In spiritual mind healing we treat to remove psychic tension by mentally viewing the patient as a spiritual being free from confusion, strain, fear, worry, etc.
12. By arraying our mental argument against a negative condition we mean that our mental treatment, which is based upon the allness of Spirit, denies the necessity of such negative condition and affirms its opposite.
13. A belief is an opinion which may or may not be true. A truth is that which is so, disregarding whatever may be believed about it.
14. A false belief can appear to be and act as though it were a truth. Our imagination makes real to us that which is believed in. For example, the imagined belief that the world was flat retarded progress, but did not flatten the world.

15. A spiritual practitioner must sense at all times that Truth has supreme power over all false or mistaken beliefs, opinions, or conditions.

Science, Superstition and Common Sense

It seems as though we were born to be superstitious because we all inherit the legacy of the entire race mind. Freud, the first man to chart the unconscious, said that neurotic thought patterns will repeat themselves with monotonous regularity throughout life unless they are changed. He was referring to what he called the unconscious and what we call the subjective state of our thought.

While there has been a great deal of controversy about Freud's life and teaching, one thing is certain: It would be impossible to write an adequate book on psychology today without its being profoundly influenced by his discoveries. We are not concerned with his philosophy of life from a spiritual viewpoint, but only with the scientific discoveries that he undoubtedly made and which caused psychological research to be recharted to conform to new patterns.

When Freud said that we are prone to repeat morbid thought patterns he was right. But Jung, his able contemporary, added to this the thought that we are subject to the influence of what he called the collective unconscious, which means the sum total of all human emotions from time immemorial.

There was a time when theology taught that there was a devil, a hell, a limbo, a purgatory, and a paradise. Because ages on end believed this, it created a pattern in the collective unconscious which influenced everyone. They were born with this idea, and as a matter at fact this theory has never yet been entirely cleared up. There are countless thousands who still adhere to this superstition.

At one time it was thought that it would be impossible to cultivate the desert and waste places, and make them productive. The thought was that it was unnatural, and so it could not be done. But some person had the courage to go ahead and make the attempt, and he was successful because he was complying with the laws of nature.

Common sense and science must be applied to religious and spiritual things as to everything else, for we can no longer monotonously repeat "Thus saith the Lord" because of certain proclamations of some of the early prophets. We must analyze their statements to see whether they are speaking from Divine patterns or from the inertia of human thought patterns which they had unconsciously inherited.

True religion, true science, and true common sense should go hand in hand, together with that other subtle something which is the essence of feeling—that which is beyond words.

It is not always easy in a world of confusion, superstition, and unbelief to maintain an independent position in one's own thought, a position based on the plain common sense that Jesus had, that Life cannot produce death, that the Universe holds nothing against us, that the gift of Heaven is eternally made but still must be received. Science is helping us to receive this gift. All the comforts and the good that have come to modern life through science are not contradictions of nature, but rather they are affirmations of the limitless resources of Life.

The very fact that two blades of grass can be made to grow where only one grew, is an affirmation that the Universe Itself did not limit the growth; it waited for someone to perceive its possibility. Poverty will one day be wiped from the face of the earth, not because God will some day decide that He is ready to change conditions but because man, cooperating with God, with nature, and with law, will proclaim an abundance that already existed.

Wars will cease not when God decides this for us, but when enough people know that it is no longer desirable, and steadfastly maintain their position. From communion with Spirit man will come to perceive the deeper reality, the broader sharing in human experience.

So disease will one day be wiped from the face of the earth, as science, sense, and the philosophy of Spiritual Truth take the place of ignorance, superstition, fear, and confusion.

You are a forerunner in this field, breaking down barriers of race consciousness, the accumulated effects of misconceptions, and the morbid fears of the universe in which we live. When science, common sense, and a right philosophy combine, the half gods will have to go.

There is no point in waiting for this consummation in human affairs, for we cannot change the thought of the whole world over night. But fortunately, we can change our reactions to it, and build a strong and impregnable barrier in our own consciousness against everything that denies the Supreme Good.

In actual practice we should daily say: *I am not bound by the superstitions of the race. I no longer fear God or the Universe in which I live. I have implicit confidence in the Supreme Good, and I permit It to flow through me and to bless everything I contact.*

Little by little there will be added to our own unconscious or subjective reactions a new body of thought which ultimately will be projected and expanded into the Universal Mind. We shall not only be freeing ourselves but we shall be helping to free the whole human race from the bondage of fear, ignorance, superstition, and thoughts based on what the past has brought forth. The past is dead.

Regression

From the Science of Mind viewpoint, emotional regression means withdrawing to a place of safety and security. When a thing regresses it goes backward. Often there is a tendency in the mind to get away from meeting objective situations which are unpleasant by withdrawing from all objective activity, and in imagination reverting to a chronologically earlier or less adapted pattern of behavior and feeling.

It is easy enough to see how one who is surrounded by confusing situations might feel inadequate to cope with them, and unconsciously might seek some place of peace or retirement where nothing could bother him.

A completely integrated person is one who has learned to meet everything as it comes along, and to make the best of it. In our science this is not a hopeless situation. When we say one should make the best of things we do not mean that one should grin and bear it, or even suffer it to be so, for we know there is a way to meet every situation through the use of the Power greater than we are.

However, we should not close our eyes to reality if there is a tendency toward regression in ourselves or in those we seek to help. We must recognize it just as we would any other error, and meet it with quiet but positive determination.

If a person finds himself apparently unable to cope with objective situations, and consequently finds his mind reverting with a certain morbid longing to the thought of getting away from it all, he is in a bad emotional state and should be helped. This is done by knowing that there is nothing to be afraid of, that we are one with an Infinite Partner, that there is nothing in the Universe designed to harm us. Confidence and faith in a Power greater than we are must be generated.

Often even in poems which make a great appeal to us we find this unconscious sense of regression creeping in. For instance the words of Elizabeth Allen: *Backward, turn backward, O Time, in your flight, Make me a child again just for tonight!* show that in writing these beautiful lines she had an unconscious desire to get away from it all. Note the first verse of *THE CRY OF A DREAMER* by John O'Reilly:

I am tired of planning and toiling
In the crowded hives of men;
Heart-weary of building and spoiling,
And spoiling and building again.
And I long for the dear old river
Where I dreamed my youth away;
For a dreamer lives forever,
And a toiler dies in a day.

In both instances you will note an unconscious desire to get away from objective reality. Something has happened to the individual that causes him to desire to revert to some former existence where there were no cares or burdens or obligations.

How wonderful to accept the thought of Jesus when he said, *Come unto me, all ye that labour and are heavy laden, and I will give you rest. Take my yoke upon you, and learn of me; for I am meek and lowly in heart; and ye shall find rest unto your souls. For my yoke is easy, and my burden is light* (Matthew 11:28-30).

This is not resignation; it is just the opposite. It is a proclamation that the mind finds sanctuary in the Spirit, and that there are no burdens when we unify ourselves with Life.

In a certain sense amnesia, or suddenly forgetting one's identity is a form of regression because it is getting away from reality. But at the base of amnesia there is fear, a sense of separation, a disunion which faith alone can heal.

The psychological approach, while scientifically correct, will never completely solve the problem of regression. For while it can uncover the cause of regression, generally speaking it lacks the spiritual faith to supply what is needed to make one more completely whole.

There is nothing to be afraid of in the past, the present, or the future. Our faith should be based on the only rock of salvation there is, which is that God is all there is, there is nothing else. *In him we live, and move, and have our being*. There is nothing to be afraid of. *Underneath are the everlasting arms*. We are cradled in Love.

Statements like these will clear the track of the mind straight back to the eternal Source of Life, where there are no fears, doubts, or uncertainties: *The Lord is my shepherd, I shall not want; He that dwelleth in the secret place of the most High shall abide in the shadow of the Almighty*. These statements are wonderful in helping to establish faith and stability, without which life is but a shambles of frustrated hopes and unsatisfied yearnings.

You might wonder why we mention these negative emotional states. The reason is that in the Science of Mind we never seek to avoid an issue, because any condition which is psychologically avoided becomes buried in the unconscious. And unfortunately it is buried alive. Thus the conflict goes on beneath the surface of consciousness, where it does more damage than it would if left objective. We must meet every situation as it comes with faith and trust, thereby avoiding regressions, escapes, and frustrations.

A Story of Growth

The Bible symbolizes the spiritual evolution of man, beginning in the Old Testament and culminating in the life and teaching of Jesus, the Christ. As we examine the spiritual symbology of the Bible we should realize that as it tells the story of a race of people it also presents the story of every man's life—yours and mine.

The Bible starts with the fundamental premise that God, the Universal Creative Spirit, is present everywhere and is within man himself. To this concept is added the great Law of Cause and Effect. Then the Bible presents the idea that man is created free, with the possibility of limitless expansion, and let alone to discover himself.

During this process of self-discovery man brings upon himself, through the operation of the Law of Mind, the experiences he images in his thought. We have on one hand the evolution of the individual life under the guidance of Divine Providence, which leads to harmony. In contrast there is the freedom to live under the false guidance of a sense of being separated from good, which leads to disaster and chaos.

But always the Bible holds before us the great promise of the final redemption of man through understanding the law of his being and his relationship to the Divine Spirit. It shows us that there is always something at the innermost depths of our being which never completely loses a sense of its spiritual nature.

Even in the midst of the confusion that followed the misuse of the Law by the Children of Israel, they produced the greatest line of spiritual prophets the world has ever known. These prophets were the ones who always remembered who they really were.

The era of the prophets cannot be divorced from the Kingdom of Israel, its development and rise to power and its division and dispersement. Nor can the Kingdom of Israel be separated from the Kingdom which each one of us represents. We can relate the development of the Kingdom of Israel to the integration of a personality or the coming into wholeness of any one being.

When the Children of Israel came out of the land of Egypt they were an unorganized people. They lived in scattered tribes, warring with other desert tribes. Necessity for self-preservation caused them to band together into greater colonies and this brought forth the need for organized leadership. Here we are introduced to one of the factors that made Israel a great nation.

The first leaders of the Children of Israel were spiritual rather than political or social leaders. The spiritual impulse was fundamental to the nature of their being. Judges were selected to rule over the people—not judges in the sense that we think of our courts of law, but spiritual judges who represented the Divine Law, the Will of God, or Jehovah. The spiritual law was, in fact, the civil law of the Hebrew people.

As the nation began to take form it passed from religious into civil leadership and the Kingdom of Israel was established. But we remember that it was a spiritual leader, the prophet Samuel, who raised Saul, the first king, to his throne, and Saul, under Divine guidance, developed the Kingdom of Israel to a power undreamed of. He organized his people so that they worked together effectively in commerce, agriculture, industry, and international relations.

When David ascended to the throne he too was anointed by Samuel the prophet, and undertook to continue the development of the kingdom under Divine guidance. David brought a quality of love to his reign to complement the organizational ability and the intellect of Saul. And the Kingdom of Israel rose to even greater heights.

David's son succeeded him on the throne, and Solomon inherited by far the richest and most powerful kingdom of the world at that time. In the early part of his reign Solomon became noted for his great wisdom and understanding. But later, to satisfy his increasing love of luxury and power it was necessary for him to increase taxation and conscript more and more slave labor. His people began to grow restless under this oppression and eventually a segment of them rebelled and seceded from the kingdom. The great nation was divided.

Here is the story of a man who, when his thought was centered on God, erected the great Temple which so perfectly symbolized the meaning of life and the relationship between the individual and the Universal. And then, when he lost the spiritual meaning of the Temple he had built and became engrossed in material force, both his wisdom and his power deserted him. Solomon began to worship two Gods—the god of temporal power and the God of his ancestors, *the one and only true God*. This marked the beginning of the disintegration of a mighty kingdom.

For hundreds of years following the fall of the Kingdom of Israel the Hebrew people were subjected to every indignity known to the human family. But as great as their plight was, never were they without a prophet of the Lord to keep hope alive, to keep before them the promise of a Messiah who would lead them out of their captivity.

> There was always an Isaiah to say:
>
> > They shall beat their swords into plowshares, and their spears into pruning hooks; nation shall not lift up sword against nation, neither shall they learn war any more (Isaiah 2:4).
>
> And in his prophecy concerning the coming of Christ:
>
> > And the spirit of the Lord shall rest upon him, the spirit of wisdom and understanding, the spirit of counsel and might, the spirit of knowledge and of the love of the Lord (Isaiah 11:2).
>
> There was always a Hosea to say:
>
> > Come, and let us return unto the Lord: for he hath torn, and he will heal us; he hath smitten, and he will bind us up (Hosea 6:1).
>
> And there was always a Micah to say:
>
> > But thou, Bethlehem, though thou be little among the thousands of Judah, yet out of thee shall he come forth unto me that is to be ruler in Israel; whose goings forth have been from of old, from everlasting ... And this man shall be the peace, when the Assyrian shall come into our land; and when he shall tread in our palaces (Micah 5:2, 5).

All of the prophets who arose during this period of captivity prophesied the final emancipation of the Children of Israel from their bondage through a return to the true knowledge of the Kingdom of God and the final triumph at spiritual power. They all pointed to the fact that somewhere in human experience some man would arise who would completely reveal the Divine Nature and the Divine Sonship.

Every man is a nation unto himself, a nation inhabited by many thoughts, feelings, appetites, and talents. Every man is a nation of consciousness. All too often, like the Children of Israel, we find it easy to build golden calves and reach with lustful hands to grasp the illusion of temporal power. It is easy for us to forget that there is a Supreme Ruler at the center of the nation of ourselves, whose sovereignty is fixed in Love and enthroned in the Sonship of God.

It is only as we turn our thoughts away from this spiritual sovereignty that our faculties and energies become dispersed. This makes us a weakened nation, subject to the invasion of every fear, doubt, disease, and temptation that presents itself at the borders of our experience.

But like the Children of Israel, there is always a prophet in our own minds that gives us hope, consolation and promise in the knowledge that Life can never destroy Itself and that *truth crushed to earth shall rise again*. This prophet is our own soul, which eternally proclaims the Messiah even though we may be lost in a wilderness of our own false concepts. We should not forget that the very power which created this wilderness is the power that builds the highway for the remnant to return to the Holy Land.

It is the personal application of these great historic symbols presented in the Old Testament in which we are particularly interested. For the ancient race of the Children of Israel has long since departed, but the lesson is as new as the latest invention.

Let us each be sure, then, that the voice of the prophet within does not go unheard or unheeded. Let us right now be still and listen as the Son of God within us proclaims the glory of his Kingdom. Let this Kingdom be real to us in a very practical way. Let us know right now that we are established in the kingdom of health, happiness, and wholeness, because we are established in the Kingdom of God.

If the Blind Lead the Blind

Jesus must have been the wisest man who ever lived. Today we can connect many of his sayings with our new outlook on the mental and emotional life.

For instance, in psychological analysis it is believed that if a physician in analyzing a patient, uncovers in the patient an unconscious hatred for his father, and if the physician had the same aversion for his own father, then the analysis might as well stop right there. This is because the physician is not able to see with clarity a block in another it he has the same type of block in himself.

In psychological terms this is expressed by saying that wherever there is an emotional bias there will be an intellectual blind spot. This means that we cannot think with truthful clarity about things that we are too emotionally affected by. Jesus understood this, and that is why he said that if the blind lead the blind they will both fall into the ditch.

We all have such emotional biases, and this is why we think it strange when someone whom we hold to be highly intelligent seems to be irrational on certain points. We often say, "How can he believe as he does when such belief contradicts common sense or reason?" But could we uncover his whole mental life we should discover the emotional bias deep down there in his unconscious where he has a block which makes it impossible for him to think straight on that particular subject.

This is where many at our theological conflicts come from. This is why people are prone to say that they alone are right or their system of thought alone is right. They have not yet gotten a clearance back to the fundamental proposition that God is One, and that every man is an incarnation of the same God. Therefore intolerance and harshness, unkindness and criticism, coldness and indifference are projected. This is one of those tricks which the mind plays on us.

When we understand these things we shall become more tolerant, more kind, more compassionate, because we shall realize that we are all on the pathway of evolution, not of the Spirit which is already perfect, but of the mind which so often is blindly groping in the dark.

We will be helped over many a difficulty if we realize that an emotional bias does create a mental blind spot. Then if we learn to overlook the differences because we understand them, we shall no longer bring condemnation to add to condemnation, or judgment to add to judgment, and our own lives will become enriched as they always must with new knowledge.

Living is an art as well as a science. It is a thing of beauty as well as form; a thing of the heart as well as of the intellect. It is a combination of all these that makes up the factors of a well-rounded life.

And again we come right back to the fundamental proposition that the problems we face are not external; they are within. They are not some other person's fault; neither are they necessarily our own fault. They are the fault of ignorance, from which enlightenment alone can free us.

No, the blind cannot lead the blind, and we all are blind in spots. Therefore no person should set himself up as the great example, but humbly following the pathway of truth as he sees it, with a good-natured and flexible tolerance for himself and others, learn to overlook all mistakes and feel his way through confusion back to the central flame from which every man's life is lighted.

Bibles of the World

Fragments from the spiritual history of the race
revealing fundamental UNITY of religious thought and experience

JUDAISM and CHRISTIANITY—I had fainted, unless I had believed to see the goodness of the Lord in the land of the living.
Blessed be the Lord; for, he hath shown me his marvelous kindness.
O taste and see that the Lord is good! Blessed is the man who trusteth in him.

CONFUCIANISM—Heaven's bounty never halteth.
The great God has conferred a moral sense even on the inferior people.

HINDUISM—Immortal One—He cares for all mankind.

ISLAM—Plenteous gifts are in the hands of God; for God is of great bounteousness.
The Lord of the world hath created me, and guideth me; giveth me food and drink; and when I am sick, He healeth me.
Surely the future shall be better for thee than the past. And as for the favors of thy Lord, tell them abroad.

SIKHISM—The Giver giveth. In every age man subsisteth by His bounty.

I have no friend like God, who gave me soul and body, and infused into me understanding. He cherisheth, and watcheth over, all creatures.

TAOISM—The Supreme produces all things. Its virtue nourishes them. Its nature gives them form. Its force perfects them.

Treating in the Consciousness of Peace

Office of the Dean

My Dear Friend,

We should like you to pay particular attention to the Supplements in this lesson. We want you to realize that a spiritual mind treatment is completely independent of the one who gives it. In giving a spiritual mind treatment you are using a Law which is independent of you or anyone else, but a Law which operates on your thought.

Your prayer, your acceptance, your affirmation, the treatment you give has no relationship to anything past, present, or future, but only to itself and the Law of Absolute Causation. The best practitioner is the one who understands this and who makes his treatment independent of even his own thinking, through realizing that it is operated upon by a Power greater than he is.

We should also like you to carefully consider the thoughts covered in the section on *Transference*, and realize that true security comes only from the individual himself, because God is within the self and there can be no security outside the Truth.

And above everything else be yourself. Everyone has to learn to accept himself for better or for worse but we do not have to accept the little isolated self. There is behind everything that we appear to be, a Reality, a real Spiritual Ego, Divinely ordained and Heaven sent. Perhaps we could call this the God-intended man, although the Bible refers to it as the Christ in us.

It is this Christ in you, the Spiritual Ego or Entity that is the true self. We need never imitate anyone else.

Sincerely,
Ernest Holmes

Lesson 36

Heart Trouble, page 238, to *Asthma and Hay Fever*, page 242

We view the heart as a center of Divine Love. Therefore in treating all forms of heart trouble we should seek to recognize the presence of Divine Love. This is done by lifting the cloud of fear from the mentality of the patient. In all cases where fear is removed and the consciousness of the patient is filled with an awareness of Divine Protection, an over-shadowing Presence, and a spiritual immortality, relief is gained.

We must know that there is no incurable disease since all things are possible to the Life Principle. The Life Principle is perfect and is already functioning at the very center of the one for whom we are working. To believe that any disease is incurable is to make it impossible to give scientific and efficient mental help. We must know that that which creates can re-create; we must be certain that the very center of man's life is spiritual, harmonious, and perfect. The pulsations of life are regular. The vitality of Spirit is at the center of man's being. From this center circulate the ideas of good, of abundance, of peace, and of joy.

The practitioner, knowing that the Truth is operating through his own consciousness but that at the same time It is independent of even his own consciousness, makes his declarations about his patient with the conviction that there is nothing in the patient and nothing in himself and nothing in any form of human belief which can hinder his word from having an instantaneous, perfect, and permanent result. Therefore there is no thought of wearing out, no belief of overdoing or of exhausting one's strength.

There is no penalty attached to any so-called broken law since the laws of God cannot really be broken; they have merely been wrongly used. The affirmation of these Divine Laws readjusts the mind to the harmony which already exists, attunes the thought to the Spirit which is ever within, and sets the captive free from the mental imprisonment in which he is incarcerated.

To treat for the elimination of fear and the recognition of perfect love is scientific in working for any form of heart trouble. Treat also to realize that there is no strain. Man's oneness with Divine Power eliminates the necessity of strain.

To take the thought, *Let not your heart be troubled, neither let it be afraid* (John 14:27), is to add the faith of countless thousands to your treatment. The consciousness and the conviction of those who have believed in the statement, *Let not your heart be troubled: ye believe in God, believe also in me* (John 14:1), has a real power arising out of the expectancy and the conviction of the spiritual-minded throughout the ages.

Heart is a Divine Idea, a central idea, an idea of harmony, of rhythm, of vitality, of circulation. At the very center of man's being, the practitioner knows that good, harmony, and joy are enthroned. There is no old age and no burden; there is no failure and no loss, no influence of fear on the body. Perfect love casts out all fear.

Again let us remember that the practitioner substitutes an idea for the physical object. His treatment is a process whereby he becomes conscious of this idea in Mind as being perfect, effective, active, never impaired, never having anything wrong with it. Whatever obstructs this vision, whatever belief of fear, doubt, or uncertainty has rendered your patient's consciousness inactive or paralyzed, must be repudiated. The practitioner must realize the Truth with a greater clarity than is his patient's false belief.

The fear of death and the sense of uncertainty attendant upon one's belief in the future life often makes it impossible for one to recover from any form of disease which human consensus has decreed to be fatal. Therefore, particularly in treating heart trouble be sure to acquire a consciousness that life is eternal, it never fails, it goes on. The removal of this restricting paralysis of fear will have a salutary effect since it tends to remove the strain and the tension, which in all probability is a part of the trouble you must heal.

Love alone casts out fear. The scientific practitioner must know that when he removes the *mental cause* of any disease, the disease will disappear with it. He must know that fear, superstition, and ignorance can be entirely obliterated. They are not indestructible verities but the suppositional opposites to spiritual verities. They are real as experience but not as eternal truths.

It is impossible to remove the effects of ignorance and fear without first dissolving the thought back of them. Man's consciousness of Divine forgiveness is necessary. Your patient really labors under the condemnation of human struggle, strife, stress, and strain; an over-burdening of the thought with anxiety occasioned by the belief in his inability to cope with situations. Life becomes too much for him to bear. He fails to bear what he calls the burden; therefore he has heart trouble.

Heart trouble is largely a result of this super-tension, this over-strain, which may be reduced to a thing of thought and dissipated. To know that evil is unreal and has no eternal law behind it relieves the sense of burden which weighs people down. The whole human race believes itself to be subject to material causation, sickness, death, and liable at any time to helplessness or to complete failure. This race consciousness, which some systems of psychology call the collective unconscious, operates more or less through all people.

The practitioner separates this belief from the believer. He does this by clearing up the belief in his own mind about the believer. He knows that there is no sin but a mistake and no punishment but a consequence (page 633, definition of *Sin*). He adjusts the mistake, and in so doing forgives the sin, thereby removing the sense of condemnation from the man's consciousness.

He removes the strain and burden from the thought of his patient, that depressing, devitalizing process of thought which has found a logical correspondent at the very center of his physical being. Most people who suffer from heart trouble are depressed mentally. The weight and the burden must be lifted. Hence, in this as in other cases, a person must build up a consciousness of good, a recognition of the Eternal Presence within his own soul, and a realization of his immunity from evil.

God, or Pure Spirit, is the Principle of all mind healing. The Law of Mind is the remedy which the practitioner uses in his spiritual work. It would be impossible for him to do this unless he were able to change things into thoughts and proceed upon the theory that Perfect Mind as original Creative Principle exists at the very center of every person's being. Mind is the one Power in the universe. It is not only the *original* Creative Principle but It is the *eternal* Creative Principle, and if a certain way of thinking produces a certain result, then it logically follows that an opposite way of thinking will produce an opposite result.

Sometimes we have to find what the mental equivalents of wrong results are in order to heal them. We find that all fear is manmade. We find that different kinds of fear assail different types of people. In some countries it is thought wrong to kill animals. Anyone living in that state of thought would feel condemned if he ate meat. In our own country we have no such mental reaction.

All laws of limitation are manmade, and man will be limited by these laws which he has created until he himself reverses them. This is why it is written, *For since by man came death, by man came also the resurrection of the dead. For as in Adam all die, even so in Christ shall all be made alive* (I Corinthians 15:21,22). Do not forget that *Adam* and *Christ* are merely two ways of looking at the same man. (Turn again to page 492 and read the section on *The Inner Man* referred to in Lesson 8.)

When we come to treating for the healing of poison (page 240) we recognize that the Spirit cannot be poisoned, the Mind cannot be poisoned, the Truth cannot be poisoned, and that our word is the law of elimination to every belief that the system contains anything which does not belong to it. The body is Mind in manifestation; it is a Spiritual Idea. There is one perfect Spiritual Body. The body is just as real as Mind since it is a manifestation of Mind. Body constitutes the evidence that man is a manifestation of God.

We declare the Truth about the spiritual body, knowing that any belief in a human body separated from the Divine is false. It would not be scientific to deny that we have a body, nor would it be intelligent to affirm that this body is evil or unworthy. We believe that there is a perfect spiritual body which we as finite beings did not conceive. Our declarations of Truth are about this spiritual body which cannot be contaminated by any form of poison. The spiritual body cannot contain any idea of poison, and our realization of the spiritual body is what heals the physical body.

Body is not to be condemned, but the Truth about body is to be recognized. The spiritual body never suffers, is never sick, because it always manifests the eternal Principle of harmony and right action. As such the spiritual body is real and we need not be afraid to declare the Truth about it.

Many people think that they deny God in affirming the reality of body, but as a matter of fact this is a subtle form of dualism, an entirely mistaken conception. Body, or objective manifestation, is the only evidence we have that there is an invisible Cause or Principle. *And the Word was made flesh, and dwelt among us* (John 1:14). Therefore it is scientific to declare the Truth about the body.

The body should be thought of as consisting of spiritual ideas which are always in harmonious accord with one another. As there is one limitless Mind which is our mind right now, so there is one infinite Body which is our body right now. The body reflects and manifests the Divine Idea of harmony and of purity. The Law of Mind operating through this body is one of perpetual harmonious action. If, then, we have a belief in a body separated from the Divine, we must reunite our concept of body with the Universal Wholeness.

In a certain sense there is no private body; there is merely a personification of the infinite Body of God, and the spiritual mind practitioner recognizes this Body of God as being manifest in all men. Wherever there is any idea of poison, of impurity, of stagnation, or of infection, he declares that his knowledge of right action dissipates this poisonous condition. He explains it away in his own thought and if he is successful in doing this, he will have a patient who will come to him and say, "My body is relieved."

At first it seems difficult to believe this, but with increasing practice a person becomes accustomed to this reaction; in fact he is disappointed if he does not receive it. He has learned to convert things into thoughts and proceed upon the assumption that thoughts are things, that nothing moves but Mind, that even disease is moved in and out of the body, so to speak, through a process of consciousness. He learns not to despise the body, nor does he seek to get rid of it; he merely affirms the presence of the Spiritual Body. Jesus said, in effect, "Destroy this body and the Principle within me will raise it up again." He must have understood body as a Divine Idea. What we need is salvation from the belief of any mind or body apart from God.

Now we come to the method of treating paralysis. We should take the thought that Life cannot be paralyzed. Life represents the eternal Principle of action and reaction which is never inhibited, congested, nor rendered useless. The body, being a Divine Idea in the Mind of God which has absolute freedom of movement, cannot be bound. Spirit is always acting through it. The Spirit is always manifested in it. In such cases we seek a realization of the body as a Spiritual Idea forever free from bondage. We must also relieve the consciousness of all sense of fear, condemnation and punishment.

What man needs to be saved from is his consciousness of evil as a reality and his consciousness of evil as an effect. For if evil of itself is not real, as reality, then neither can evil be real as effect. Both ends of the false proposition are erased through a knowledge of the Truth.

The Principle within man transcends any particular use of the Law of Cause and Effect he may ever have made, and the practitioner must never forget this. When he says, “My word is the law unto this thing whereto it is spoken,” there must be no question whatsoever about the power of his word, for his word will have only as much power as he believes it to have. We all know that the Spirit cannot be paralyzed, and it is not difficult for any of us to feel that the Spirit is free. We must now realize that the Spirit of God is also the spirit in man. Therefore we couple this conception of freedom with our consciousness of man.

The Principle of Freedom flows through every nerve center, activates every atom of man's being. Freedom is a principle; bondage is the limitation of thought. Freedom is perpetual, eternal; bondage is a temporary mistake. The knowledge at freedom dissipates the idea of bondage just as the knowledge of any truth dissipates the illusion about that truth. So the practitioner not only realizes the principle of freedom at the center of his patient's being, but he declares that this principle of freedom is now active and operative through every organ of his patient's physical being.

The body is a spiritual idea activated by the consciousness of God, dominated by Pure Spirit, re-created instantly and eternally. It has never lost any faculty. No center within it has ever been destroyed because every center within it is a center of God's consciousness. This leaves nothing to be paralyzed. When Jesus healed the paralyzed man and told him to take up his bed and walk, he certainly could not have been thinking of bondage as a real law, but rather as no law; that freedom alone has the right to be.

We must know that the Universe holds nothing against us. Read again the paragraph on page 470 referred to in Lesson 11. There is no sin but a mistake and no punishment but a consequence; hence both mistake and consequence may be reversed. If this were not true spiritual mind healing would be impossible.

In physical paralysis we have an objective form of mental bondage, and we must get rid of this belief in mental bondage if we hope to heal the physical form. We destroy any particular experience of bondage by acquiring a sense of freedom greater or higher than the consciousness which produced the bondage. In order to do this we must turn entirely from the objective effect to the opposite state of consciousness.

Summary

In treating heart trouble we seek to recognize the presence of love.

In spiritual mind healing we do not think of a curable or an incurable disease because all things are possible to the Life Principle. The Presence of God and the activity of Spirit already are at the center of everyone's being. The practitioner knows that there is nothing in him, in his consciousness, or in anyone else that can prevent his word from working, because his word is the Presence, the Power, and the Activity of the Living Spirit within him.

It is always scientific to treat for the elimination of fear and the recognition of love. Heart is an idea of harmony, the rhythm, the vitality, and the circulation of the Spirit.

Every spiritual mind treatment is filled with the idea that the Spirit is immortal here and now, and perfect here and now.

It is necessary that we have a consciousness of Divine forgivingness or a feeling that the Universe holds nothing against us. Otherwise we shall continue in our superstitions, fears, and the morbid beliefs of the whole human thought.

The practitioner removes every sense of burden and strain, and realizes for his patient freedom, love, and joy. He declares the Truth about the spiritual body, which is right where the physical body appears. From this standpoint the idea of body is not to be condemned, but is to be interpreted spiritually.

Freedom is the true state of the universe. Bondage is a limitation of thought. Freedom is triumph. There is a spiritual center in man that has never been touched by any external fact.

Questions

Brief answers to these questions should be written out by the student after studying the lesson, and the answers compared with those which will be included in next week's lesson.

1. In what symbolic way do we view the heart?
2. What spiritual realization should we have in treating heart ailments?
3. Why should the mental practitioner know that there are no incurable diseases?
4. What is the Life Principle which can remold, remake, and reform?
5. Where Is the Life Principle?
6. How does the Life Principle operate through us?
7. To what degree can we consciously use the Life Principle?
8. What do we mean by saying the practitioner's realization of Truth must transcend his patient's belief in its opposite?
9. What do we mean by a decree of human opinion?
10. If the belief about our patient is that he suffers from a fatal ailment how should we mentally treat?
11. Why is it that people who suffer from heart ailments so frequently have mental depression?

12. Why is the *original* Creative Principle also the *eternal* Creative Principle?
13. What is the proper method of mental treatment for the elimination of poison?
14. Do we deny or condemn the body?
15. In mentally treating paralysis what spiritual realization should be supplied?
16. Upon what spiritual realization do we base our declaration that evil has no power?
17. If evil has no power how do we explain that which we call evil in experience?
18. What do we mean by saying, "Both mistake and consequence can be reversed"?

Answers to Questions on Lesson 35

1. In mentally treating affections of the skin, the spiritual realization should be that man's outward manifestation corresponds to his inward harmony and admits of no irritation, inflammation, or separation from the pure stream of life activity.
2. To mentally practice the presence of perfection means that the practitioner should at all times recognize the presence of Pure Spirit at the center of all form, and man as a manifestation of this Spirit.
3. A practitioner never treats disease as though it were a thing of itself because he realizes that all causation is invisible. Therefore he mentally removes the thought obstruction and supplies the recognition of the presence of perfection.
4. The arms and hands represent man's ability to grasp ideas. They are a result of a desire or spiritual urge to express the Universal Self.
5. The metaphysical term, *The Divine Urge*, means the *Universal urge toward self-expression* manifest in nature, animal, and man. From our viewpoint the psychological term, *Libido*, means the *Universal Urge as it expresses through man*.
6. Spirit must have self-expression as well as desire toward self-expression because desire unexpressed remains a dream. Life to be complete must be both idea and manifestation.
7. When a craving for self-expression is repressed or inhibited the psychic energy generated by such desire remains in an active subconscious state and tends to create some undesirable physical condition.
8. If a person willed himself to go somewhere while his emotion strongly desired him to remain where he was, his lower limbs might become paralyzed. This process would be unconscious.
9. An unconscious compromise is a subjective reaction arising from the opposing tendencies of conscious intention and unconscious desire. (This is illustrated in Answer 8 of this lesson.)
10. The feet and legs represent the spiritual capacity to move about, to go from one place to another.
11. In mentally treating feet and legs we should seek to embody the spiritual realization of freedom to move about, freedom of progress and understanding, freedom from bondage.
12. We do not deny physical manifestations of disharmony; we affirm that all physical manifestation is an effect of an invisible cause. Therefore such effect can be changed by changing its cause.
13. In mentally treating to remove false growths we work to know that man is Spirit, there are no false growths in Spirit, anything of discordant nature which appears in or upon our patient's body is now removed. Everything not a part of the harmonious expression of body is now removed.

14. A psychological complex is a group of ideas, largely subconscious, which tend to cause irrational actions and emotional attachments to oneself, to others, and to certain fixed beliefs about one's relationship to life. All people have psychological complexes, and unless they are abnormal or pathological they are not necessarily destructive to health or happiness.
15. The subconscious can have no will or intention of its own because it is an impersonal law reacting alike to all who use it. It cannot refuse to act, and like the soil it is a neutral, creative medium. It is a law and not a person.
16. The subconscious is both individual and Universal. It is Universal in that it is everywhere. It becomes individual through our use of it.
17. When we consciously impress subjectivity with a definite desire we are providing a definite thought pattern or channel through which its creativity may flow into definite form for us. In this manner our thought becomes its intention for us.
18. The psyche or mental man may receive its impressions through intuition (which is omniscience in man), through science, knowledge, experience, and through opinions, beliefs, and philosophies.
19. Spiritual mind healing is based upon the Principle of the unity of all life, the omnipresence of Spirit or Infinite Wisdom, the omniscience of the Law of Cause and Effect, and man's ability consciously to use this Law.
20. The truth known automatically produces freedom; is the knowledge of man's unity with God and with right action. This knowledge consciously used for definite purposes specializes the Law toward freedom rather than bondage.
21. By separating the belief from the believer we mean that since a belief operates only when it is believed in, and since belief is mental and can be changed, it follows in mental treatment that we should reverse all negative beliefs, knowing that they can no longer operate through our patient.

What Do We See in the Mirror?

I once read an article called *The Scent of Fear*, in which it was claimed that fear exudes a scent that an animal can smell. The author claimed that this scent of fear arouses an antagonism within the animal, and he often attacks in self-defense.

A geologist friend told me he was sitting on a rock one day out in the desert, drawing a map. He happened to glance down and noticed a rattlesnake coiled under the edge of the rock on which he was sitting. I asked him what he did when he saw the rattlesnake and if he was afraid of it. He said, not at all. I had no desire to hurt the snake, and it had no desire to harm me. So he sat there and leisurely completed his plans.

This reminded me of a passage in the Bible which says: *Behold, I give unto you power to tread on serpents and scorpions, and over all the power of the enemy; and nothing shall by any means hurt you.* And in another place: *They shall take up serpents; and if they drink any deadly thing, it shall not hurt them; they shall lay hands on the sick, and they shall recover.*

Dogs feel our personal atmosphere, and if it is one of trust and confidence, if it is one of understanding and love, they respond to it. And I wonder if it is not true that when we feel antagonism for others, they in turn feel it and their response to us becomes antagonistic. Perhaps this is why the Bible says that a soft answer turneth away wrath.

There is a subtle atmosphere around us which unperceived by us is silently attracting people to us or repelling them from us. I have no doubt that some form of fear is the cause of most of our troubles. What the animal smells, because of its acute instinct, we humans feel when we contact each other.

An atmosphere of failure attracts failure. The person who always has the feeling that no one likes him, surrounds himself with an atmosphere that pushes people away from him. It seems as though our mental attitudes are contagious, as though we go around more or less enveloped in them. The silent influence we exercise on others is something that takes place automatically. Friendship attracts friends, while antagonism not only repels people, it actually awakens a feeling of distrust and dislike within them.

Here is one of the keys to successful living and right relationships among people. It is only when we are whole within ourselves that we can help others. It is only when we have faith that we can instill faith. It is only when we have hope and enthusiasm that others respond to us with an equal hope and enthusiasm.

You have often noticed that when you spend considerable time with people who are depressed and afraid, you feel as though the weight of the universe were on your shoulders, as though everything were hopeless. On the other hand, in company with those who are buoyant and confident, you feel a lightness, a sense of joy, a feeling of enthusiasm.

It is almost as definite as going from fog to sunshine, and from sunshine back into fog again. It is as definite as the wind in your face. Sometimes, as you talk with people who are depressed, and try to bring them comfort and courage, you feel their atmosphere lift as though a fog were clearing away. You feel the sun coming out again. Almost invariably these people will tell you how much better they feel for having talked with you.

If we could come to see that life is like a mirror, tending to reflect back to us the images of our own thinking, then we should realize that by changing our thinking we can change the reflections in the mirror.

Next we should ask: What do we want to see in this mirror? And have we the courage to admit that what we are looking at in the mirror is a reflected image of our own outlook on life? Are we looking at antagonism, resentment, confusion? Are we looking at fear, failure, unhappiness? And are we actually willing to look into this mirror of life and say, "That is I"? And then, if we do not like what we see, have we enough confidence to believe that we can change it? If so, we have made the right start.

Our starting point is to recognize God at the center of our own being, to have faith in this Divine Presence within us, and to have an equal faith in the Divine in everyone else. We must come to see that

God is the one eternal Presence in everyone and in everything and we must learn to think from this basis.

How wonderful it would be if we were never afraid of anything. We fear people because we think that in some way they can harm us. So the very antagonism we have for others arouses a like antagonism in them for us. But turn the proposition around, change fear into faith and antagonism into love, and we shall have reversed the whole process.

You see, the mirror is merely something that reflects. You cannot scratch the reflection out of the mirror, but you can change the image in front of it. And you are the image maker. So let us create new images which will reflect new patterns. And we must be definite in our conviction, and deliberate in our aim if we expect happy results, for theories are no good unless they are applied.

Let us take the case of an individual who feels that everyone is against him. He always seems to be at cross purposes with people and with events. This has gone on until people avoid him, because they feel the resentment in his mind and it arouses an equal antagonism in their thoughts about him.

Let us make believe that we are teaching this person what is actually taking place, and that he is accepting our explanation. We understand what is wrong with him. We know that his suffering is self-imposed and we wish to help him. So our explanation will have to be very kind and considerate. It will have to be like leading a child or helping an invalid, for he really is a sick person. We are acting as a doctor to his mind, and doctors should not harshly judge their patients. They should try to help and encourage them to the place where the great restoring power of nature can resume its natural function.

We are acting as physician to this person's mind. We, too, will have to be kind and considerate and willing to let him explode a little, because we understand what is eating at the vitals of his being. Deep inside him he is afraid, scared to death, and unconsciously he is reacting in self-defense. This we must explain to him.

He is longing for love and friendship. He would rather have it than anything else in the world. He wants people to like him, but he is afraid of them. So we tell him how the mind works and how it is that he must come to have faith in something bigger than he is. This he will like, because he is looking for strength; he longs for happiness even as blind men long for light.

We must be very gentle about this, with the simple, sincere desire to be helpful and with no criticism whatsoever. We might even be able to say to him that there was a time when we felt exactly as he does; a time when we thought everything was against us. But one day the light broke, and gradually a transformation took place in our lives. This will cause him to feel that we are sharing our innermost secrets with him, and when we take him by the hand he will respond with confidence.

The change may not take place in a day, a week, or a month, but it will take place if we persist. Let us give him certain affirmations to make for himself each day, similar to the ones we use at the close of this article. Let us help him to make them; let us make them with him. He will begin to feel that he has a partner, and this is a feeling we all need; someone understands him. It will not be long before he will be working with us with an enthusiasm equal to our own, and by and by the signs will begin to follow. His mirror will begin to change its reflection.

This will create hope, and it is only a short step from hope to faith. Through this experience we shall learn the great lesson of life, that the good we have must be shared with others if it is be increased. For when we have made a friend of a person who is friendless, and have made it possible for him to acquire friends, we have multiplied our own friendship by that number of persons. When we have brought good to some person, and have shown him how to extend that good in his own experience, we have brought that much more good into our own life.

Meditation

As I look out into my world I, see that there is nothing to fear. And as I look back into my own mind I know there is nothing in me that is afraid. My thought is filled with confidence, with hope, with trust, and with the acceptance of good.

I expect the mirror of my experience to be filled with joy, and as I turn the magic lantern of my mind into the great Mind and Spirit of the Universe in which all things exist, I know that I am one with all peace, all power, and all good.

I affirm the presence of good in everything I do, the guidance of love everywhere I go. I affirm that strength, enthusiasm, and vitality forever flow through me from the all-sustaining Life of the Universe.

I affirm my union with God, and I know that there is nothing in the entire Universe to be afraid of, nothing to avoid, nothing to run away from. I am at home in the Universe—one with God, one with people, one with that perfect and abiding faith that knows no fear.

Transference

The mental and emotional analysis of the mind as practiced in psychology, particularly in the analytical field, is supposed to carry the patient from where he is back through his entire life history, even to the place of birth, and some have already advanced the theory even to the period of conception.

In the process of clearing the passageway of the mind from the present, straight back through all experiences to the place of beginning of the individual experience, a point is reached in the analysis where the feeling that the patient once had toward his own parents becomes transferred to the one conducting the analysis. In other words, the patient reacts to the analyst as he did to his own parents, since the analyst by substitution or by proxy takes the place of the parents.

If the original feeling of the patient toward his parents was one of hostility, there may be what is called a negative transference; indeed he could even come to despise the analyst and wish to do him harm. It is evident that this could become a difficult situation, and unless overcome, the analysis would become futile.

On the other hand, if the original feeling of the patient toward his parents was one of confidence and trust, the transference is what is called positive, and the patient might even fall in love with the analyst. This is why it has been suggested that men should be analyzed by women, and women by men.

Generally speaking, the patient is apt to have either a sense of hate toward the analyst or one of warm affection. The theory is that the patient will now feel as he did earlier in life toward his parents; therefore the emotions he felt toward them will more quickly come to the surface to be self-seen.

It is believed that this transference of the emotional reactions of earlier life to the analyst is necessary, but at once we are faced with another proposition, and a difficult one. The patient could not go through life with the feeling that he must depend on the analyst, so there comes a time when the transference must be broken.

This means that the patient's possibility of happiness must return to himself and not be imposed in the analyst, for where the treasure is, there will the heart be also. Consequently the transference must be broken in order that the patient may be made whole psychologically, which in this instance means emotionally. He must find within himself the stability and security that he needs. This is called breaking the transference, and the analysis is not complete without it .

Now we have no doubt that this theory in the main is true but from it we should draw a broader generalization, which is this: No matter what the external object may be in which we place our security or possibility of happiness, we shall never become whole until we have separated all negative reactions from that object, because wholeness is within the self and nowhere else.

Even the idea of salvation through some particular religion constitutes in a certain sense a kind of unbroken transference. People believe they can be saved or healed only through certain formulas, certain methods of procedure, through certain prayers or incantations. This is not wholeness; rather it is just the opposite. For it is a complete dependence on a form, or a word, or a person, or even an institution, rather than upon the self.

There are people who depend upon certain books, perhaps even the Bible, for their happiness. Without in any way discrediting the value of these books or the supreme value of the great Bibles of the world, or of those great teachers who have brought to us the highest and the best the world knows, even these transferences must be broken if we are to become whole, for nothing should stand between us and the Universe.

It is not necessary that someone else do this for us. We merely have to go back through our entire lives and say:

> *Bless my father and my mother, my brothers and sisters; everyone whom I have ever depended on. I love and appreciate them. I recognize the good I received from them at the time when it was necessary that I receive that good, but now, without thinking any less of them, I am whole within myself. There is finally only*

One Father and One Mother, which is God, and in this One we are all brothers and sisters.

I love everyone, but depend upon no one. Nothing can rob me of this love I have for others. It cannot be rejected, because I am Love and that which never rejects its own creation.

People, things, institutions, methods, sciences, philosophies, all are good. From each I shall learn everything that I can and with deep gratitude acknowledge the good I am receiving from whatever source, but I am still whole within myself, dependent upon nothing, and yet always interdependent with all things.

Breaking the transference does not mean isolation from Life. Quite the opposite. It means being whole in Life, so that we may discover the love and the friendship of all people without seeking to destroy them or permitting them to destroy us.

The individual security is within the self. Recognizing the same security within others, we work and play with them in gladness. We are whole and they are whole, because God in us is whole.

Be Yourself

People are the most interesting things in the world. While it is true that we do not always get along with them as well as we might, it is also certain that we could not get along without them. We need each other more than we realize. The world is made up of people, and human relationships are merely reactions of people to each other. Many business firms maintain human relations departments for the purpose of helping their employees to appreciate each other and get along together in their work.

We are told that the two things people are most interested in are love and personality. This is not strange, because everyone wants to love and be loved; everyone wants to feel needed. Every individual wishes to feel that he plays an important role in life. All are attracted to the person who has a winning personality.

One thing is certain—whatever our personality may be, or whatever it is to become, is wrapped up in the one idea that there is a Spirit in man, and God Himself is incarnated in every living soul. This Spirit within us is the gift of heaven and without it we would not be alive. It is a recognition of this Spirit within us that is the true starting point for the development of personality.

We often think we have to pattern our lives after the lives of others. But personality, no matter how winsome it may be, or how convincing, or how dominant, is more than a mask we wear; it is a manifestation of an inner, hidden principle, a Divine spark within us which uses both the mind and the body for its own self-expression.

We could think up all the beautiful things to say and the most wonderful and best method of approaching people, and study all the arts of personality development that have ever been taught, and still fall flat on our faces as far as the real personality is concerned. For personality is not the clothes we wear, nor is it our physical appearance alone. It is not just a dominant or domineering something so powerful that it brushes everything else aside.

Personality is the flowering of the Spirit within us, the coming forth of a secret relationship that we all hold to God. The people who have most completely influenced the human race throughout the ages are those who have known this, and who have made but little effort to influence others. They are the ones who have had the deepest feeling of the Divine presence within them.

No one will ever be satisfied or happy or secure in developing a dominant personality. For those who win their way through life by force eventually become weary with the struggle, the purpose of which never reaches its final goal. Personality is not an external thing, for everything we do and say and think, and everything that we appear to be outwardly, is always the result of some hidden fire burning at the center of our being, some Divine Reality which we did not create but which we may discover.

I think we can say without hesitation that the person who finds himself in God, will discover at the center of his own being something which dominates without effort, something which does not have to assume a false front, something which, by the very nature of its being, is both human and Divine.

But someone may say, "Now you are introducing religious ideas that we don't want to be bothered with. What we want is something that can take us into the activities of life in a triumphant manner."

Now this is both right and wrong; right in that we wish to be successful in living; wrong if we think that of ourselves we can add to or take from what God already has given. For while we can, and should, develop an outer personality, back of this there is something you and I never thought up—we did not plan it, we did not create it. Finding this something is like exploring new land. This country already existed before we discovered it. There are heights and depths to our own being which we have not plumbed.

There is a Divine Person back of our personality—a unique manifestation of the Living Spirit. It is never alike in any two people. This is proved by the fact that no two person's thumbprints are alike, no two blades of grass are alike, no two anythings are identical. And yet everything is rooted in one Life, one Presence, and one Power. Why, then, should we expect that any two individuals should be alike? God Himself has placed a unique stamp on everyone. We should not study to be alike, but rather to develop what we really are.

Unity does not mean uniformity. Our unity with other people does not mean that we must think and act as they do. All it means is that we should get along with them. We should unify with everything, while at the same time keeping intact and whole that God-given something at the center of our being which is the Spiritual Ego.

To find this true center is the end and aim of our search. This Divine Person within us has, in a sense, one hand placed in the hand of God and the other outstretched to humanity, for the person who finds himself in God will discover God in others. He will see things in a different light than will the one who thinks he is alone. He will draw strength and inspiration from Life Itself, for no man can live without God and be whole.

Since everything is included in God—for God is the only Presence and Power that there is—the person who wants to be the most himself will have to be the one who has discovered more of himself in that which is greater than he is. Our capacity to think, to live, and to move is nonphysical. There is an invisible Presence hidden within us which has Its Source in a higher Power, and which acts through our actions, wills through our minds, and reveals Itself in what we are doing.

At the center of our being there is a Divine Person, a unique incarnation of God. This is the source of all real inspiration; here, and here alone, at the center of our being, is the real creative power. The question is whether or not we are living from this center, or whether we are thinking of ourselves as detached, separate, divided, alone, and inadequate. We all have direct access to the Infinite Presence, the Universal Person. There could be no more beautiful thought than that the Divine Spirit Itself, infinite as It is, is also within us.

And with this acceptance of God there must come an acceptance of the real self, that self which blossoms in our relations with others and finds fruit in its own action.

Treatment Is Independent of the One Who Gives It

Spiritual mind healing is based on definite Principle and one that works mathematically. In no way should this concept interfere with the beauty of it, or whether or not it is spiritual. The Universe is a system of law and order plus Infinite Presence or Person, and from the standpoint of the human being, personalities. We are persons living in a Mind Principle that reacts mathematically upon our acceptance. Throughout the ages this has been the secret of faith and the answer to prayer.

Just what is the position of the person in this Principle and how does a spiritual mind treatment operate in such a way as to be independent even of the one who gives it? This consideration is of deepest importance, for we should never feel that when we give a treatment we must compel it to operate, any more than we feel that if we plant an acorn we must compel it to become an oak tree. The personal element is volition which makes it possible for us to plant an acorn instead of an apple seed, and with complete certainty know that the answer will be an oak tree and not an apple tree.

As far as the creation of the tree is concerned we have nothing whatsoever to do with it. We have merely used a law of nature that responds to us, that operates upon the particular concept or the seed we buried in the ground, that some invisible force might operate upon it to produce the exact correspondence to the idea of our seed, and not something else. We plant and cultivate the ground but we do not really grow the garden. Nature does this for us.

We cannot expect when we come into the field of spiritual mind treatment that we have entered a field of chaos where nothing happens in accord with law. If this were true we could place no reliance upon our treatment, or the Principle operating on it. We should be dealing with some whimsical fancy or the caprice of some law in nature that might or might not respond to us mathematically and with complete certainty. It is in this sense that the treatment is independent of the one who gives it.

You can plant a garden for someone else in his plot of ground and it will grow provided he cultivates it and waters it. You can plant one in your own ground and it will grow. You can scatter seeds by the roadside and they will grow. All about us in nature we see the variations of such plantings. Perhaps the wind has blown the seed, perhaps it has been accidentally dropped, possibly it has been consciously planted, but always the creative Law produces in complete independence of the avenues through which the seed was planted.

A person giving a spiritual mind treatment should know that he is using such a Law. There is no argument against the existence of this Law because It is invisible, any more than there could be a valid argument against the operation of any law in nature. All laws are invisible. We see only the effect, never the cause. We know that certain effects will follow certain uses of the laws of nature, and we place complete reliance on the operation, not of our will or our desire but of the actual operation of a law.

Now there is such a law as Mind in Action, and it is this law that we use when we give a treatment. Our word is operated on by a Power greater than we are, an Intelligence superior to ours, which is entirely independent of us as personalities. Therefore a practitioner, when he has said that his word is for a certain person or a specific situation or condition, gives his treatment feeling that it is entirely independent of precedents or anything that has happened before; that in a certain sense it becomes an actual entity in the field of Universal Mind that operates upon it.

Every sense of personal responsibility or individual obligation other than the obligation to do one's work to the best of one's ability, must be dropped from the mind. There should be no thought of anxiety, even as there should be no feeling of uncertainty. The Law operates on the word you speak, not because of your wishing or willing, but because that is the way the Law works.

This is the Principle you are dealing with. This is the Power you are using, and this is the certainty upon which you can rely.

There is a vast difference in our mental reaction when we know that we are dealing with a Law that operates upon our word, than there would be if we felt we had to push that word to make it do something or go somewhere or become something. And so again we come right back to the very foundation of the whole theory upon which this practice is built; that we live in a Universe which sustains Itself by Itself, out of Itself, within Itself.

Every scientist must follow this same rule. He uses a certain law. It is the nature of the law that he uses to respond in the way he uses it. We have the obligation to do the best we can. The responsibility rests in the Law of Good.

Made in United States
North Haven, CT
21 April 2023

35714655R00111